INTERNATIONALIZATION IN CENTRAL AND EASTERN EUROPE

T0315915

Internationalization in Central and Eastern Europe

Edited by

MARIN ALEXANDROV MARINOV
Gloucestershire Business School, England

Routledge
Taylor & Francis Group

LONDON AND NEW YORK

First published 2002 by Ashgate Publishing

Reissued 2018 by Routledge
2 Park Square, Milton Park, Abingdon, Oxon OX14 4RN
711 Third Avenue, New York, NY 10017, USA

Routledge is an imprint of the Taylor & Francis Group, an informa business

Publisher's Note
The publisher has gone to great lengths to ensure the quality of this reprint but points out that some imperfections in the original copies may be apparent.

Disclaimer
The publisher has made every effort to trace copyright holders and welcomes correspondence from those they have been unable to contact.

A Library of Congress record exists under LC control number: 2001095868

ISBN 13: 978-1-138-72652-9 (hbk)
ISBN 13: 978-1-138-72644-4 (pbk)
ISBN 13: 978-1-315-19135-5 (ebk)

Contents

List of Contributors   *vii*

The Internationalization Process
Marin Alexandrov Marinov   1

**PART I: INTERNATIONALIZATION OF NATIONAL
           ECONOMIES**   17

1 Economic Restructuring and Internationalization of Slovenia
   Yoji Koyama   19

2 Internationalization through Outward Foreign Direct Investment:
   The Case of Slovenia
   Marjan Svetličič and Andreja Trtnik   47

3 Internationalization of a Post-Communist Economy -
   Opportunities and Threats: The Case of Poland
   Marian Gorynia   76

4 Internationalization of the Albanian Economy through Foreign
   Investments: The Italian Case
   Donata Vianelli, Patrizia de Luca and Roland Kajca   105

**PART II: INTERNATIONALIZATION OF ECONOMIC
            SECTORS**   131

5 Internationalization of the Estonian Economy: Foreign
   Direct Investment and Banking
   Mart Sõrg, Mait Miljan and Hans Künka   133

6   The Internationalization of Grocery Retailing in Poland after 1989
    John A. Dawson and John S. Henley   169

PART III: INTERNATIONALIZATION OF COMPANIES   181

7   Local Expansion Processes of Dutch Firms in Central and
    Eastern Europe
    Rian H. J. Drogendijk   183

8   Internationalization of Interbrew in Eastern Europe:
    A Case Study
    Marin Alexandrov Marinov and Svetla Trifonova Marinova   204

Name Index   *233*

Subject Index   *237*

List of Contributors

John A. Dawson – University of Edinburgh, Scotland

Rian H. J. Drogendijk – Tilburg University, The Netherlands

Marian Gorynia – University of Economics, Poznan, Poland

John S. Henley – University of Edinburgh, Scotland

Roland Kajca – University of Tirana, Albania

Yoji Koyama – Niigata University, Japan

Hans Künka – University of Tartu, Estonia

Patrizia de Luca – University of Trieste, Italy

Marin Alexandrov Marinov – Gloucestershire Business School, England

Svetla Trifonova Marinova – University of Birmingham, England

Mait Miljan – University of Tartu, Estonia

Mart Sõrg – University of Tartu, Estonia

Marjan Svetličič – University of Ljubljana, Slovenia

Andreja Trtnik – University of Ljubljana, Slovenia

Donata Vianelli – University of Trieste, Italy

The Internationalization Process
MARIN ALEXANDROV MARINOV

Introduction

The internationalization process started at the business level as transactions taking place between developed Western countries have largely similar levels of environmental characteristics and economic development. Alternatively, the conditions of internationalizing were dominated by Western countries, politically and economically supreme, that allowed them to inflict ways of conducting international operations on less developed nations. Currently, the conditions under which international business is conducted are far more complicated. The internationalization process encompasses countries on different level of their economic development, with various political structures, and other environmental characteristics. The democratization of societies and liberalization of business activities create conditions for convergence in circumstances under which international business operations take place. The likelihood that an economically strong country can readily inflict its ways of conducting international business is continuously diminishing. This means that the economic interdependence of businesses, countries, and regions has been constantly reducing the relative power of more developed businesses and countries.

Businesses have been internationalizing their operations worldwide in an attempt to leverage their competencies, capabilities, and expertise. The internationalization process has facilitated the overall economic globalization (Ohmae, 1992; Sassen, 1996). This exercises a positive impact on the scope and intensity of international competition. Internationalization of business brings benefits to firms and regions where it takes place. The growing pace of internationalization has occurred within the boundaries of regional economic integrations, national economies, economic sectors and individual businesses.

It can be argued that through the internationalization of production and markets the world is moving away from an economic system in which national markets are distinct entities with certain degrees of isolation from each other by barriers of different nature towards a system in which national markets are merging into a global marketplace. Hence, a most notable characteristic of current economic integration is the process in which regions, countries, and companies have become increasingly interdependent, representing intrinsic parts of the world economy (Auerbach, 1996).

Brief Outlook on Internationalization Theory

The foundations of the internationalization theory were laid down by Coase (1937). He introduced the notion that there may be conditions under which a firm may find it more efficient to create an internal market rather than enter foreign markets. Those conditions are identified as transaction costs of foreign activities. Williamson (1975) developed the internalization perspective that coupled with the transaction cost theoretical approach emphasized the minimization of transaction costs and the conditions underlying market failure. When adopting the internalization perspective, a firm considering internationalization is faced with the dilemma of either internalizing within its own boundaries (a subsidiary) or forming a collaborative venture with an external partner (externalization). The key issue is to decide upon the most efficient governance mode minimizing transaction costs.

The approach to internationalization introduced by Penrose (1959) focuses on the firm's core competences and the opportunities provided by the foreign environment (Prahalad and Hamel, 1990). The cost-focused view of this tradition is based on the concept that a firm has to have a 'compensating advantage' to counterbalance the 'cost of foreignness' (Kindleberger, 1969). The application of this approach resulted in the identification of technological and marketing skills as key factors for successful internationalization.

A strong body of publications has been developed covering theoretical aspects of the internationalization process (Johanson and Vahlne, 1977; Bilkey and Tesar, 1977; Buckley and Casson, 1979), methods of foreign market servicing (Hedlund and Kverneland, 1983), problems caused by internationalization (Tesar, 1985), the internationalization processual characteristics (Turnbull, 1987), organizational issues of internationalization (Bartlett, 1981), and strategic aspects of internationalization (Joynt, 1989).

The concept of internationalization has evolved over time. For example, Melin (1992) views internationalization as an ongoing process of evolution whereby the firm increases its international involvement as a function of knowledge creation and market commitment. Welch and Luostarinen (1993) support the view that internationalization may include outward and inward patterns of international expansion. Beamish (1990) argues that internationalization should be analyzed in its behavioral and economic aspects. In increasing the understanding of the processual aspects of company internationalisation, the creation, development, and experimentation of process models have played an important role (see, Andersen, 1993; Czinkota, 1982; Cavusgil, 1980; Johanson and Vahlne, 1977).

Vernon (1966) introduced the sequential modes of internationalization. According to him firms initially engage in exporting before adopting foreign direct investment (FDI) with either market-seeking or cost-focused motives. The theory of internationalization supports the idea that exporting is a first step in internationalizing and often plays the role of a 'spring board' to more substantial international involvement. Further internationalization takes place through FDI when its benefits exceed its costs. In mid-1970s Buckley and Casson (1976) included licensing as a mode of internationalizing. Internationalization through contractual modes of market entry such as licensing jeopardizes the know-how and technology of the licensing firm and is regarded as risky in this respect. Joint ventures have been explicitly considered as a mode of internationalization since the mid-1980s (Kogut, 1988).

The Scandinavian Uppsala model of internationalization is typically gradual and sequential, based on the knowledge acquired by the company as it expands from a country-to-country (e.g., Johanson and Wiedersheim-Paul, 1975; Johanson and Vahlne, 1977; Luostarinen, 1979; Luostarinen and Welch, 1990; Vahlne and Nordstrom, 1988). Its supporters bring forward the evolutionary substance of internationalization. Theoretically, the Uppsala model emphasizes the slow and progressive pattern of internationalization that ensures a gradual process of organizational learning.

Dunning (1988) proposed the eclectic paradigm trying to draw on several lines of economic theory. He has brought together the issues of advantages in ownership, location, and internalization. When a firm possesses all advantages its propensity to internationalize increases.

In the late 1980s the network approach to internationalization was introduced emphasizing the fact that individual firms are dependent upon resources that are not under their control. Hence, the existent domestic network of a firm can be utilized for providing connections to networks abroad thus, helping firm's internationalization (Johanson and Mattsson, 1993).

Approaches to Internationalization

There are two principally different approaches to internationalizing, still complementing one another. Countries, economic sectors and companies can either be passively impacted by the internationalization activities or get actively involved in internationalization. Both approaches suppose the application of different modes of international market entry (Cateora and Graham, 1996) that are subdivided in three major groups.

The first group refers to international trade and includes *export* and *import*. Some economists (e.g., Marin, 1992) have researched the concept of internationalization through international trade and its positive or negative impact on gross domestic product (GDP). Through export-led activities, a nation may improve its internationalization eventually resulting in upgraded economic well-being and societal prosperity. This means that ameliorated export performance has a positive effect throughout a country's economy in a variety of advantageous externalities, mainly in the form of technological spillover effects. The involvement in internationalization through export increases the exposure of national economies to international markets. This requires increased efficiency, and innovation activities in technological and marketing areas. Although the international trade is the easiest and most common approach to internationalization, it can enhance GDP and produce positive effects on national economies through upgrading the economic viability of industries and individual companies.

The second group of market entry consists of the contractual modes of *licensing* and *franchising*. Similar to exporting, they are low-risk involving approaches to internationalization in a new market environment. They represent granting the rights and methods for production of goods or services to a host-country firm for a royalty fee. Through applying these modes of market entry in their internationalization processes firms assume low capital involvement and achieve a speedy market entry.

The third group of market entry includes a variety of investment modes. The market imperfection theory supports the notion that firms look constantly for market opportunities. Hence, they are prone to invest abroad, and their decision to do so is explained as a strategy to capitalize on particular capabilities that are not possessed by competitors in foreign countries (Hymer, 1970). International production theory (Dunning, 1980; Fayerweather, 1982) proposes that the tendency of a firm to engage in foreign production depends upon the specific attractions of its home country compared with resource implications and benefits of locating production in another country. Subsequently, the international production theory makes it explicit that investment decisions overseas are dependent not only on resource differentials and potential advantages, but also on government foreign policies of host countries. Internationalization theory puts an emphasis on the assumption that firms strive to develop their own internal markets whenever transactions can be made at lower cost within the firm. According to the internationalization theory the internationalization process involves some forms of vertical integration providing the firm with new opportunities and activities.

The investment modes of market entry involve the formation of *international joint ventures (IJVs), consortia, partially-* or *wholly-owned subsidiaries.* IJVs are either extensions of an existing strategic alliance or formations of new partnerships between two or more partners under a new corporate name. Consortia merge resources for the execution of large projects through forming a group of companies joining to benefit of one participant's location or expertise. The formation of a partially- or wholly-owned subsidiary is through either acquisition or greenfield investment. This mode allows ripping most benefits from internationalization. However, it involves the highest possible risk as it represents the most substantial exposure to environmental factors.

The applied mode of market entry is dependent upon the characteristics of the company intending to get involved in internationalization and the environmental features of a chosen context of internationalization. Companies with greater capabilities and more substantial international experience are more likely to undertake a mode that assumes higher involvement and risk. The less risky the environment, the more likely it is for a firm to undertake a market entry mode that assumes substantial involvement in international business operations. The type of business activities a company decides to implement in its internationalization can also impact the mode of market entry. For instance, companies intending to get involved in sales activities will probably do this through direct exporting, while those considering involvement in manufacturing and assembly activities will most probably choose an investment mode of market entry. The timing of market entry is mostly associated with the provision of a first or early mover advantage (Patterson, 1993; Ryans, 1988). Some research brings evidence that late entrants may perform better than early movers (Olleros, 1986) and no single timing strategy can bring best results (Schnaars, 1986). Competition and number of competitors affect both the mode of market entry and subsequent satisfaction with economic performance (Aaker and Day, 1986). A large market potential by itself can account for a more substantial involvement in internationalizing in a particular national context and impact the decision on a mode of market entry. The anticipated economic performance in a new market relates to the business outlook and impact the amount of dedicated resources and level of involvement (Daniels, 1970). Many factors, among which most important is the mode of market entry (Green and Ryans, 1990), affect the economic performance and the satisfaction from it.

Since the end of World War II there has been a substantial shift, constantly gaining pace, in the way in which businesses have been performing their international operations. The traditionally strong exporting and importing operations have been increasingly supplemented by the overwhelming growth of the contractual and investment modes of foreign market entry. In the period 1982-1998 the volume of the world international trade has risen slightly more than two times, whereas the growth of FDI flows has increased more than eleven-fold (Hill, 2001). The liberalized conditions for undertaking FDI, adopted by the majority of countries worldwide, and seeing foreign investment by international businesses as an appropriate approach of circumventing trade barriers, have been among the most important reasons for the rapid growth in foreign investment. The radical changes in the national environmental characteristics in political, economic, social, legal, and financial aspects have facilitated this dramatic shift in the characteristics of the internationalization process. These changes have spurred spectacular economic restructuring and innovation resulting from economic deregulation and introduction of privatization programs on a great scale allowing foreign capital participation across Latin America, most of Asia, and the whole of Central and Eastern Europe.

The traditional export/import characteristics of international trade have undergone substantial change. An ever increasing amount of exports is only between the headquarters and/or the subsidiaries of one and the same firm operating outside its home base.

Internationalization Forces in Central and Eastern Europe

A variety of forces drive the internationalization process of business activities worldwide. Using the list of factors provided by Lovelock and Yip (1996) their significance for the Central and Eastern European (CEE) context can be evaluated. Forces like common customer needs, economies of scale, government policies and regulations, and transferable competitive advantage are well represented in the contemporary internationalization process in the CEE region and exercise positive impacts on its course.

While common customer needs are mostly unified across CEE, government policies and regulations vary significantly from a country to country and in a particular country over time. The forces of global channels, favorable logistics, and information technology are represented in the activities of a relatively small number of businesses, most of which tend to involve foreign participation in their ownership structure. Because of the collapse of the former state owned distribution channels, comprising wholesalers and retailers, guaranteeing adequate distribution of consumer products represents a challenging task in separate countries and across the region. Logistics is more a barrier rather than a driving force throughout the region. It is a very substantial constraint in the countries less advanced in their transition to market. The development and positive impact of information technology on the internationalization process has recently been boosted, especially in telecommunications through privatization with the participation of foreign capital.

The internationalization of domestically owned CEE businesses is somewhat restricted by their size, experience, capabilities, and resource base. There is a clear trend towards the internationalization of such business within the CEE region. The reasons for this limited internationalization are mostly inherited from the recent communist past or due to restricted transition changes to market-led.

The CEE subsidiaries of multinational corporations (MNCs) have been provided with a better chance to internationalize. Apart from the internationalization of their production activities, those companies tend to be more engaged in export operations, especially the ones manufacturing industrial products. CEE countries with very cheap production bases are used for the manufacturing of consumer goods mainly for export.

Government policy has played a crucial role in the internationalization of CEE countries, economic sectors, and companies. The favorable conditions provided by some CEE countries for the massive penetration of foreign capital and business practices have played a crucial role in the internationalization process. Initially, Hungary, followed by the Czech Republic, Poland, Estonia, and Slovenia are best examples in this respect. The high amounts of FDI inflows in these countries provided their national economies with better opportunities to restructure and innovate. This fact is looked upon favorably by businesses and politicians, and is one of the positive preconditions for the accession of these economies to the European Union (EU).

CEE has been providing MNCs and business investors with strategic opportunities. Many economic sectors received major boosts through FDI. Among the beneficiaries are food, beverage and consumer good providers; electronics; transportation; pulp and paper; pharmaceuticals; oil; mining. Mighty global players have established their presence across the region, such as McDonald's, Philip Morris, Coca Cola, Heineken, Interbrew, IBM, Matsushita and General Motors.

Both MNCs and business investors have shown permanent interest in investing in CEE regarding it as a rapidly expanding market with high potentials. Current investment opportunities vary from country to country. These opportunities encompass possible privatization of most of the companies in the national economies of Albania, Bulgaria, Romania, Slovakia, Ukraine still owned by the state. In most of the Central European economies and the Baltic countries the existing opportunities are in creating new businesses and privatization of utilities and service sectors.

Initially, the internationalization activities of foreign companies in CEE have been negatively impacted by the volatility of the environment in general, including political, economic and social aspects, and currency instability in particular. With the expansion of international business operations in some CEE countries the environmental characteristics and financial stability of the economy have gradually improved providing a better climate for further internationalization on the country level.

For CEE businesses with FDI that have gone international the lessons have been twofold. On the one hand, they have been involved in the internationalization of production and markets on a large scale using the experience, expertise and networks of the foreign investors. On the other hand, their involvement in the decision making process and role in the process of internationalization has been somewhat limited. This is particularly true for former state owned companies that have become targets of hostile acquisitions or for companies that post-acquisition serve mostly or exclusively the domestic market.

Internationalization of Central and Eastern Europe since 1989

Since the collapse of the communist economic order, symbolically represented by the fall of the Berlin Wall, the region of Central and Eastern Europe has embarked on a process of radical political and economic changes. During the recent communist past this part of the world had been developing inward political and economic interdependency materialized in the creation and functioning of the Warsaw Pact and the Council for Mutual Economic Assistance (CMEA). These two international structures seized their existence in the early 1990s. It has become necessary for the countries in the region to find alternative ways and solutions for their political and economic systems and development.

With varying degrees of success, CEE countries have been departing from their totalitarian political systems, state ownership of productive assets, and central planning of the economy. This process has been coupled with the introduction of democratic principles for the functioning of society and economic reforms focused on liberalization providing more freedom for private business initiatives. On the whole, market oriented policies have reduced the constraints and lowered the barriers for domestic and international business activities thus, radically changing the environment of recent totally regulated economic activities.

The shift of ownership from state to private has been legally guaranteed and introduced through various methods of privatization. The emphasis on a specific method or methods has varied geographically across the region and over time in a particular national economy. National economies have been in great need of foreign investment for their economic restructuring and renewal. After the introduction of liberalization of economic activities, FDI has entered the economies of the region mainly through participation in privatization and greenfield activities.

The degree of FDI penetration in any particular CEE country has been dependent on the environmental conditions, progress made in transition, historical affiliation, cultural links, psychic distance, market size and growth and natural resource base. The stock of FDI in some CEE countries is presented in Table 1. Data show uneven spread of cumulative FDI skewed towards the Central European and Baltic countries. The major deterrent to FDI inflows into a specific country has proved to be the level of country risk. However, risk has been perceived differently by various multinational corporations depending mostly on country of origin and corporate culture. While the structure of cumulative FDI in terms of country of origin varies from country to country, the dominant players are MNCs from Germany and the US German investment has been triggered among other factors by geographic proximity and historical relationships. US MNCs have been risk takers seizing new exciting opportunities.

From the very early years of implementation of political, economic and social reforms CEE countries have tried to change the pattern of their international trade. After the collapse of the CMEA market and the consequent financial insolvency of many of the countries in the region changes in international trade became a must. On the initiative of the then Hungarian prime minister, top government representatives of ex-Czechoslovakia, Hungary, and Poland met in the Hungarian town of Visegrad in early 1991. They adopted the declaration on cooperation between the three countries on the path for advancing towards European integration facilitating international economic exchanges. The purpose of the declaration was to mobilize joint efforts for the integration of the participating countries in institutions of the EU and through this, to join political, economic, security, and legal systems of the Union. The Central European Free Trade Agreement (CEFTA) was signed in Krakow, Poland on December 21, 1992 including Hungary, Poland, and then splitting Czechoslovakia into the Czech Republic and Slovakia. Gradually, CEFTA incorporated other countries into the Agreement. Thus, Slovenia joined CEFTA in 1996, Romania in 1997, followed by Bulgaria. Membership in CEFTA became a prerequisite for eventual accession to the EU. The impact of CEFTA on inter-regional economic relationships, mostly international trade, has been positive. Additionally, CEFTA membership eases economic relations of CEE countries with the EU. All CEFTA member countries have applied for full EU membership. This creates conditions for expanding the internationalization of CEE economies in and outside the region. The structure of exports of CEFTA member countries in 1997 is presented in Table 2. Data in Table 2 show that the exports of CEFTA countries in 1997 were highly concentrated. The first five partners accounted for between 49.8 per cent of Romanian exports up to 67.3 per cent in the case of Slovakia. Germany was the major export partner of the Czech Republic, Hungary, Poland, and Slovenia accounting for 37.3 per cent of Hungarian exports.

Table 1 Cumulative FDI in CEE (in US$ billion)

Country	1990	1993	1996	1999	FDI per capita in 1999 (US$)
Bulgaria	0.0	0.1	0.4	2.3	285
Croatia	n/a	0.1	0.9	3.6	873
Czech R.	0.0	3.6	8.5	17.5	1,720
Estonia	n/a	0.4	1.0	2.5	1,950
Hungary	0.6	5.6	15.0	19.3	1,990
Latvia	n/a	0.1	0.9	3.9	1,695
Lithuania	n/a	0.1	0.7	2.1	595
Poland	0.1	2.3	11.5	28.0	740
Romania	0.0	0.2	1.2	5.4	240
Russia	n/a	1.2	6.3	18.6	125
Slovakia	n/a	0.5	1.4	2.1	395
Slovenia	n/a	1.0	2.1	3.0	1,590
Ukraine	n/a	0.4	1.3	3.2	60

Source: Business Central Europe (January 2001).

Table 2   Structure of exports of CEFTA member countries in 1997

Country	First partner	Second partner	Third partner	Fourth partner	Fifth partner	Others
Czech R.	Germany 35.7%	Slovakia 12.9%	Austria 6.4%	Poland 5.7%	Italy 3.7%	35.6%
Hungary	Germany 37.3%	Austria 11.5%	Italy 6.2%	Russia 5.1%	France 3.8%	36.1%
Poland	Germany 32.9%	Russia 8.4%	Italy 5.9%	Holland 4.7%	France 4.4%	43.7%
Romania	Italy 19.5%	Germany 16.8%	France 5.5%	Turkey 4.2%	US 3.8%	50.2%
Slovakia	Czech R. 26.7%	Germany 22.3%	Austria 7.2%	Italy 5.6%	Poland 5.5%	32.7%
Slovenia	Germany 29.4%	Italy 14.4%	Hungary 10.0%	Austria 6.8%	France 5.5%	33.9%

Source: CEFTA Official Statistics.

Table 3   EU and intra-CEFTA exports to the first five partners of CEFTA member countries in 1997

Country	Exports to EU member countries	Exports to other CEFTA member countries
Czech R.	45.8%	18.6%
Hungary	58.8%	0.0%
Poland	47.9%	0.0%
Romania	41.8%	0.0%
Slovakia	35.1%	32.2%
Slovenia	56.1%	10.0%

Sources: CEFTA Official Statistics.

Data considering EU and intra-CEFTA exports taking into account the first five partners of CEFTA member countries are given in Table 3. Hungary and Slovenia managed to direct more than 50 per cent of their exports to EU countries. While Hungary, Poland, and Romania did not have an export partner from CEFTA member countries, the Czech Republic and Slovakia were substantially dependent on intra-CEFTA trade mainly taking place between themselves.

Meanwhile, each CEE country started to reorient its international trade shifting from high dependency on the CEE region towards gradual involvement in economic exchanges outside CEE. Table 4 reveals the degree of internationalization of certain CEE countries in and outside the region in 1996.

The countries most advanced in their transition to market have managed to reduce successfully their dependence on the CEE region and attract the largest stock of FDI. The leader has been Estonia, followed by the Czech Republic, Latvia and Slovenia. Bulgaria and Romania have experienced great difficulties in increasing their involvement in international trade and in internationalizing outside the CEE region. Hungary and Poland have also found it difficult to expand their international trade but have successfully shifted their trade relationships towards partners outside CEE.

Table 4   Internationalization of CEE countries through foreign trade

Country	Ratio of the average of total exports and imports to country's GDP in 1996	Ratio of the average of exports and imports outside the CEE region to country's GDP in 1996
Bulgaria	32	11
Czech R.	60	42
Estonia	80	62
Hungary	33	28
Latvia	50	39
Lithuania	30	23
Poland	26	21
Romania	30	12
Slovakia	63	25
Slovenia	49	41
Ukraine	44	14

Sources: UN/ECE, East-West Investment News, World Bank, EBRD.

There are clear trends in the internationalization of companies of industrialized countries in the CEE context. In the first years of transition, modes of market entry assuming less involvement in internationalization of companies were implemented. Depending on the national context they varied from exporting to countries like Ukraine and involvement in IJV formation as in Hungary. Over time the choice of market entry modes started to develop and involved more substantial application of mode of market entry presupposing higher involvement in internationalization. Such were acquisitions and greenfield investments gradually spreading all over the region starting from Hungary and going to the Czech Republic, Poland, Estonia, and beyond. While the speed of development and degree of involvement have been substantial in the countries more advanced in their transition to market-led, the extent of passive involvement in the countries less advanced in their internationalization has been not very significant.

Table 5   Internationalization of some CEE countries through outward FDI in million US$

Country	1994	1995	1996	1997	1998	1994-8	Per cent out of CEE	FDI per capita (US$)
Czech R	116	37	155	28	55	391	27	39.3
Hungary	49	43	n/a	433	478	1,003	36	99.3
Poland	29	42	53	45	316	485	29	12.5
Russia	101	357	770	2,604	1,025	4,857	26	32.5
Slovakia	14	10	48	95	134	301	11	51.9

Sources: IMF and UNCTAD.

Apart from experiencing the impact of passive internationalization the economies of the Czech Republic, Hungary, Poland, Russia, Slovakia, and Slovenia gradually started to be involved in outward FDI activities. Table 5 contains data for the outward FDI from some CEE countries. The most substantial FDI outflow in absolute terms in the period 1994-1998 was made by Russia and Hungary. Taking into account the countries' populations the best performing outward investing countries were Hungary, Slovakia, and the Czech Republic. While Slovakia invested mainly in the CEE region the other countries made substantial efforts to internationalize through outward FDI outside CEE.

Future Trends

What can be said about the internationalization of CEE businesses in the foreseeable future? What will be the impact of internationalization on the competitiveness of the regional and national economies, and individual businesses? There is clear evidence that the internationalization process in CEE has fostered international competitiveness on regional, national, industry and company levels. What is still unsure is whether the future development of competitiveness on regional level will become uniformal. To what extent will the different industrial sectors become internationally competitive. Will that result in a clear cut divide between loser and winner countries, economic sectors and businesses?

The scope and magnitude of activities for further development of internationalization is enormous and difficult to be currently embraced. However, the decision for the expansion of the European Union will benefit the internationalization of those CEE countries that have managed to internationalize their economies significantly during the transition period. There will be nations left behind that will remain beyond the embrace of the European Union (e.g., Ukraine, and Albania).

There are universal tasks for further internationalization, though the degree of change required varies from country to country. These are: the overall modernization of national economies, guaranteeing law enforcement, development of internationally competitive financial sectors and other business support structures, the establishment of adequate regulatory institutions and practices. Countries like Hungary, the Czech Republic, Poland, Slovenia and Estonia have made substantial progress in these respects.

References

Aaker, D. and Day, G. (1986), 'The Peril of High Growth Markets', *Strategic Management Journal*, vol. 7, no. 5, pp. 409-421.

Andersen, O. (1993), 'On the Internationalization Process of Firms: A Critical Analysis', *Journal of International Business Studies*, vol. 24, no. 2, pp. 209-231.

Auerbach, P. (1996), 'Firms, Competitiveness and the Global Economy', in M. Mackintosh, Brown, N. Costello, G. Dawson, G. Thompson and A. Trigg (eds), *Economics and Changing Economies*, London: The Open University, pp. 393-425.

Bartlett, C. (1981), 'Multinational Structural Change: Evolution versus Reorganization', in L. Otterbeck (ed.) *The Management of Headquarters Subsidiary Relationships in Multinational Corporations*, London: Gower, pp. 79-96.

Beamish, P. (1990), 'The Internationalization of Small Ontario Firms: A Research Agenda', in A. Rugman (ed.) *Research in the Global Strategic Management - International Business Research for the Twenty First Century*, Greenwich, Connecticut: JAI Press Inc., pp. 77-92.

Bilkey, W. and Tesar, G. (1977), 'The Export Behavior of Small-Sized Wisconsin Manufacturing Firms', *Journal of International Business Studies*, vol. 8, no. 1, pp. 93-98.

Buckley, P. and Casson, M. (1976), *The Future of the Multinational Enterprise*, New York: Holmes and Meier.

Buckley, P. and Casson, M. (1979), 'A Theory of International Operations', in *European Research in International Business*, Amsterdam: North Holland.

Cateora, P. and Graham, J. (1996), *International Marketing*, Tenth Edition, New York: McGraw-Hill.

Cavusgil, S. (1980), 'On the Internationalization Process of Firms', *European Research*, vol. 8, no. 11, pp. 273-281.

Coase, R. (1937), 'The Nature of the Firm', *Economica*, vol. 5, pp. 386-405.

Czinkota, M. (1982), *Export Development Strategies: US Promotion Policies*, New York: Praeger Publishers.

Daniels, J. (1970), 'Recent Foreign Direct Manufacturing Investment in the United States', *Journal of International Business Studies*, vol. 1, no. 1, pp. 125-132.

Dunning, J. (1980), 'Towards an Eclectic Theory of International Production: Some Empirical Rests', *Journal of International Business Studies*, vol. 11, no. 1, pp. 9-31.

Dunning, J. (1988), *Explaining International Production*, London: Irwin.

Fayerweather, J. (1982), *International Business Strategy and Administration*, Cambridge, Massachusetts: Ballinger.

Green, D, and Ryans, A. (1990), 'Entry Strategies and Market Performance: Casual Modeling of a Business Simulation', *Journal of Product Innovation Management*, vol. 7, pp. 45-58.

Hedlund, G. and Kverneland, A. (1983), 'Are Entry Strategies for Foreign Markets Changing? The Case of Swedish Investments in Japan', *Working Paper Series 1983/12*, Stockholm: Stockholm School of Economics.

Hill, C. W. L. (2001) *International Business: Competing in the Global Marketplace*, Third Edition, New York: McGraw-Hill.

Hymer, S. (1970), 'The Efficiency (Contradictions) of Multinational Corporations', *American Economic Review*, vol. 60, pp. 441-448.

Johanson, J. and Mattsson, L.-G. (1993), 'Internationalization in Industrial Systems', in P. Buckley and P. Ghauri (eds) *The Internationalization of the Firm: A Reader*, London: Academic Press, pp. 16-31.

Johanson, J. and Vahlne, J.-E. (1977), 'The Internationalization Process of the Firm - A Model of Knowledge Development and Increased Foreign Market Commitment', *Journal of International Business Studies*, vol. 8, no. 1, pp. 25-39.

Johanson, J. and Wiedersheim-Paul, F. (1975), 'The internationalization of the Firm: Four Swedish Cases', *Journal of Management Studies*, vol. 12, no. 3, pp. 305-322.

Joynt, P. (1989), 'International Strategy: A Study of Norwegian Companies', in S. Prasad (ed.) *Advances in International Comparative Management*, Volume Four, Greenwich, Connecticut: JAI Press Inc., pp. 179-201.

Kindleberger, C. (1969), *American Business Abroad*, New Haven, Connecticut: Yale University Press.

Kogut, B. (1988), 'Joint Ventures: Theoretical and Empirical Perspective', *Strategic Management Journal*, vol. 9, pp. 319-332.

Lovelock, C. and Yip, G. (1996), 'Developing Global Strategies for Service Businesses', *California Management Review*, vol. 38, no. 2, pp. 64-87.

Luostarinen, R. (1979), *Internationalization of the Firm*, Ph.D. Thesis, Helsinki: Helsinki School of Economics.

Luostarinen, R. and Welch, L. (1990), *International Business Operations*, Helsinki: Helsinki School of Economics.

Marin, D. (1992), 'Is the Export-Led Hypothesis Valid for Industrialized Countries', *The Review of Economics and Statistics*, vol. 74, pp. 678-688.

Melin, L. (1992), 'Internationalization as a Strategy Process', *Strategic Management Journal*, vol. 13, no. 1, pp. 99-118.

Ohmae, K. (1992), *The Borderless World: Power and Strategy of in the Global Marketplace*, London: Fontana.

Olleros, F. (1986), 'Emerging Industries and the Burnout of Pioneers', *Journal of Product Innovation Management*, vol. 3, pp. 5-18.

Patterson, W. (1993), 'First-Mover Advantage: The Opportunity Curve', *Journal of Management Studies*, vol. 30, no. 5, pp. 759-778.

Penrose, E. (1959), *The Theory of Growth of the Firm*, London: Basil Blackwell.

Prahalad, C. and Hamel, G. (1990) 'The Core Competence of and the Corporation', *Harvard Business Review*, May, pp. 71-97.

Ryans, A. (1988), 'Strategic Market Entry Factors and Market Share Achievements in Japan', *International Journal of Business Studies*, vol. 19, pp. 389-409.

Sassen, S. (1996), *Losing Control? Sovereignty in an Age of Globalization*, New York: Columbia University Press.

Schnaars, S. (1986), 'When Entering Growth Markets, Are Pioneers Better than Poachers?', *Business Horizons*, vol. 29, pp. 27-36.

Tesar, G. (1985), 'Assessment of Perceived Problems Related to Direct Investment by Small and Medium-Sized Western European Firms in the Upper Midwest as an Alternative Strategy to Direct Export', *International Symposium on the Interrelationships between Exports and Imports*, National Center for Export-Import Studies, Georgetown University, Washington, D.C., USA, November 13-15.

Turnbull, P. (1987), 'A Challenge to the Stages Theory of the Internationalization Process', in P. Rosson and S. Reed (eds) *Managing Export Entry and Expansion*, New York: Praeger, pp. 123-139.

Vahlne, J.-E. and Nordstrom, K. (1988), 'Choices of Market Channel in a Strategic Perspective', in N. Hood and J.-E. Vahlne (eds) *Strategies in Global Competition: Selected Papers from the Prince Berlin Symposium*, New York: Croom Helm, pp. 256-281.

Vernon, R. (1966), 'International Investment and International Trade in the Product Cycle', *Quarterly Journal of Economics*, vol. 80, pp. 190-207.

Welch, L. and Luostarinen, R. (1993), 'Inward and Outward Connections in Internationalization', *Journal of International Marketing*, vol. 1, no. 1, pp. 46-58.

Williamson, O. (1975), *Markets and Hierarchies: Analysis and Antitrust Implications*, New York: The Free Press.

PART I:

INTERNATIONALIZATION OF NATIONAL ECONOMIES

1 Economic Restructuring and Internationalization of Slovenia[1]

YOJI KOYAMA

Introduction

Contemporary Slovenia is located in the northwestern part of the Balkan Peninsula, and has borders with Italy, Austria, Hungary, and Croatia. It is a small country with an area of 20,251 square kilometers and population of two million. With 90.1% of its inhabitants being Slovene, the country was ethnically the most homogeneous among the republics and autonomous provinces of former Yugoslavia. Slovenia was the richest republic in ex-Yugoslavia and its per capita GDP was more than two and a half times higher than the Yugoslav average. At the beginning of the 1980s with only 8.3% of the population of then Yugoslavia, Slovenia was producing 18% of the Yugoslav GDP and accounted for 25% of Yugoslavia's total exports. Some 33% of all Yugoslav goods exported to Western markets were produced in the Republic of Slovenia. Slovenia's contribution was 25% of the total revenue of the Federal Budget[2].

Historically speaking, the Slovene nation had been under the rule of foreign super powers for more than eleven hundred years, and from the second half of eighth century to the end of the World War I under the rule of Germany and Austria[3]. In 1918, owing to the defeat of the Austro-Hungarian Empire, Slovenia became a part of the Kingdom of Serbs, Croats, and Slovene that was renamed Yugoslavia in 1929. Tito re-established Yugoslavia as a socialist country, including Slovenia, after World War II. Since 1950 ex-Yugoslavia constructed a decentralized self-managed socialism that was based on 'social ownership' of the means of production, and had been developing with a comparatively high growth rate until the late 1970s. As long as the Yugoslav economy was developing satisfactorily, the various nationalities within Yugoslavia lived together happily. But at the beginning of the 1980s the Yugoslav economy began to stagnate and was mired with crises during the mid-1980s. The League of Communists of Yugoslavia (LCY) failed to produce any effective solutions for overcoming the economic crisis[4].

This is why the LCY, which had aimed at binding the various republics and nationalities into a country, gradually lost its prestige. Antagonism among republics became reflected in the LCY, and finally in January 1990, the LCY split. From April through December 1990 free elections based on multi-party system were carried out successively in each republic. Slovenia conducted the first free election in April. As a result, a noncommunist government was formed, however, the newly elected President was the 'Socio-Democratic Communist', Milan Kucan.

With the passage of nearly 50 years since World War II, which was a unifying experience for the nationalities of Yugoslavia who fought for the liberation of their country, the international environment has drastically changed. For example, Gorbachev, who promoted *Perestroika*, practically abandoned the principle of limited sovereignty in 1988, and subsequently from 1989 to 1990 socialism collapsed in Central and East European countries one after another. Thus, the Yalta regime had collapsed and the cold war came to an end. Also disappearing was the menace of the Soviet Union, a factor that had united nationalities in the former Yugoslavia into a single country. In addition, the fear of German and Italian expansionism, which was traditionally a great threat to the Slovene nation, came to an end. Additionally, the European Union (EU) was pursuing a further integration. 'The end of the Cold war made the previous deep political, ideological and military gap along Slovenia's Western and Northern borders with Italy and Austria politically obsolete and economically harmful. The Slovenes were the most exposed and sensitive within the former Yugoslavia to the demonstration effect of the West's growing affluence, its economic liberalism and political democracy' (Bebler, 1997).

Therefore, Slovenes became eager to return to Europe and join the stream of the European integration[5]. In June 1991 Slovenia declared its independence. It introduced a new currency the tolar (SIT) on October 8, 1991. This aimed at de-linking Slovenia's monetary policy from that of the Yugoslav Federation, thus breaking the links with the hyperinflation trends of the past (World Bank, 1999b). EU membership became a primary goal for both the Government and opposition parties. On June 10, 1996 the Government of Slovenia concluded the Association Agreement with the EU, and at the same time applied for EU membership.

In this chapter I would like to address the following points:

- First, when I visited Slovenia in April 1991, that is, immediately before the Federation's breakup, I was skeptical about its independence on the grounds that Slovene industries, which were competitive in the Yugoslav markets, were less competitive in European markets. It is said that at that time many Slovene businessmen represented by the Chamber of Commerce were also skeptical[6]. Eight years later, however, the performance of Slovene economy seems good in spite of the previous anticipation. What is the reason for its success?

- Second, Slovenia faces the tasks of transition to a market economy in the same way as other transition countries. Of course, as Slovenia had a decentralized self-managed socialism that was quite different from the Soviet type, the transition is from semi-market economy to complete market economy. However, Slovenia had to tackle many tasks in the process of transition. In what way were these tasks accomplished?

- Third, Slovenia aims to become a member of the EU by 2003. For that purpose, Slovenia accepted *Acquis Communautaire*, the whole of a number of laws that EU member countries have accumulated on the basis of its basic treaty[7]. This obligates Slovenia, among other requirements, to restructure its economy and improve its legal framework in order to satisfy the requirements of the EU. To what extent have these tasks been completed so far and what tasks remain?

Slovenia's Strategy for Survival and Development

Aspirations by Slovenia to join the EU were expressed as early as 1989, when the country was a part of former Yugoslavia. In 1989, soon after 'the program Europe 1992' was adopted, studies were made in the former Yugoslavia on how to prepare for the new Europe. A special Coordinating Commission for Europe 1992 was established in Slovenia in order to coordinate all adjustment activities. After its independence, EU membership became Slovenia's first priority. However, gaining EU membership is not easy. To begin with, Slovenia joined the EFTA. According to Svetličič, the EFTA has been a 'waiting room' for the EU. Joining EFTA basically means the application of EU standards and rules (de facto economic harmonization), but not having the opportunity to participate in their creation. In other words, it is the second-best solution to the EU option (Svetličič, 1998).

Then, Slovenia tried to cooperate with CEFTA countries (initially comprising Poland, Hungary, the Czech Republic, and Slovakia). Gradually, with the development in CEFTA and with the difficulties Slovenia encountered in negotiating the Association Agreement with the EU, joining CEFTA became a more attractive means of substituting the lost markets from former Yugoslavia. CEFTA is on a macro-strategic level perceived a 'breathing space' for those parts of Slovene industry that are losing competitiveness. In November 1995, the Accession Agreement of Slovenia to CEFTA was signed with membership from January 1, 1996.

At first a simple yearning toward the EU (Euro euphoria) was dominant in Slovenia. Later, however, a skeptical viewpoint (Euro skepticism) became a little bit stronger. This change was related to disillusionment as a reflection of the European incompetence to resolve the war in Bosnia and Herzegovina, and the 'siding of the EU with Italy' as understood by the general public when Italy blocked the Slovene Association Agreement (Svetličič, 1998). To supplement the latter point, in 1994 Berlusconi Government of Italy demanded compensation for Italian citizens' properties which were confiscated by the Yugoslav Government immediately after World War II. Possession of land by foreigners is in contravention of the Slovene Constitution. This problem was finally resolved by the 'Spanish compromise'[8]. The Constitution was revised as a result of a referendum. Article 68 of the Constitution has been revised so that foreigners now have the right to acquire the right of possession of real estate as the law and international contract stipulates provided that there is reciprocity in the country of the foreigners concerned (Svetličič, 1998). The removal of barriers made it possible for Slovenia to conclude the Association Agreement with the EU in June 1996.

After independence, the Slovene Government felt it necessary to envisage various long-term strategies and visions. In mid-1993 the Government requested the Institute for Macroeconomic Analysis and Development to create a long-term economic development strategy. In April 1995, the Institute produced an elaborate report titled 'The Strategy for Economic Development: Approaching Europe, Growth, Competitiveness and Integration'. The main goals of this strategy are:

- faster economic growth and catching-up with developed European countries;
- higher competitiveness of the Slovene economy;
- inclusion into European integration;
- permanent sustenance of economic growth from the ecological, social and ethnic stand-points[9].

To achieve these main goals, Svetličič states that increasing competitiveness can be achieved only in stable macroeconomic conditions along with development of an adequate social infrastructure. The quality of labor force, faster technological progress, and the growth of entrepreneurship are regarded as essential for development. The role of the state is regarded as complementary. Companies are to function independently in market conditions (Svetličič, 1998). Competitiveness should not be taken simply as reduced prices. The major objective is not to strengthen competitiveness by reducing prices, but to improve the quality, marketing, technological development, and to redirect into production of goods in higher prices classes (Svetličič, 1998).

It is very interesting to learn that Svetličič compared Slovenia with Japan. He reports that a link between liberalization and competition policy similar to that made by Japan, for instance, is not contemplated. What Japan did was to shield certain industries from foreign competition, but simultaneously stimulate competition among local companies within sectors. Today globalization and particularly the small size of the national economy of Slovenia make such policy infeasible (Svetličič, 1998).

Svetličič's hypothesis is that the costs of staying outside are higher. Costs of non-integrating basically are the costs of fragmented small markets which are now operating below minimum efficiency, and all kinds of related inefficiencies (Svetličič, 1998).

In parallel with the application for EU membership, the Slovene Government applied for NATO membership. A majority of the population supported the Government's line. In public opinion poll in March 1997, 62 percent of the respondents supported the government policy in terms of NATO (an increase from 44 percent in 1994/95 period). This percentage is higher than the support for the EU membership (53 percent), which was expressed at the referendum in April 1997 (Svetličič, 1998). In NATO's eastward enlargement Slovenia was placed in the first group of candidates together with Poland, Hungary, and the Czech Republic. Slovenia was not made a member of NATO as it did not to get the support of the US.

Next I would like to examine what considerations the strategy for survival and development is grounded on. In this regard, Svetličič's paper 'Small Countries in a Globalized World: Their Honeymoon or Twilight?' is highly informative. His opinion can be summarized in the following two points:

• First, fundamental technological changes, the information revolution and related changes, have made small countries (SCs) more viable today than they were 'yesterday', the external environment is enhancing smallness. In view of globalization tendencies and the increasing importance of economies of scale and scope, the thesis is that SCs cannot survive and should be rejected.

* Second, the viability of a SC in the globalized economy depends to a large extent on its ability to swiftly adapt to the changing external environment (Svetličič, 1997).

Table 1.1   Strengths and weaknesses of small countries

Strengths   Weaknesses

Strengths	Weaknesses
a. Advantages of a small social and political area in which social cohesion is more easily achieved, policies better implemented and the system more stable;	a. Weak position international relations due to the lack of different kinds of power (influence);
b. Absence of responsibility for the international order which might be costly to large states;	b. External policy/system and conditions (e. g., growth rates, demand conditions) create dependency;
c. Stronger and swifter adjustment capability (flexibility, speed of adjustment, selection of right policies);	c. Lack of natural assets, labor, local factor conditions, or, better put, the whole complex of national diamond of competitive advantages;
d. Better possibilities for specialization (gains from international trade, investments and specialization also by stronger internationalization);	d. Inability to realize economies of scale;
e. Gaining the difference between higher world prices and lower national ones (price takers);	e. Limited financial funds. No possibilities for more ambitious innovation-led strategies;
f. Increasingly important gains of better educational systems in view of the increased importance of human capital and human relations as a production factor;	f. Easy monopolization of local industries;
g. High technologies are relatively more powerful weapons for small firms and countries than for large ones.	g. Weak possibilities for equal partnership in strategic alliances as a growing modality of international integration.

Source: Svetličič, 1997.

In order to support these arguments, the strengths and weaknesses of small countries can be compared and examined (see, Table 1.1). On the one hand, weaknesses of small countries include: a weak position in international relations due to the lack of different kinds of power; lack of natural resources, labor and local factor conditions; an inability to realize economies of scale due to a small domestic market; limited financial funds and R&D capacities, etc.

On the other hand, strengths of small countries include: more easily achieved social (cultural and religious) cohesion, better implemented policies and more stable system; absence of responsibility for the international order which might be costly to large states; stronger and swifter adjustment capability; better possibilities for specialization; computerization and telecommunications which are relatively more powerful weapons for small firms and countries than for large ones, etc.

Similarly Svetličič (1997) compares and examines threats (Table 1.2) and opportunities for small countries (Table 1.3). He stresses that despite the weaknesses and threats mentioned above small countries have now strengths and opportunities that surpass their weaknesses and threats. In his opinion, smallness of domestic markets is not important. Access to the world markets is decisively important. Small countries like Slovenia need not have a whole set of industries. Instead, they should find good areas appropriate to them, that is niches, and specialize in those areas. For that purpose, they should thoroughly internationalize all kinds of activities.

Table 1.2   Threats for small countries

a. Erosion of sovereignty with all resulting consequences for political and cultural autonomy (threats of cultural homogenization);

b. Securities risks, higher vulnerability to external political influences, high dependency on external conditions;

c. Oligopolization of the world market in which the powerful have advantages of setting prices and general conditions;

d. Homogenization of consumer patterns which increases the importance of economies of scale and scope;

e. Weaker potential of establishing private (firm) standards after being taken over by public authorities (states, regional groupings) and their related public standards.

Source: Svetličič, 1997.

Table 1.3 Opportunities for small countries

a. Strengthening democracy in the world opens possibilities for the creation of even more small states; b. Integrating with other countries compensating for otherwise weak security positions with strong collective security systems; c. The relative weakening of the importance of military rather than economic power gives SCs a chance to increase their influence in international relations since they have potential for promising economic growth; d. Achieving an influential position in one (specialized) area, gaining influence in other areas; e. The possibility of swift adjustment and better forecasting; f. Better access to world markets as a result of liberalization of international trade. What is important is not so much a large national market, but smooth access to the world market; g. Enjoying free rider benefits and externalizing costs; h. Benefits by imitating other R&D (free rider). By employing time-based competition, by speedy imitation of technological leaders in view of very fast technological changes, SCs can improve their profit-making capacities; i. By globalization (outward FDI, strategic alliances), enabling realization of economies of scale and scope and gaining access to the knowledge of others; j. Employment of productive combinations of imitation and innovation development strategies gives opportunities to exploit ever steeper learning curves; k. Decreasing transportation and communication costs today enables SC participation in the global economy also in areas which were previously limited to large countries; l. increasing importance of created assets; SCs' capacity to create such assets is relatively stronger than in case of natural or physical assets; m. Application of flexible technologies decrease the relative importance of economies of scale; n. Through the increasing importance of international trade in intermediate products, SCs/firms can more easily find appropriate niches as suppliers to large ones; o. Increasing the importance of differentiated products and services and customizing them to local needs make FDI in SCs more attractive and opens up opportunities for more local R&D driven FDI; p. Access to integrated financial markets presents an opportunity to overcome (at least in the short- and medium-term) the limitations of restricted national savings capacity.

Source: Svetličič, 1997.

The Research Center for International Competitiveness of the Ministry of Economic Affairs has been creating a series of industrial policies. 'Strategy for Increasing the Competitiveness Capabilities of Slovenian Industry', which was produced by the Center, was based on the same awareness of the problems involved in Svetličič's paper. I can not afford to explicate it here, but its essence can be summarized as follows: As a rule, Slovenian companies have too wide a portfolio of products, a result of which are low economies of scale and an inadequate emphasis on the development of technology and research, and on the commercialization of new products. Henceforth, Slovenia should lay more emphasis on marketing. The development of Slovenian trademarks is the most important requirement for competitiveness on a world scale. Companies should expand their presence on existing markets and penetrate new market segments and niches. The level of technological complexity of products and production processes is in direct proportion with value added per employee. As for the technological complexity measured by value added, in 1978, its level of Germany was 3.1 times that of Slovenia and the gap has since increased to 5.02 times. In this view, the raising of the technological complexity level must be made an important goal. Measures to attain it include: technological modernization of Slovenian industry; introduction of information technology in companies; financing of modernization in companies; management education and industrial training; reconstruction of technostructure (those groups between top management and workers, who work out information and on the basis of it make decisions in their capacity as a company's brain); increase of the share in GDP of investment in fixed assets (from 18% in 1993 to more than 25% in the year 2000); stimulation of small and medium-sized companies; promotion of inward foreign investments. (Dimovski, 1996).

To what extent have these strategies succeeded? Let us examine the economic performance.

Economic Performance

The Costs and Benefits of Secession and Independence

Slovenia has experienced 'double transition, from a socialist to a market economy and from a regional economy to a national economy' (Mencinger, 1996). The country shared advantages of an early start in making market-oriented reforms in the former Yugoslavia (the first in mid-1960s), maintained some advantages of its own, and was therefore in a better position than other former socialist countries to implement economic reforms, to adapt to 'European values', and to adhere to sound economic policies. The famous Hungarian economist, Janos Kornai, explains causes of serious depression in transitional countries using what he calls a 'transitional depression'. In his opinion, a transitional depression is caused by the transformation from supply-constrained economies to demand-constrained ones (Kornai, 1995). In the case of Slovenia, however, the transitional recession was not so serious. Because the coordination of the economy had been for many years decentralized, the impacts of insufficient demand had prevailed over those of supply shortages in the 1980s, and most of its exports had been oriented towards Western Europe. More serious were costs the caused by its secession and independence (Mencinger, 1996).

The costs of secession and independence have been as follows:

- The Slovene economy has been badly hit by the secession itself and, even more so, by the subsequent political and economic developments in the remnants of the former Yugoslav Federation.
- The 'supply shock' added considerably to inflationary pressures in the first months after independence.
- Slovenia also suffered damage because of hostile actions against business units in other Yugoslav republics, particularly because of asymmetry of ownership. In 1990, there were 2,710 business units and 62 companies owned by Slovene companies in other republics compared to only 690 units and 9 companies owned by other republics in Slovenia.
- The links with the rest of the world have remained hindered by other unresolved issues such as responsibility for the Yugoslav foreign debt and foreign currency reserves, the non-financial assets, 2,500 different bi- and multi-lateral agreements on export quota, transport licenses, etc. (Mencinger, 1997).

However, these issues proved to be relatively less important. It was the near disappearance of the Yugoslav market of 23 million people that has been most important and difficult to overcome. In terms of the structure of sales and purchase in 1990, 57.3% of total sales of the Slovene companies were sold to Slovene markets, 17.9% was sold to other countries, and

24.8% was sold to other republics of former Yugoslavia. More than 63% of total purchases made by Slovenes originated in Slovenia, 15.2% in other countries, and 21.6% in other republics of former Yugoslavia. Mencinger calculated 'normal' value of 'exports proper' in 1992. Multiplying this value by the proportion of sales to other republics of Yugoslavia to sales to other countries (24.8/17.9), he got value of 'normal' exports to Yugoslavia in 1992. He has estimated losses by deducting actual exports from 'normal' exports. According to his estimates, Slovenia lost 74.1% of 'normal' exports to Yugoslavia, 18.8% of 'normal' exports proper, and 45.2% of 'normal' total exports (Mencinger, 1997).

Such a drastic reduction of trade with the former Yugoslav republics was the principal cause of the depression. The GDP declined in 1991 and 1992 by 8.9% and 5.5% respectively. The unemployment rate, which was 2.6% in 1989, rose to 7.3% in 1991, and 9.1% in 1993. The most seriously affected groups were young job seekers and the unskilled. While the overall rate of unemployment in 1993 was 9.1%, it was 24.2% in the age group 15 to 24 years (Svetlik, 1997).

Slovene companies endeavored to increase their exports to West European markets in order to substitute for plummeting exports to the former Yugoslav markets. In 1992 exports increased by 33% and imports by 28%. The results in 1993 were far less impressive. Total exports decreased by 9% while total imports increased by 5.9%. The drastic decline in total exports was caused mainly by the collapse of trade with the former Yugoslavia that plunged by 37% (from US$ 1,508 million to US$ 963 million). Particularly important in this difficult period was the relative openness of the German market (Mencinger, 1997). The share of the EU in the total exports of Slovenia increased from 60.9% in 1992 to 67.2% in 1995, and its share in the total imports increased from 59.6% to 68.9% in the same period. The driving force behind Slovene exports to the EU were those manufactured goods that were redirected from the former Yugoslav markets. Specifically, they were footwear, chemicals, textile, metalworking, and paper. In the second quarter of 1993 the economy reached bottom and then production started to increase. In 1993 the GDP increased by 2.5%, and since then it has been growing (World Bank, 1999b).

Slovene economy seems to be competitive in spite of the previous pessimistic anticipation. What is the reason for it? The reasons can be attributed to the following factors:

- First, Slovene companies have endeavored to modernize themselves

under the pressure from market forces.
- Second, Slovenia succeeded in inheriting the whole quota of exports that the EU had assigned to ex-Yugoslavia.
- Third, Slovenia has formed with Germany and Austria division of labor similar to the one that exists between Southeast Asian countries and Japan. For example, some Slovene companies produce parts (i.e., car seats for BMW), and other companies produce and export textile products under foreign companies' brand names.

Four years after the secession and independence, Mencinger concluded, 'The benefits of secession appear to prevail over its costs. Namely, while the costs of re-orientating trade from protected to competitive markets were significant, the secession intensified economic restructuring, produced sound economic policy, and permitted the construction of a 'normal' economic system' (Mencinger, 1997).

Tendencies in Recent Years

Since 1993 Slovene economy has been continuously developing, and in 1996 it exceeded its level of 1990. In 1997 per capita income equaled US$ 9,161, which corresponded to about US$ 13,000 as measured in purchasing power parity (World Bank, 1999a). Now Slovenia is the richest country among all transition countries of Central and Eastern Europe.

Slovenia was already highly dependant on foreign trade, but the secession and independence from Yugoslavia made this dependency much higher. Its exports and imports of goods and non-factor services account jointly for over 100% of GDP. For example, in 1997 the share of exports of goods and services in GDP was 57.1%, and the share of imports 58.3%. Slovenia's small open economy is therefore vulnerable to external economic fluctuations (World Bank, 1999b).

The share of trade with the EU, which had already accounted for the bulk of Slovenia's external trade even before independence, increased on both the export and import side, amounting to more than two-thirds of the trade turnover by 1995. The share of the EU in Slovenia's total exports increased from 60.9% in 1992 to 67.2% in 1995, while its share in Slovenia's total imports increased from 59.2% in 1992 to 69.2% in 1994. Since then the trade share with the EU fell on both the export and import side (in 1997, 63.6% and 67.4% respectively). From 1992 to 1997, the share of EFTA in Slovenia's total exports maintained the same level (1%).

In the same period the share of CEFTA in Slovenia's total exports increased from 3.5% to 5.7% while the share of the countries of former Yugoslavia decreased from 22.6% to 16.6% (of which Croatia's share from 14.2% to 10%). The share of EFTA in Slovenia's total imports fluctuated between 1.8% and 2.6%. The share of CEFTA in Slovenia's total imports increased from 4.7% to 7.5% while the share of countries of the countries of former Yugoslavia drastically decreased from 19.8% to 6.3%, of which Croatia's share from 13.9% to 5% (World Bank, 1999b).

As we have seen, export penetration into the EU has run out of steam. After a three-year spell of double-digit growth rates over 1993-95, the value of total exports remained flat for the 1996-97 period. This was due to the lull in Europe's economic growth in the second half of 1995. In this period and through 1996, export performance was maintained, in large part, owing to the depreciation of the tolar. The stagnation of exports affected Slovenia's economic performance. Output growth decreased from 4.1% in 1995 to 3.3% in 1996 (World Bank, 1999b).

The trade balance recorded a slight deficit every year. As the deficits were covered by surpluses in invisible trade, the current balance recorded surplus every year except in 1995.

Restructuring of the Economy

Privatization

Since the former 'owner', which was the state, was legally known, centrally planned economies with state ownership of the means of production (for example, Poland and Hungary) seemingly had less difficulty in their privatization process. So in these countries the state could easily decide how to organize the transformation to private ownership. In contrast, in the case of Slovenia, the state did not formally own the means of production, and it was a matter for national consensus to decide on how privatization should be organized (Kumar, 1993).

Preparation for privatization had already begun at the existence of former Yugoslavia. The amendment to the 1974 Constitution in November 1988 and the enactment of related laws enabled gradual transformation of socially owned companies into mixed ones, and 'internal shares' enabled management/employee buy-outs through the purchase of shares at a discount. In 1990, responsibility for privatization was shifted to the republics. In Slovenia the first draft of privatization was announced in November 1990.

It is said that there was a heated controversy between two approaches over the method of privatization. The first group proposed a gradual, decentralized, and commercial privatization. The term 'decentralized' implied that firms themselves initiate the process of transforming into private companies; the government's role was, consequently, limited to determining the rules and monitoring the process. The term 'gradual' implied the possibility that initial privatization (by the sale of existing equity or by raising additional equity) might be full or partial, while the term 'commercial' implied that there was no free distribution of shares at the beginning of the process. Instead, the citizens of Slovenia would be entitled to discounts on the purchase of shares up to a certain value, and the employees would, as mentioned above, enjoy additional discounts. Joze Mencinger represented this approach. In his opinion, the experience of self-management had merits, and it would be useful for management of companies in the future.

The second group proposed mass, centralized, and distributive privatization. This approach was represented by Jeffrey Sachs, who is famous for his 'achievements' of having eradicated vicious inflation in South America, and instructed the shock therapy to governments of Poland and Russia. In his opinion, the political, social, and economic legacies of the past should be destroyed. The term 'centralized' related to the big role of government in carrying out privatization procedures. The term 'mass' implied that enterprises were to be immediately converted into joint stock companies by the free distribution of shares to the population.

At that time, Mencinger was Vice Prime Minister in charge of economic reform. Jeffrey Sachs was invited by the Government of Slovenia in April 1991 and became an adviser to the Prime Minister. He criticized the proposal of 1991. His argument was that spontaneous privatization would lead to an undesirable delay and result in too much control by employees and managers over companies and that there would be no guarantee for actual privatization of loss-making companies. Being criticized from within the Government, Mencinger and the Finance Minister resigned from their positions. Thus, the controversy between the two approaches resulted in a stalemate lasting for a year and a half. However, the process of privatization was not completely stopped. In November 1991 the second draft of privatization law was not adopted. In November 1992 the privatization bill, the Law on the Transformation of Social Ownership was finally passed. It was a compromise encompassing features of both methods of privatization, a decentralized and gradual approach, and a predominantly distributive privatization using vouchers distributed to all citizens (Mencinger, 1996).

According to Stiblar, the content of the privatization law and the related laws can be summarized as follows:

- First, it regulates the transformation of enterprises in social ownership into enterprises with known (private) owners, as well as the role of the Agency for Privatization, the Reimbursement Fund and the Pension Fund.

- Second, certain legal entities are excluded from regulation with this law (public enterprises, banks, insurance companies, cooperatives, enterprises in bankruptcy procedure).

- Third, social capital is defined in the law as the difference between assets and liabilities of social enterprises plus permanent investments and stocks belonging to the enterprise. Its value is established by the 'opening balance', for which methodology is prescribed by the Privatization Agency and Social Accounting Service. It is not a book value, because this value is usually far from reality.

- Fourth, the rights of previous private (natural and civil persons) owners and their heirs are also prescribed. The denationalization law prescribed the restitution of private property rights in kind (if possible) or value (shares) to those who were stripped of ownership with the nationalization procedure by the socialist regime after World War II.

- Fifth, all agricultural land and forests in social ownership are transferred to the Fund for agricultural land from the day of enactment of this law. The company may continue to use and manage agricultural land and forest until an authorized body decides on denationalization (restitution) or concession (Stiblar, 1993).

In 1993, in order to promote privatization process, an ownership certificate, a kind of voucher, was distributed to each Slovenian citizen. Unlike the voucher in Russia, the ownership certificates had different face values between SIT 200,000 (DM 2,500) and SIT 400,000 (DM 5,000) depending on the age of the citizen. The total amount of ownership certificates represented 40% of the book value of social capital as of December 31, 1992. The certificates were not transferable to other persons, but could be used to purchase shares of privatized companies. They were used in the internal distribution and buyouts, public sales, or were transferred to the privatization investment funds (World Bank, 1999b).

Mencinger summarized the intention of the privatization law in the following equation:

$$(10\% + 10\% + 20\% + (1\text{-}x) \times 40\%) + (20\% + x \times 40\%) = 100\%$$

According to him, this equation delimits institutional owners in the first set of parentheses from the likely individual owners in the second set. He explains this equation as follows:

- 10% of social capital left after restitution to former owners and debt-equity swaps is transferred to the Pension Fund, 10% to the Restitution Fund (the first two items in the equation).
- 20% of the capital is transferred to the Privatization (Development) Fund, which is to 'sell' its shares to investment funds, which in turn, 'sell' their shares to citizens in exchange for their ownership certificates (the third item).
- Up to 20% of a company (the first item in the second set of parentheses) is to be allocated to employees in exchange for their ownership certificates.
- The remaining 40% of the equity capital is sold through management and employees buy-outs, public tenders, public auctions, public offerings of shares, or transferred to the Development Fund as preferential or common shares, depending on the decision by the company – if bought in 'internal buy-outs' the employees receive a 50% discount.
- 'x' - determines whether individual or institutional owners will prevail. It depends on the value of ownership certificates of the employees and their willingness to 'buy' shares in their company. If these certificates exceed 20% of the company's value, employees can use them to acquire shares out of the remaining shares transferred to the Development Fund (Mencinger, 1996).

From 1993 to 1997 almost 1,500 socially owned enterprises went through the process of ownership transformation. By November 1998, 1,369 companies have registered in the Court Register, and have begun to operate as private companies. The World Bank report saw a strong self-management tradition in Slovenia in the way of privatization. Insiders control the majority of companies. More than 90% of enterprises chose to transfer ownership via internal distribution/buyout. In terms of value of capital, however, total value of capital held by insiders amounted to only 26%, while 29% was held by the state, and 31% by institutional owners (World Bank, 1999b).

Insider buyouts were, in most cases, implemented in labor-intensive small- and medium-sized companies with a lower value capital. In 67% of approved programs, employees acquired more than half of the enterprise's ownership, although these enterprises accounted for 16% of the value of total capital in Slovenia. In the case of more capital-intensive enterprises, the shares were to be sold in public offerings for either cash or owner certificates after obtaining the approval from the Slovenian Security and Exchange Commission. Only 12% of companies used public sales as their preferred privatization method, although the share of their capital in total social capital amounted to almost 30%. At the time of purchase, Slovenian citizens had a pre-emptive right to purchase the companies. In this sense, public sales to foreign investors were limited (World Bank, 1999b).

Attention should be paid to the big role that is still played by the state in the process of ownership transformation. For example, the agricultural lands and woods previously used by socially owned companies were nationalized. Also nationalized were public utilities and three large banks and steelworks that have been rehabilitated under state guidance to avoid bankruptcy. The public services sectors in which the state retained its participation include: (a) energy supply and distribution; (b) transportation; (c) telecommunications and postal services; (d) water distribution and other municipal public services; and (e) urban and environmental infrastructure (World Bank, 1999b).

By 1996, private sector participation in GDP reached only about 40%, well below the levels observed in other Central and Eastern European transition countries, which were already over 60% of GDP in 1996. Even in 1999 the private sector is estimated to generate only 50-55% of GDP and to employ about 50% of the labor force (World Bank, 1999b). Thus, as the World Bank report stresses, paradoxically, for a country in which in the past state ownership was non-existent, after privatization, the state became a prime owner of the former socially owned enterprises, with insiders following closely. In only about 30% of the firms, incentives changed significantly. More than two thirds of the privatized companies face incentives that are not different from those in the period of self-management. In effect, the worst performance in terms of profitability is found in companies that are not privatized yet and those that are in the hands of insiders (World Bank, 1999b).

Except for Renault's investment and the more recent Goodyear Tire & Rubber joint venture with Slovenia's Sava Group, producer of car tires, companies investing in Slovenia have been only small to medium in size. Foreign companies have invested mostly in manufacturing – 43% of total FDI stock at the end of 1996, financial institutions – 17%, electricity production – 14%, and trade and service – 12% (World Bank, 1999b). Information on a comparative country basis of the cumulative FDI per capita in some CEE countries, including Slovenia, is presented on Table 1.4.

Given its superb location, its high level of industrial development, the quality of its labor force and its political stability, Slovenia should have attracted a sizable amount of FDI. Nevertheless, FDI in Slovenia has not reached its potential. The World Bank Report mentioned several reasons:

- First, Slovenia's reform agenda has been slower than in other first-wave EU candidates.
- Second, Slovenia's privatization program favored insider (manager and worker) buyouts over outsiders, both foreign and domestic. Insider ownership rarely results in the aggressive shedding of excessive employment, and adjustment to increased competition. It does not contribute to better corporate governance, as it retains the old corporate power structure. It produces a powerful lobbying group with a strong interest in frustrating attempts by foreign investors to buy into firms.
- Third, as shares acquired through vouchers in the mass privatization could not be sold for two years the privatization program explicitly reduced the scope for trading.
- Fourth, there are various regulations that have restricted access by foreign firms to some sectors of the economy. The existing regulatory framework has reduced the rights of investors to select the management of their companies, thus erecting an extra barrier to FDI. For example, the purchase of 25% or a controlling share of a company requires prior approval by the government. Such a requirement discourages some investors. Limits that are imposed on foreign participation exist in auditing (49%), investment companies dealing with the management of investment funds (20%) and stock brokerage firms (24%).
- Fifth, in February 1997 the Central Bank introduced restrictions on the acquisition of securities by foreigners. This regulation compels non-residents to use custodian accounts with authorized domestic banks to

conduct portfolio investments in Slovenia, thereby increasing the costs of these transactions. The measure was subsequently softened in mid-1997 and again early 1999, but not eliminated. Although the regulation was aimed at reducing Slovenia's vulnerability to short-term capital flows, it segmented equity market and increased costs for foreign investors (World Bank, 1999b).

Restructuring of the Financial System

Slovenia has inherited the banking system with its defects from former Yugoslavia. In the period of ex-Yugoslavia, especially in the regime of the 1974 Constitution, banks were given a character of financial institutions, which ought to serve self-managed enterprises. Banks were established by these self-managed enterprises. They owed banks a large amount of debt and local political circles were interested in financing the local self-managed enterprises for the purpose of development of regional economies. Thus, banks were actually managed by big debtors. Such a defect was one of the causes for the economic crisis that surfaced in 1980s.

The Constitutional Amendment in 1988 redefined banks as independent self-managed financial institutions, and socio-political communities such as communes came to join founders of banks. After the independence of Slovenia, the financial system, including banks, was essentially restructured.

According to the World Bank report, at the time of independence, Slovenia's banking sector faced four major problems:

- First, 30 to 40% of bank loans were non-performing.
- Second, there was no real competition in this sector.
- Third, the regulatory and supervisory regime was poor, lagging behind international standards.
- Fourth, Slovene banks lost assets in the rest of the former Yugoslavia.

Nonetheless, Slovene banks retained liabilities, especially with the London Club creditors.

In order to tackle the most pressing problem of bad loans, the authorities nationalized three major banks that were close to bankruptcy – Ljubljanska Banka (LB), Kredina Banka Maribor (KBM), and Komercialna Banka Nova Gorica (KBNG), and launched a rehabilitation plan for these banks. In January 1995, KBNG and KBM merged.

Table 1.4   Cumulative foreign direct investment, 1990-97 (per capita US$; figures in parentheses denote contribution to GDP)

	1990	1991	1992	1993	1994	1995	1996	1997
Estonia	0	0	55	163	305	440	513	620
	(0.00)	(0.00)	(2.17)	(6.64)	(12.20)	(16.59)	(18.89)	(22.03)
Czech R.	12	61	153	216	301	549	683	809
	(0.38)	(2.48)	(5.86)	(7.97)	(10.41)	(16.15)	(19.10)	(21.81)
Hungary	29	168	308	531	639	1,068	1,256	1,439
	(0.98)	(5.55)	(9.71)	(16.01)	(18.87)	(29.40)	(33.98)	(38.26)
Poland	2	10	27	71	119	213	329	411
	(0.16)	(0.56)	(1.36)	(3.37)	(5.39)	(8.48)	(12.06)	(14.48)
Slovenia	0	0	56	112	154	239	328	476
	(0.00)	(0.00)	(0.88)	(1.77)	(2.36)	(3.27)	(4.19)	(5.67)

Source: World Bank, 1999b.

It is the newly created Bank Rehabilitation Agency (BRA) that has been playing the most important role in the rehabilitation of the banking sector. The process began by writing off current bank losses against their capital and by replacing their non-performing assets for bonds issued by BRA. A total of DM 1.9 billion of bonds was issued for this program. This amount was equivalent to just under 10% of Slovenia's 1993 GDP. The swap removed two thirds of the bad assets of the banks.

Afterwards, LB and KBM were each split into two, with the old banks taking over all claims and liabilities to the former Yugoslavia and the new banks Nova Ljubljanska Banka (NLB) and Nova Kreditna Banka Maribor (NKBM), created in mid-1994 retaining all the rest. The remaining regional banks were originally owned by socially owned enterprises. The degree of ownership was directly related to the amount of lending the bank had with the enterprise. When the socially owned enterprises were transformed into joint stock companies, the associated regional banks were not separated as independent entities. As a result, when a socially owned enterprise was privatized, the associated bank was also privatized with the firm. Since many firms partially owned regional banks, the degree of ownership concentration in many of the banks was thus limited. In addition, new banks were established, foreign banks were allowed to participate in the Slovene banking system, both through acquisition of shares in Slovene banks and through the opening of new foreign banks in Slovenia (World Bank, 1999b).

By the end of 1997, there were 28 banks, 6 of which were saving banks. Commercial banks maintain 98% share of the market while saving banks have only 0.4%. The World Bank Report also finds it paradoxical that public ownership in the banking sector significantly increased during Slovenia's transition to a market economy. For example, before independence state ownership was limited to 12% of shares in the parent group of Ljubljanska Banka Group, which then owned the majority shares in the 12 regional banks. By 1997, however, the Government of Slovenia was the most important shareholder in the banking sector. Besides having 100% ownership in two of the three major banks, NLB and NKBM, the Government indirectly has majority control over 6 previous LB Group banks through the new NLB Group. The state also owns 100% of Postna Banka Slovenia, the post office bank (World Bank, 1999b).

Besides, the World Bank Report pointed out some problems: weak competition among banks, high operational costs, and the necessity of encouraging competition.

Table 1.5   Annual percentage change in GDP and employment, 1993-97

Year	Czech Republic		Hungary		Poland		Slovenia	
	Real GDP	Employment	Real GDP	Employment	Real GDP	Employment	Real GDP	Employment
1993	-0.9	-1.6	-0.6	-5.9	3.8	-2.4	2.8	-1.8
1994	2.6	0.8	2.9	-2.1	5.2	1.0	5.3	-0.4
1995	5.0	2.6	1.5	-1.9	7.0	0.3	4.1	-0.3
1996	4.8	1.7	0.2	-1.9	6.0	-0.1	3.1	-0.7
1997	1.0	-0.3	4.4	0.5	6.9	1.4	3.8	0.2
1993-97	13.0	3.2	8.6	-10.5	32.5	0.2	20.6	-3.0

Source: World Bank, 1999.

The banking rehabilitation has so far been successful, and it has contributed to the significantly improved financial position of the banking sector as a whole. However, taking into account the country's size, it is imperative that the restructuring of this sector should continue (World Bank, 1999b).

Other Sectors

Labor markets in Slovenia experienced at first a steep decline in real wages that was followed by a reversal that generated an increase in real wages well above productivity. The fast turnaround of real output has not been followed by recovery in employment as expected (see Table 1.5). Thus, an asymmetry emerged in output and employment, creating what is now called structural unemployment. This has been partly the result of a skill mismatch between what labor markets demand and what workers can offer. The unemployed workers have lower education and/or skills, while labor demand is moving away from unskilled labor and toward more skilled workers. Moreover, traditional skills are no longer in demand as they once were, while new skills are sought in the market.

High labor cost, through taxes, social security contributions and expensive redundancy costs, a lack of flexibility in labor markets, particularly as a result of both the prevailing wage settling mechanisms and overprotective labor legislation further hinder labor market restructuring. The lack of job opportunities for first-time job seekers, young workers, and people coming out of inactivity, rather than job loss itself, is the most important reason for unemployment. On the basis of this perception, the World Bank Report recommends that Slovene Government should re-focus its concern towards making the market more flexible and facilitating job creation, rather than mainly pursuing job preservation.

Also serious is the problem of 'early retirement programs', which were used in the early 1990s to protect workers from increased hardship brought about by transition reforms and to 'make room' for the employment of young workers. Under these programs, women qualified for early retirement at the age of 50 and men at the age of 55, five years before the regular retirement age. Although active programs of early retirement were terminated and although conditions for early retirement were made stringent, the impact on the government's fiscal accounts will prove lasting. In 1996, pension expenditures represented 14% of GDP, almost twice as much as before the transition. This level of pension expenditure implies a

3.5% of GDP deficit in the pension system. Without comprehensive pension reform, it is expected to deteriorate even more during the coming years (World Bank, 1999b).

According to the World Bank Report, the agricultural sector can be characterized as follows:

- The share of agricultural sector in GDP is about 4.4% while its share in total employment is about 10%.
- Slovenia is a net importer of agricultural and food products. Its exports of agricultural and food products equal almost a half of the imports.
- Slovene farms supply the country with much of its need for food consumption in dairy products, eggs, pork, potatoes, fruit and vegetables.
- Slovene agriculture has a dual structure in the farming sector with a large number of small, often labor intensive, family farms, and some large farms from the former 'social sector'.

Labor productivity in agriculture is estimated about half what it is in the Slovene industry. Slovene agriculture is currently protected at about the same level as in the EU. In 1995, the Producer Subsidy Equivalent (PSE) in Slovenia was about 42% while the PSE in the EU was 49%. But the instruments of protection differ. In Slovenia these differences are related to the relative absence of efficient marketing channels at the wholesale level. Moreover, they are constrained by:

- direct intervention by the State Reserve Administration;
- weak marketing cooperative industry;
- lack of incentives to add value to agricultural products;
- lack of incentives to export as domestic market is artificially attractive.

With the objective of harmonizing the Slovene legislation with the EU regulations in agriculture, it would be appropriate to progressively open the domestic markets to foreign competition and, to take into consideration the on-going discussions on the reform of the Common Agricultural Policy. In this regard, the government policy toward self-sufficiency is unsustainable. In the coming years, Slovenia faces a difficult challenge.

On the one hand, Slovenia must strengthen its agriculture and food sector, preparing it for the new and increased competition in the single EU market. On the other hand, Slovenia must protect fragile eco-system against potentially negative consequences of an intensification of its agriculture and a poorly managed land consolidation process. This is important because the image of Slovenia, an ecologically protected garden of Europe, is already being promoted to develop tourism in the country. In this respect, support to rural development should become progressively de-coupled from agricultural development (World Bank, 1999a; 1999b).

Conclusion

Although 'the costs of re-orientating trade from protected to competitive markets were significant' (Mencinger, 1997) for Slovenia, it has so far succeeded in entering the EU markets. It seems that for the time being the small country's strategy to find good areas appropriate for it and to specialize in these areas has been successful. In addition, the tides in the world, such as end of the Cold War, globalization and regionalism are running in favor of Slovenia.

It should be added that Slovenia had advantages when compared with other transition countries. Slovenia as a part of the former Yugoslavia, had decentralized market economy during the period of socialism. It seems that the decentralized coordination mechanism, which Slovenia inherited from this period, facilitated transition to a market economy. The country has also experienced a long period of self-management.

The World Bank Report negatively points out tradition of self-management in the process of restructuring of enterprises. However, I also that there must be advantages in the experience of self-management and that they will be helpful for Slovenia's future economic development. Owing to the experience of self-management, Slovene workers have strong sense of belonging to their enterprises as Japanese workers have. This point can be applied also to enterprises' management. In contrast to highly centralized planned economies, where state enterprises' management did not truly act as managers but simply administrators, enterprises' management in Slovenia acted as managers who accumulated experience and know-how of market economy.

Slovenia has difficult challenges ahead. It has to solve many problems that are associated with the structural adjustment required by the process of harmonization with the EU standards. I hope that the strengths of Slovenia as a small country, that is, a country able to achieve social cohesion more easily, stronger and swifter adjustment capability will ease the pain of structural adjustment.

Notes

1 This chapter was originally written to submit to the international conference 'International Trade and Capital Flows in Economic Restructuring and Growth: European and East Asian Experiences', which was held at the Inha University, Inchon, Korea, on October 5-6, 1999, jointly organized by the Inha University and the University of Le Havre (France). This paper is a result of my research trips to Slovenia. When I made short visits to Slovenia in April 1997 and in July 1998 I was able to meet and discuss with many researchers in the field not only of economics but also of sociology and political science. I would like to express special thanks to Dr. Danica Fink-Hafner, who arranged my visit while she was in the US and whose book (Fink-Hafner and Robbins, 1997) was very useful to my understanding of Slovenia, to Dr. Marko Lah and Dr. Bogdan Kavcic, both of whom arranged my discussion with researchers in Slovenia. Also special thanks to Dr. Marijan Svetličič (Dirctor of Center for International Relations at the University of Ljubljana, the next year Dean of Faculty of Social Sciences) and to Dr. Joze Mencinger (Director of the Economic Institute of Law Faculty at the University of Ljubljana, the next year Rector of the University of Ljubljana). In description of this paper I am greatly indebted to their opinions and papers provided by them. I would like to say that results of the discussion with many Slovene researches are reflected in this paper, though I cannot afford to mention the names of all of them. Finally, I would like to add that I am greatly indebted to the World Bank reports in description of this paper. Needless to say that all possible errors belong exclusively to me.

2 As for Slovenia's contribution to the Federal Budget, I quoted the figure mentioned by Mr. Slavko Mihelic in my interview on April 24, 1991. Koyama, 1996.

3 For detailed history of the Slovene nation, see Bederly and Kraft, 1997; Prunk, 1996.

4 For mutual relationship between economic crisis and nationalities conflicts, see Koyama, 1996 and Koyama, 1997.

5 For Slovenia's 'European orientation', see Brinar, 1999.

6 Nakamura, 1995 describes the skepticism of the Slovene Chamber of Commerce about independence at that time.

7 A concise explanation of 'Acquis Communautaire' is from Ikeda, 1999.

8 The term 'Spanish compromise' is used by Svetličič, 1998; Brinar, 1999, but I found no explanation on why this is called so. Nakamura reports that in 1994 Spain as the chairman country of the EU made a proposal of compromise, but no concrete explanation about it is given (Nakamura, 1995). Perhaps the term derived from this.

9 'The Strategy' is briefly introduced by a Japanese diplomat in Nakamura, 1995.

References

Bebler, A. (1998), 'Slovenia and South-Eastern Europe', *Sudost Europa*, 47, pp. 3-4.

Bederly, J. and Kraft, E. (eds) (1997), *Independent Slovenia: Origins, Movements, Prospects*, Basingstoke: Macmillan.

Brinar, I. (1999), 'Slovenia from Yugoslavia to the European Union', in K. Henderson (ed) *Back to Europe: Central and Eastern Europe and the European Union,* London: UCL Press.

Dimovski, V. (ed.) (1996), *Strategy for Increasing the Competitiveness Capabilities of Slovenian Industry,* Republic of Slovenia, Ljubljana: Ministry of Economic Affairs.

Fink-Hafner, D. and Robbins, J. (eds) (1997), *Making a New Nation: The Formation of Slovenia,* Aldershot: Dartmouth.

Henderson, K. (ed) (1999), *Back to Europe: Central and Eastern Europe and the European Union,* London: UCL Press.

Ikeda, T. (1999), 'Discord in Czech Republic Concerning European Integration: Mainly on the Negotiation of the EU Membership', Typescript, (in Japanese).

Kornai, J. (1995), 'Transformational Recession: A General Phenomenon Experienced through the Example of Hungary's Development', in J. Kornai (ed), *Highway and Byways,* London: MIT Press.

Koyama, Y. (1992), 'Enterprises and Workers in Slovenia Which Is Urged to Do Restructuring: Situation on the Eve of the Federation's Breakup', *Studies in Socialist Economies,* no. 19.

Koyama, Y. (1996), *A Study of Yugoslav Self-managed Socialism: Movement of the Regime of 1974 Constitution,* Tokyo: Taga Shuppan.

Koyama, Y. (1997). 'Causes of Nationality Conflicts in the Former Yugoslavia', *Japanese Slavic and East European Studies,* vol. 18.

Kumar, A. (1993), 'Slovenia – Developments and Transition', in M. Senjur, *Slovenia: A Small Country in the Global Economy,* Ljubljana, Slovenia: CICD and ICEG.

Majcen, B. (1999), 'Measurement of Costs and Benefits of Accession to the EU for Selected CEECs: Country Report Slovenia', *Research Report,* no. 256, Vienna: WIIW.

Mencinger, J. (1994), 'From Socialism to the Market – The Case of Slovenia', in A. Bibic, Adolf and G. Graziano (eds) (1994), *Civil Society, Political Society, Democracy,* Ljubljana, Slovenia: Slovenian Political Science Association.

Mencinger, J. (1996), 'Privatization Experiences in Slovenia', *Annals of Public and Cooperative Economics,* vol. 67, no. 3.

Mencinger, J. (1997), 'Costs and Benefits of Secession', in D. Fink-Hafner, and J. Robbins, (eds) (1997), *Making a New Nation: The Formation of Slovenia,* Aldershot: Dartmouth.

Nakamura, Y. (1995), 'The State Strategy of a Small Country Slovenia', *Monthly Research Report of Ministry of Foreign Affairs,* no. 4.

Prunk, J. (1996), *A Brief History of Slovenia: Historical Background of the Republic of Slovenia,* Ljubljana, Slovenia: Zalozba Grad.

Rojec, M. (1993), 'Theses for Slovenia's Inward Foreign Investment Strategy and Policy', in M. Senjur, *Slovenia: A Small Country in the Global Economy,* Ljubljana, Slovenia: CICD and ICEG.

Senjur, M. (1993), *Slovenia: A Small Country in the Global Economy,* Ljubljana, Slovenia: CICD and ICEG.

Sevic, Z. and Wright, G. (eds) (1997), *Transition in Central and Eastern Europe,* Beograd: Yugoslav Association of Sasakawa Fellows.

Svetličič, M. (1993), 'The Competitive Position of Slovenia to Attract Foreign Direct Investment', in M. Senjur (1993), *Slovenia: A Small Country in the Global Economy*, Ljubljana, Slovenia: CICD and ICEG.

Svetličič, M. (1997), 'Small Country in a Globalized World: Their Honey Moon or Twilight?', Paper prepared for ECPR Workshop on Small States in the Transforming European System.

Svetličič, M. (1998), *Slovenian State Strategy in the New Europe*, Ljubljana, Slovenia: University of Ljubljana.

Svetličič, M. and Bucar, M. (1993), 'The Strategy of International Economic Cooperation of Slovenia', in M. Senjur, *Slovenia: A Small Country in the Global Economy*, Ljubljana, Slovenia: CICD and ICEG.

Svetlik, I. (1997), 'Re-shaping the Labor Market', in D. Fink-Hafner, and J. Robbins, (eds) *Making a New Nation: The Formation of Slovenia*, Aldershot: Dartmouth.

World Bank (1999a), *Slovenia: Economic Transformation and EU Accession*, Volume I: Summary Report, Washington, D.C.: the World Bank.

World Bank (1999b), *Slovenia: Economic Transformation and EU Accession*, Volume II: Main Report, Washington, D.C.: the World Bank.

2 Internationalization through Outward Foreign Direct Investment: The Case of Slovenia[1]

MARJAN SVETLIČIČ and ANDREJA TRTNIK

Introduction

In the globalized world economy and with simultaneous tectonic technological changes, the internationalization of firms has become the key to sustained growth. It is not only important in order to compensate for a small national market that cannot offer efficiency through economies of scale and scope but also in order to tap the knowledge and technology created abroad. International trade is, with the growing globalization and oligopolization of market structures, no longer an efficient way for firms to earn profits on the basis of their advantages that are increasingly becoming intangible. The market is failing to adequately reward the owners of such knowledge. Therefore, firms are 'forced' to internalize their operations, to invest abroad so as to be remunerated for their intangible knowledge. With the advancement of transition, the firms of Central and Eastern European countries (CEECs) will have to develop their own specific knowledge/technologies in order to survive and fend off growing foreign competition.

Internationalization is broadly defined as the process of a firm's involvement in international business operations (Welch and Luostarinen, 1988) and encompasses different types of operations from imports and exports through to foreign direct investment (FDI) and strategic alliances. The depth and variability of business operations are increasing. With the exception of foreign investment, no other type of international operation has matched the growth and volume of FDI.

Internationalization through FDI has a very short history in CEECs compared to other smaller European countries like Portugal[2], Finland[3], and other Scandinavian countries. In the last decade, the processes of liberalization, deregulation and privatization have, together with democratization, been 'pushing' firms from CEECs to invest abroad. Confronted with the increased need for internationalization in a globalized world economy, the lack of relevant experience makes such internationalization under time pressure a major challenge. To cope with international competition and to benefit from globalization, they will have to internationalize in a much shorter period. This shortness of time prevents firms from CEECs to benefit gradually from the cumulative learning process of sequential internationalization. This is one explanation why the process of internationalization is faster at the company level, but is not necessary parallel to the similarly intensive expansion in terms of number of countries of penetration. Firms tend to concentrate their foreign operations only in a few countries.

Outward internationalization cannot be completely separated from inward internationalization. We should be aware of the possible interrelations (interdependencies) between inward FDI and outward FDI, and take into account the inward dimension in any other kind of firms' outward activities. Although outward FDI recently gained importance in CEECs, inward FDI remained by far more important. Outward investment by CEECs remains almost negligible, compared with the global outflows of FDI.

The theory of the development implications of FDI, which should be the most important objective of the study of outward internationalization, is less developed and, to that extent it is dominated by host country perspectives. 'Feedback effects of large outward investment on the home base remains a seriously under-researched area.' (Chenessis, 1995). The same applies to the potential link between inward and outward investment. Dunning's investment development path or Ozawa's FDI-facilitated-development paradigm, Vernon's (and others') product life cycle theories and Cantwell and Lall's theories on technological accumulation and localization technological changes are the few exceptions. The lack of awareness of the potential positive effect on a home county (strengthening competitiveness, restructuring role) and the quite common public belief that outward FDI (OFDI) is anti-patriotic since it exports the jobs and capital so badly needed for domestic investment discourages the more rapid development of such direct investments abroad by CEECs.

This chapter concentrates on the *Slovenian experience of the internationalization process through outward foreign direct investment* after its independence gained in 1991. The current pattern of the operations of Slovenian firms, the characteristics, modes of operation and geographical orientations will be studied primarily within the framework of a modified version of Luostarinen and Welch's (1988) internationalization model. Other theories relevant to evaluating foreign direct investment will also be used to explain Slovenia's outward FDI when appropriate. They include in particular Dunning's investment development path, Ozawa's dynamic paradigm and Scandinavian sequential internationalization approach.

We tested the following hypotheses:

- Despite the fact that outward FDI in Slovenia started before inward FDI, which conflicts with the sequential internationalization process (Luostarinen, 1979) and investment development path (Dunning, 1993), companies are following a gradual internationalization approach that can be explained by traditional theories.
- Foreign operations are today crucial to the success of firms from small countries; therefore traditional export operations should be upgraded so as to involve further internationalization. Of all diversified operational methods, outward foreign direct investment is probably the most important vehicle for firms to strengthen their competitive edge, acquire knowledge and gain markets.

Empirical evaluation will be performed at both macro- and micro-economic levels. Since outward FDI is a relatively new phenomenon the related statistical coverage and data availability are limited. Reluctance to report information on FDI seems to be present at all levels and many data sources should be combined to gather in valuable information. We used official statistical sources from the central bank, national accounts and a special company-based survey, and case studies.

This chapter presents the results of the first in-depth study of Slovenian outward investments. The brief historical overview will be followed by a presentation of recent experiences of direct investing abroad. Firstly, FDI stocks and flows will be studied and then their geographical concentration. This aggregate empirical analysis[4] based on the Bank of Slovenia's figures is complemented by the results of a survey[5] among companies that are investing and this has provided primary data on several issues. Firstly, the focus is on the underlying motives for investing abroad. Secondly, attention is paid to the effects of investment at the company level.

The Outward Foreign Direct Investment from Slovenia

Brief History before Slovenia's Independence

Firms from the former Yugoslavia were the first from socialist countries to start investing abroad back in the 1960s[6]. In spite of this early start, levels of investment abroad were relatively modest before Slovenia became independent in 1991. The rationale for this early internationalization in the socialist era was not the same as it was for firms from market economies. By establishing affiliations abroad or through other forms of long-term contracts, due to the foreign exchange and international trade regimes of the then Yugoslavia, Slovenian firms did achieve a kind of privileged position. Namely, firms having long-term contracts with foreign partners gained a privileged position in terms of changes to foreign trade and foreign exchange laws. By internationalizing their activities they gained stability in their international trade relations, as well as certain autonomy since changes to the legislation did not affect such long-term arrangements with foreign companies. Firms were thereby able to secure the necessary foreign currency to pay for requisite raw materials, intermediate products, machinery and equipment. That is why we suggested a special name for such outward FDI, *system escape investments* (Svetličič et al., 1994). Later on, outward FDI became increasingly an instrument for the promotion of exports. The specific reasons for such early outward investment from Slovenia, or from Yugoslavia for that matter, did not allow the conclusion that such investment contradicts the traditional explanation of outward FDI following investment development path or sequential internationalization models although such investment started before inward investment in Slovenia (then within Yugoslavia) was permitted and before the country achieved a certain development level.

Institutionally, the possibilities for outward FDI were opened by the gradual elimination of the state monopoly over foreign economic relations in the then Yugoslavia by increasing the autonomy of enterprises and by introducing certain market elements into the economic system (see, Svetličič, Rojec, and Lebar, 1994).

Because of this early start and experience in investing abroad, greater FDI outflows were expected after Slovenia's independence in 1991 and after a fully-fledged market economy started to be introduced. However, the firms did not adapt as fast as expected. Instead of stepping up the making of direct investments abroad, such investment almost stopped.

Initial uncertainties regarding formal recognition of the new state of Slovenia, how the rights and obligations and financial and other succession matters would be resolved posed a serious barrier to strengthening and upgrading the international economic cooperation of Slovenian firms. Political instability and later wars in former Yugoslav republics of Croatia followed by Bosnia and Herzegovina and, finally, Kosovo also prevented the faster marketization of firm activities on the world market.

The first priority after gaining independence was to find the ways and means for replacing the lost Yugoslav market in which Slovenian enterprises had formerly realized around 50% of their sales. Survival of firms, keeping the existing Western markets and increasing market share in Europe were collectively priority number one. Another factor preventing bolder steps in developing new strategies was managers' initial preoccupation with the privatization process. This was the first strategic task. Legislation itself prevented firms from investing abroad before their privatization process had been completed or at least before they had permission from the Privatization Agency. Parallel unfavorable public opinion on direct investment abroad also discouraged managers from embarking on development of this form of international economic cooperation. Such investment, meaning an outflow of capital, was regarded as anti-patriotic in a situation in which the priority was to attract foreign capital to assist restructuring of the Slovenian economy. Managers were frequently accused of privatizing the public assets of companies by establishing so-called by-pass firms abroad in which the good, profit-making parts of companies were became owned by such managers while the loss-making ones remained socially owned. It was not surprising that in this general climate outward FDI did not get off the ground. The exceptions were only *'window dressing'* firms established mostly in Austria, Italy, and Hungary through which Slovenian firms tried to continue to do business with Republic of Serbia that had refused to do business with Slovenian firms.

Transition was also accompanied by the disintegration of many big and internationalized companies into a host of small companies that were unable to internationalize, especially not through outward FDI due to the lack of knowledge (labor force and experience) and capital. Due to limited resources, recession and uncertain economic circumstances, many companies were forced to stop expanding their international operations or even to do away with their affiliates abroad. Annual FDI outflows up till 1993 were negative (divestment). Outward FDI stock increases were predominantly due to the increased net claims of Slovenian investors on companies abroad. Affiliations outside Slovenia were a good source for getting cheaper loans abroad[7] since foreign banks considered Slovenia as a risky new country, whereas foreign affiliations had a better reputation based on past records.

Alongside the disintegration of Yugoslavia, many Slovenian companies became foreign direct investors 'overnight'. After disintegration, all of the assets or sales units of Slovenian firms in the former Yugoslavia became foreign investment. Slovenian firms unintentionally became multinational (*'forced internationalization'*) or foreign investors even though such investment had not initially started as a foreign operation but a purely domestic one. Therefore, the most important share of outward investments abroad of Slovenian enterprises represented 'inherited' investments located in former Yugoslav republics (Svetličič *et al.*, 1994).

Those companies becoming multinational overnight without being able to develop know-how about investing abroad in a more evolutionary way and not possessing internationalization capabilities were often unable to preserve these affiliations abroad. The first response was divestment, which was the combined outcome of external circumstances and internal factors within companies themselves.

With the introduction of a market economy after Slovenia's independence, *system escape investments* lost their importance while other motives gained in importance. 'Normally' (in terms of theory) motivated outward direct investments began to emerge after Slovenia gained international recognition, when the main problems with at least the financial succession of Yugoslavia had been resolved, and after the main wave of privatization and the market reforms had concluded. The loss of the Yugoslav market and the small domestic market with slow or even negative growth rates in the first years of transition were the dominant push factors of internationalization.

Outward Foreign Direct Investment in the 1990s

Outward FDI started in Slovenia or, more accurately, in the then Yugoslavia, before the inward variety. It however soon started to lag behind inward FDI after the passing of the first joint-venture law in 1967, allowing foreigners to invest in Yugoslavia. Slovenia then started to follow the investment development path model. Such a situation has persisted until today. After independence when Slovenia achieved macro-economic stability and resumed growth, inward FDI picked up in momentum although it is still lagging behind other transition economies like Hungary, Poland and the Czech Republic. Outward FDI stock in 1998 represented approximately one-fifth of inward FDI (see, Figure 2.1 and Table 2.1). Inward FDI generally increased over the past decade, but the net investment position fell suggesting that Slovenia is in the second stage of Dunning's investment development path.

A greater volume of inward FDI and loss in export competitiveness should, according to Ozawa's dynamic paradigm of TNC-assisted development, be followed by increased outward FDI flows into countries with lower labor costs. We cannot find strong support for this in the case of Slovenia. The level of direct investment abroad is increasing very slowly. Geographical orientation also does not follow the Ozawa paradigm since such OFDI was initially not predominantly directed to low-cost locations and not in manufacturing where low labor costs are crucial. Affiliations abroad are established mostly as sales units. Lately, there has been a very strong push to (re)-establish manufacturing and marketing units in some former republics of Yugoslavia, namely Croatia, and Bosnia and Herzegovina. However, the biggest explanations are not only the differences in labor costs but also previous business ties, knowledge of the market and language. In other words, such investment could be explained by both the Ozawa model as well as by network theory.

The short time series make it impossible to do reliable analysis trend or investment development path tests. Parallel to the increasing, although oscillating, trends in the stock of OFDI, the number of companies investing abroad has stagnated. The share of companies with OFDI within the total corporate sector is very modest, at slightly over 1%, and is also decreasing.

Table 2.1 Inward FDI stocks in Slovenia and Slovenian outward FDI stock in US$ million

Stock of FDI	1993	1994	1995	1996	1997	1998
Inward stock	954.3	1,331	1,759.6	1,980.8	2,194	2,907
Outward stock	280.6	280.8	500.4	426.7	428	563

Source: Bank of Slovenia.

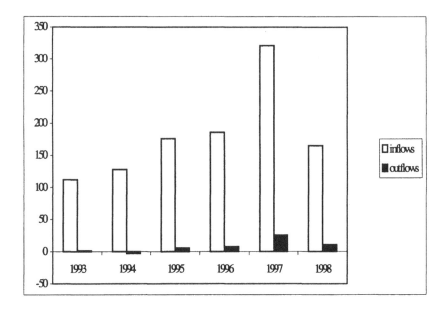

Figure 2.1   FDI inflows and outflows in Slovenia in US$ millions

Source: Bank of Slovenia.

Of all first-wave candidates for the EU, Slovenia is in last place in terms of inward FDI stock as a share of GDP (14.9% in 1998). In terms of per capita share, the lagging behind other candidate-countries is slightly less pronounced which reflects the fact that Slovenia is the most developed (in terms of per capita GDP) of all of them. By cooperating with transnational corporations (TNCs), firms should create their assets and thus become able to invest abroad later. Therefore, the influence of inward FDI (the inward – outward linkages explained in Ozawa's dynamic paradigm and investment development path) has not yet started to work. Inward FDI has substantially begun to assist restructuring of the corporate sector[8]. This process has not yet been supplemented by a similar role that outward FDI could also assume.

The restructuring role of outward FDI is however explained differently by the Ozawa model compared to Dunning's investment development path. In Dunning's case, the national income level is the most important determinant, while for Ozawa changing competitive and comparative advantages are in the forefront. The investment development path model would predict that Slovenia is the leading CEEC likely to invest abroad due to it having the highest level of development. The share of outward FDI stock in GDP in 1998 was 2.9% and was the highest among CEECs. That is also a result of the relatively longer tradition in FDI compared to other CEECs and the many more 'inherited' investments abroad[9].

Trends in Slovenian outward FDI also clearly demonstrate the relevance of stage development models claiming those previous experiences with exporting are important. Those Slovenian firms that were major exporters (or direct investors) in the past, in the socialist era, were among the first to start internationalizing their activities after the transition started. Exceptions to this rule are certain new small - and medium-sized enterprises (SMEs) that were established after the transition and started operations abroad in this new period. Some of these firms may be regarded as having been *'born global'*, although their level of internationalization is still very limited (in terms of the geographical direction of their activities and level of such investment). They are exceptions.

At the same time, it has to be stressed that the managers of many such newly established firms came from large (socialist) companies where they acquired basic knowledge about internationalization. After the transition started they created their own enterprises and later initiated their own operations abroad, based to a large extent on the experiences and networks established while they worked in socially owned enterprises. Companies may be *'born multinational'* but not their management.

Since the number of companies investing abroad is stagnating, there are not many new companies starting internationalization through outward FDI. The survey of the main exporters and fastest growing firms carried out in 1999[10] showed that more than 60% intended to invest directly abroad in the next three years. The result of a comparable study in 1995 was similar; more than 50% of firms planned to invest abroad (see Krašovec *et. al.*, 1995). Obviously, the realization of such plans has lagged behind considerably; there were only a few 'newcomers' among companies with FDI.

Companies were either too optimistic in their plans or unable to materialize such plans. Clearly, companies are aware of the need for further internationalization but lack the capacity to engage in it. It seems that they also underestimate the complexity of the first entry through outward FDI that has proved in practice to be more difficult than expected by the managers. Foreign operations are especially difficult tasks for smaller companies that dominate in the Slovenian corporate sector and have limited resources.

It is therefore not surprising that respondents in our survey spontaneously claimed (in open questions) that the major barriers to such undertakings were lack of experience, high risks and lack of knowledge and information on how to invest abroad. Companies lack knowledge about administrative procedures as well as international business operations, foreign market entry, marketing and management. General economic instability, systemic changes and legal regulation of some of the former Yugoslav republics were also mentioned as investment barriers.

The ranking of impediments was similar when companies assessed the importance of particular impediments stated in the questionnaire (see Figure 2.2). Lack of personnel able to undertake outward investment was estimated as the most important impediment followed by high risk, difficulties with insurance (reinsurance), and lack of both information and knowledge. Many companies also lacked funds or did not have easy access to outside finance or the costs were too high (interest rates). Companies also assessed governmental support as insufficient.

Legislation and the general climate at home and in the host country were also considered unfriendly. Corruption in a host country was a relatively less important obstacle to outward investment. The least important investment impediments were assessed as being cultural differences and national attitudes of customers and public authorities that is certainly a reflection of the concentration of Slovenian outward FDI in Croatia and, and lately also in Bosnia and Herzegovina.

Attitudes of customers and public authorities and the general cultural vicinity to former Yugoslav markets are well known to Slovenian managers and cannot represent a barrier.

In spite of the general assessment of stagnation or the very slow progress of outward FDI of Slovenian firms, companies that started investing abroad at the beginning of the 1990s have made quite significant progress in their internationalization process in terms of the expansion of their international network by countries.

The number of foreign affiliates grew faster than the number of companies investing abroad. According to our survey, among companies the average Slovenian company investing abroad expanded the number of foreign affiliates from 2 in 1992 to 4 in 1998 (see Table 2.2).

The majority of companies surveyed (62%) intend to increase outward investments either by expanding existing foreign affiliates or establishing new ones.

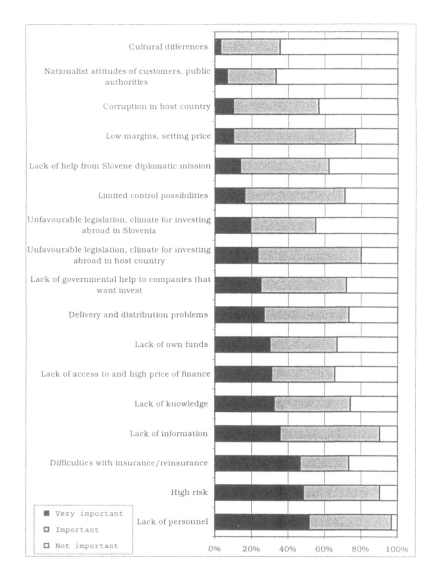

Figure 2.2   The importance of individual barriers to investing abroad

Source: Survey on OFDI of Slovenian companies, June-October 1999.

Table 2.2 Number of investors and their companies abroad

Information about Investors	1992	1995	1998	Index 95-92	Index 98-95
Number of investors (current year)	25	29	32	116.0	110.3
Number of affiliations abroad	67	91	137	135.8	150.5
Average number of companies abroad	2.1	2.8	4.3	133.3	153.6

Source: Survey on OFDI of Slovenian companies, June-October 1999.

More dynamic increase in the number of companies investing abroad in the first half of the 90s, and the growth in the number of foreign affiliates in the second half of the 90s demonstrates that intensification of internationalization is more pronounced than the broadening of the process to newcomers. Companies that succeeded in reorienting to new markets and quickly reached high foreign market sales after the disintegration of Yugoslavia did so in the first half of the past decade and only then expanded their foreign operations from traditional exports through a direct presence in a foreign market via FDI. Those that lost their competitiveness and did not succeed with OFDI closed down their international operations.

Companies that spread their international network of foreign affiliates do so in order to gain economies of scale and scope, to increase efficiency and make the best use of their, albeit limited, ownership specific advantages[11] in different locations. Thereby they try to strengthen their strategic position. Case studies also showed that the first step in the internationalization process is also the most difficult.

This certainly confirms the basic assumptions of Johanson & Vahlne's model that lack of knowledge about foreign markets and operations is an important obstacle to the development of international operations and that the necessary knowledge can be acquired mainly through doing such operations abroad. This applies to internationalization in the form of increasing involvement of the firm in an individual foreign country as well as for the successive establishment of operations in new countries (Johanson & Vahlne, 1977). In the internationalization process, firms gradually increase their international involvement by acquisition, integration and use of knowledge about foreign markets and operations. Considering the internationalization process as an accumulation of knowledge, the recent geographical concentration of Slovenia's outward FDI in countries emerging from former Yugoslavia is not surprising.

Geographical Dispersion and Concentration of Outward FDI

In the same way that Slovenian exports are too dispersed, nearly capillary (Trošt, 1993), outward direct investments are also dispersed over a number of countries. The network spread index[12] for Slovenia exceeds 21.9%, which is an extremely high value in comparison to other developed countries. A similar network spread index value is held by the USA (21.8%), while Japan has a lower one (18.4%), although these two countries are the world's biggest foreign direct investors (WIR, 1998). A high network spread index may be accompanied by higher costs of managing far-flung operations (transaction costs). It may also indicate risk dispersion and high levels of ownership advantages including knowledge of market conditions in many countries, or a combination of ownership and internalization advantages. The network spread index is only a partial measure of internationalization, neglecting the magnitude of business activity in a host country and counting each host country only once, independent of the amount of assets, sales, production or employment located in it. Slovenia's high network spread value index is consistent with the expectation that companies from small, open economies should be more internationalized and should have a broader foreign affiliate network spread. Increasing internationalization could be a substitute for slower growth rates and possibilities to achieve efficiency in the home market alone.

The average surveyed company with foreign operation has affiliates in four different countries. A quarter of sample companies has a foreign affiliate in only one country. One-eighth (12.5%) of them has affiliates in at least ten countries. For every sample company, the number of its export markets is bigger than the number of markets in which they have established their affiliations abroad. The export and OFDI markets do overlap. OFDI succeeds export operation as the first market entry mode, which again confirms the stage internationalization approach.

The geographical concentration of export and outward FDI confirms that minimal physical and cultural distance and past experience are the most important determinants of OFDI by Slovenian firms. While Slovenian exports are mostly concentrated in Western European countries (more than two-thirds of exports within the European Union), foreign direct investments and sales are predominantly oriented to CEECs and especially to ex-Yugoslav countries with Croatia[13] being the main destination. In the period studied from 1993 to 1998, the latter receive from 50 to 70% of total OFDI. This is more a reflection of inherited investments than the result of new FDI flows into this region (with the exception of Bosnia and Herzegovina, which is truly becoming an increasing net receiver of Slovenian OFDI in 1999 and 2000). As many Slovenian firms possess rich experience and knowledge about these countries as well as comparative advantages over local firms, FDI entry to these markets is not so risky. Companies also tend to follow the leading competitors in those markets (Knickerbocker, 1973) or want to assure their market shares even before their competitors enter (especially in the rebuilding phase of these countries). They want to achieve a *first-mover advantage*. The sequential internationalization pattern of entering neighboring countries with minimal physical and cultural distance first, already confirmed by many countries[14], has proven to apply also in the case of Slovenia.

The second most important country grouping involves CEECs that are increasingly attracting Slovenian investors abroad. Due to its market size, Poland is especially attractive, followed by the Czech Republic and Hungary. These two groups of countries are gaining in importance while EU countries are, to our initial surprise, losing in their attractiveness. This relocation to less developed markets suggests that knowledge, experience, and especially the firm ownership specific advantages of Slovenian companies are only sufficient to outperform such ownership advantages in less demanding markets.

Among the EU countries Germany, Austria, and Italy dominate both in terms of the location for OFDI and as trading partners. The importance of Austria as a location for Slovenian OFDI could be explained not only by traditional internationalization patterns (neighboring country with strong historical ties), but also by the *'origin disguising'* reason. By investing in Austria, Slovenian firms have tried to disguise the origin of goods to be exported to Serbia since it started to ban 'imports' from Slovenia already within the integrated Yugoslavia. This has continued even after the disintegration of Yugoslavia. Therefore, Slovenian firms try to maintain business in former markets by 'origin covering investments', by establishing trade affiliates mostly in Austria.

According to the plans of sample companies investing abroad, such a geographical allocation of OFDI will not change significantly in the near future.

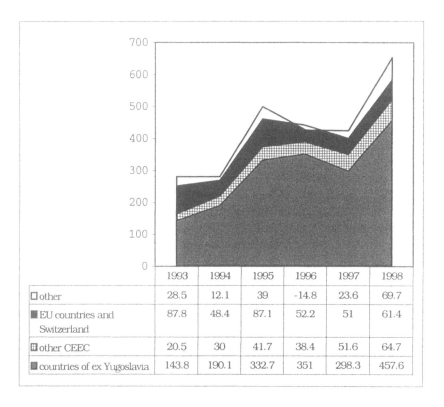

	1993	1994	1995	1996	1997	1998
☐ other	28.5	12.1	39	-14.8	23.6	69.7
▇ EU countries and Switzerland	87.8	48.4	87.1	52.2	51	61.4
⊞ other CEEC	20.5	30	41.7	38.4	51.6	64.7
▩ countries of ex Yugoslavia	143.8	190.1	332.7	351	298.3	457.6

**Figure 2.3 Regional concentration of Slovenian OFDI - end-year
stock in US$ million**

Source: Bank of Slovenia.

Ex-Yugoslav markets will still be the most attractive location for Slovenian
OFDI, especially Bosnia and Herzegovina, where more than a fifth of
interviewed companies intends to establish a foreign affiliate in the next
three years. The countries of CEE are more frequently cited as a planned
destination than Western European or EU countries. Among planned
locations we can also find many distant countries (such as Japan, the
USA, South America, Malaysia, etc.). The shift in emphasis from product
to geographical diversification, intensifying of a more global distribution of
production and sales for companies entering internationalization through
OFDI is therefore already at work. All presented countries are mainly
chosen because of the size of their markets and not as a springboard to
other markets. More than 81% of foreign affiliates of sample companies are

market-seekers realizing most of their sales in local markets. Only about 15% of foreign affiliates (of the sample companies) further export their goods and services to neighboring countries. Host country determinants play the major role in a location decision.

The principal determinants of locating FDI are (WIR, 1998) the policy framework, business facilitation measures and economic factors. When companies choose investment locations they combine their ownership-specific advantages with the location specific advantages of host countries and internalization as the best way of maximizing their return on the assets they possess. The relative importance of different location-specific FDI determinants depends on the motive and type of investment, the industry, and the size and strategy of the investor. Different motives, for example, can translate into different location patterns depending on the investor's strategy. Before motives are presented in the next chapter, we first present an evaluation of the host county determinants of FDI.

The survey showed that the most important factors influencing the location decision of direct investment abroad are economic and are closely related to market characteristics. To preserve an existing market share was the most frequently mentioned factor behind a location decision. Through mere traditional export operations companies cannot keep let alone increase foreign market shares. Costs of increasing foreign market shares are attainable to Slovenian companies, if 'they play it alone' only in less demanding markets with less competition. Ex-Yugoslav markets are relatively very convenient because Slovenian companies and their brand names are very well recognized and do not need substantial additional investments to establish market recognition.

In terms of the importance of individual factors behind location decisions (host country determinants), the sample companies indicated as the most important economic determinants of a host country the size and growth of the market (see Figure 2.4). Purchasing power was the second most important factor influencing an investment decision. Vicinity of a country and lower transport costs were the next important location decision factors, showing that transport and communications between the parent company and foreign affiliate are still an important consideration. The majority of sample companies also assessed low operation costs as an important factor. Ex-Yugoslav countries being a major destination of Slovenian OFDI confirm the importance of labor and other costs.

Relatively less than economic determinants but still important in a host country decision were factors referring to the policy framework for FDI and business facilitation (an FDI-friendly environment) such as low country risk, the tax environment and FDI regulation, administrative procedures and incentives. This is in accordance with the general trend that a friendly FDI policy framework is a necessary but insufficient determinant of FDI location. It is also becoming relatively less important with liberalization and globalization trends around the world.

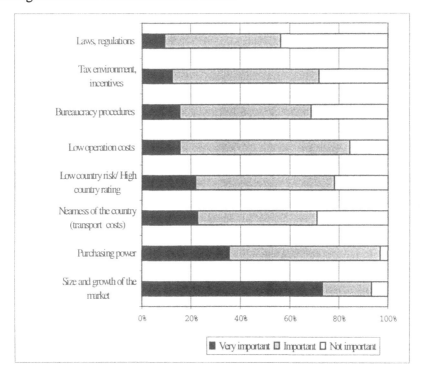

Figure 2.4   The importance of host country determinants

Source: Survey on OFDI of Slovenian companies, June-October 1999.

Motivation

Motives for direct investment abroad could be very heterogeneous and also intertwined. Dunning distinguishes four main groups of motives: resource seeking, market seeking, efficiency seeking and strategic asset seeking (Dunning, 1993). Despite overlapping, these groups reflect historical developments in the country as well as at the firm level. Economic development of a country and a firm's growth and strategy influences the motives for outward investments. At the firm level, these groups of motives are usually developed gradually. In our survey, several individual motives listed in the questionnaire have been merged into these groups of motives (see Figure 2.5).

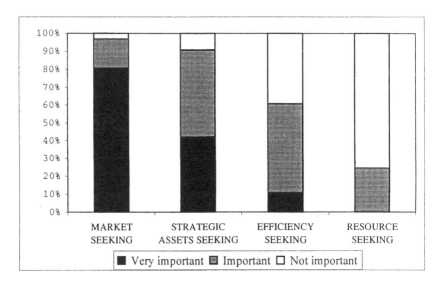

Figure 2.5   The importance of a particular group of motives

Source: Survey on OFDI of Slovenian companies, June-October 1999.

Although Slovenia is small and therefore, in terms of factor endowments, a poor country, incentives related to resource seeking have proved to be the least important. Regardless of the type of production factor, production factor costs were assessed as an unimportant motive for most sample companies. Unit labor costs were seen as being slightly more important compared to other factors.

That is surprising especially in view of Ozawa's paradigm and the general opinion that Slovenian labor costs are relatively high. Countries providing the main destination have quite lower labor costs, but also lower productivity. The first explanation could be that the sample companies actively involved in the internationalization process have already passed the stage of major resource allocation (although one could counter that since permanent resource reallocation is needed to stay competitive) and are now predominantly following other motives.

Most Slovenian OFDI is certainly market seeking. This can easily be explained by the loss of the Yugoslav market after Slovenia gained independence. A small domestic market with increasing inward internationalization and competition and the stage of economic development further support the reason that outward FDI is predominantly market seeking. The continuous trade balance deficit in the 1990s and current account deficit in 1998 remind firms that export capability has to be further developed and enriched through a direct presence in foreign markets. This suggests that Slovenian affiliates abroad are more trade- than local-production oriented (production relocation). Only 11% of foreign affiliates (of the sample companies) are in manufacturing, almost 95% of them are in sales and marketing. The modest share of resource-seeking motives is consequently understandable.

Strategic asset seeking has proved to be the second most important incentive. Growth of a company and strengthening its overall competitive position were evaluated as especially important incentives for OFDI. As these investments are, according to theory, long-term oriented (assets and competitiveness enhancing), it is encouraging to find this group of motives as the second most important incentive of sample companies.

The strategic-asset-seeking investment orientation is a reflection of the international strategy of multinational companies. Often, strategic asset-seeking motives are closely related to efficiency-seeking motives, which in our survey follow asset-seeking motives in terms of importance.

Strategic-asset-seeking motivated investments are frequently carried through mergers and acquisitions, which are recently the most important form of FDI growth. Although mergers and acquisitions save time in the processes of a firm's growth and assets creation and offer quick technology and knowledge transfer, companies are at the beginning of the internationalization process unable to cope with mergers and acquisitions. They are quite rare in the case of Slovenian OFDI. Still, greenfield investments are predominating (85.4% of foreign affiliates of the sample companies were established as greenfield, 11.7% through acquisitions and 2.9% through mergers).

After strengthening market position and acquiring market knowledge, we can expect that the group of investors mainly motivated by strategic reasons will expand. For improving international competitiveness, this type of investment requires some already developed firm specific advantages but, on the other hand, it offers to first-time foreign direct investors the opportunity to gain competitive strength in an unfamiliar market. Strategically, OFDI goes hand in hand as firms restructure their assets to meet their objectives (Dunning, 1993).

The efficiency-seeking incentive for outward FDI as the third most important group of motives can only be realized after a parent company has established some foreign affiliates. They facilitate the further relocation of resources (by using differences and similarities of factor endowments and economic systems and institutional agreements in different countries) pursuing the maximum-efficiency objective. Through central supervision of geographically spread activities, this type of investment aims to increase yields with specialization, economies of scale and scope, and risk diversification.

Although we have seen that the affiliate network of the average sample company is expanding, there are only a few *star companies* in a position to invest abroad for this reason. The important explanatory variable in this respect is the size and international experience of a company. Although Slovenian multinational companies are on average bigger and more experienced than companies without direct investments abroad they are still relatively small and inexperienced compared to Western multinationals. Since economic integration (and liberalization) usually stimulates this type of investment, we can expect their growth after Slovenia joins the EU.

Effects

The realized positive effects are the best guarantee for furthering the internationalization process. Experience of Slovenian direct investment abroad is in general good. According to our survey, 85% of sample companies assess the success of OFDI as expected; 10% are even positively surprised. Only 6% reported negative outcome.

Failure of OFDI is mostly attributed to management failures, particularly the poor choice of personnel, followed by the lack of capital and an unfavorable political climate. Particularly important factors of success are the quality of products and knowledge about competition and the foreign market (see Figure 2.6). Cooperation with foreign partner(s) is a less influential factor behind foreign investment success[15]. Firm specific advantages cannot be substituted by a partner's advantages, merely complemented.

The effects of OFDI on parent companies go hand in hand with the predominant motives. Evaluating the importance of outward investment's effects on parent company sample firms stressed in particular the exports and sales increase and growth of a company, which itself reflects the importance of the market-seeking motive. This was expressed through case studies as well as in the survey (see Figure 2.7). Cheap imports from affiliates abroad proved to be unimportant. Resource-seeking investments were considered least important.

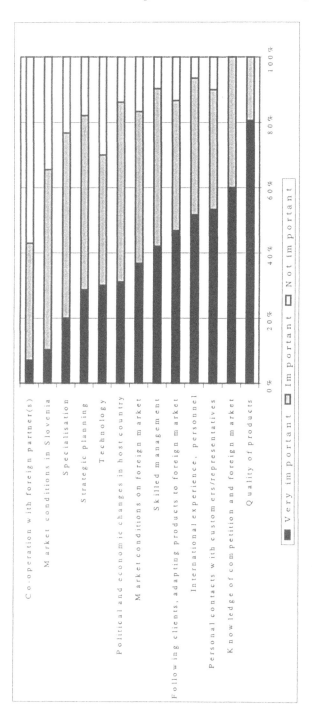

Figure 2.6   The importance of factors influencing the success of direct investment abroad

Source: Survey on OFDI of Slovenian companies, June–October 1999.

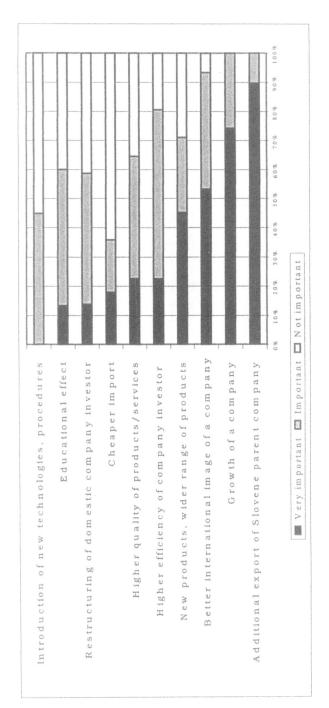

Figure 2.7   Importance of the impact of direct investment abroad

Source: Survey on DIA of Slovenian companies, June-October 1999.

Since induced export was the main result of direct investment abroad in a parent company, export and outward investments do not seem to be substitutes, but are in a complementary relationship. Investments with the objective of at least partly substituting previous exports with local production as predicted by the theory of the life cycle are very few. Not all firms yet realize that export markets could be lost if local production is not started as a consequence of the technological upgrading of local capabilities, along with increasing development aspirations of local companies and progress in general.

A complementary relationship between OFDI and exports may also exist in the other direction; that is, an increase in exports may lead to an increase in OFDI. For instance, after increased exports have established a certain level of demand for a product in a foreign market, firms may decide to invest abroad in order to retain and secure a stable level of demand in that market (Kim *et al.*, 1997). Sales in ex-Yugoslav markets (and later exports) were certainly so big that a stable level of demand was guaranteed. On the basis of such arguments, outward investment can also be expected in the future in the main current export markets, especially if we take into account the future investment plans of Slovenian exporters.

A better international image and higher efficiency of the parent company were also assessed as an important consequence of investing abroad. The important result for the majority of sample companies was the introduction of new products or a wider range of products as well as their higher quality. International competition thus motivates the parent company to develop a firm's specific advantages with direct investment abroad. This confirms Dunning & Narula's thesis that today companies invest abroad not only to use the existing advantages but also to strengthen them. Today, firms start investing abroad not only because they possess firm specific advantages, but also 'from the position of weakness' (Dunning and Narula, 1996); that is, because they seek to obtain advantages they do not have currently but are available abroad to strengthen existing competitive advantages or to speed up their process of catching up to the competitors. This was also the case in the past as demonstrated by the eclectic paradigm. Firms were strong in one area (firm-specific advantages), but weak in terms of local factor conditions. By investing abroad, companies can use available factor endowments abroad and thereby strengthen their factor conditions (see Rugman's critique of Porter's diamond, 1991). Therefore, they went abroad in order to benefit from the 'foreign diamond'. Since natural assets are nowadays losing their relative importance and the human factor (created assets) is becoming crucial, knowledge-seeking OFDI is gaining in importance. Firms tend to start investing abroad much earlier than they used to (see also Tolentino, 1993) in order to gain assets abroad.

In the survey, the majority of respondent companies regard learning effects as important. It seems however that knowledge spillover occurs only at the level of products (product adaptation and innovation), but not yet in the production process. Introduction of new technologies or procedures was namely evaluated as not having an important effect for most companies. If outward investments from medium-income countries such as Slovenia increased in the future, the function of acquiring foreign (created) assets not only in product innovation but also production processes and technology (innovation) will increase in importance.

A slight discrepancy between the important motives and effect was only noticed in terms of efficiency and restructuring. Higher efficiency and restructuring of a parent company were evaluated as being more important effects of OFDI than among motives. Even market-seeking motives stimulate companies to raise efficiency and competitiveness.

The significant impact of outward FDI is not only perceived on the firm's level but also at the national, macroeconomic, level. Export, sales and efficiency increase next to higher growth of companies directly investing abroad reflect also through importance in total Slovenian corporate sector. Although investing abroad companies represent a very modest share within the total corporate sector (approximately 1%), they have a substantial influence in the total corporate sector and create significant qualitative growth. The share of companies with OFDI within the total corporate sector fell slightly from 1994 to 1998, yet the share of selected balance sheet or income statement items generally increased (Figure 2.8).

Companies with direct investment abroad held 38% of the equity and 32% of all assets in 1998. They employed 27% of all employees and realized 25% of total sales and even 37% of the exports of the entire corporate sector. It is similar with value added and operating profit where investors realized 30% of value added and operating profit of the total corporate sector. The net profit share of investors in the total corporate sector is even higher (56.9%), so such a high share in investment outlays is not surprising. Such high shares in selected balance sheet and income statements proved that although small in number, companies with direct investment abroad are significantly influencing and improving the performance of the total Slovenian corporate sector. Successful business indicators are probably also results of internationalization through OFDI, though not the only one.

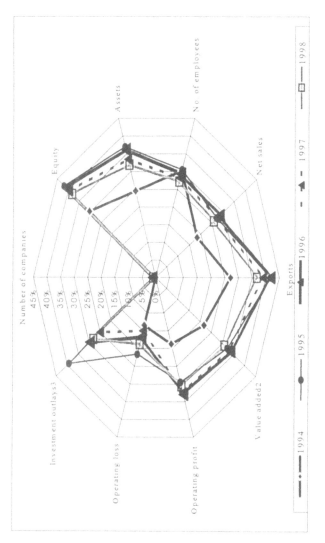

Figure 2.8 **The importance of companies with direct investment abroad within the total corporate sector**

Source: Survey on DIA of Slovenian companies, June–October 1999.

Conclusions

Slovenian companies started outward investment already under the previous regime. Such investment started even before inward foreign investment was allowed. During the transition and under the influence of globalization and EU integration trends, as well as increased competitive pressures from global markets, Slovenian companies are increasingly undertaking OFDI. They regard such moves as an efficient way to keep their market shares and strengthen their competitiveness. Their internationalization seems to be taking off. However, at the firm level it follows the traditional sequential approach in many dimensions, especially as concerns geographical concentration, foreign entry mode, and functional orientation.

Neither the different 'investment starting position' (very early system escape type of OFDI) nor the substantially changed international economic environment (globalization) have altered the investment development patterns of Slovenian companies at the macro-economic level.

Internationalization among companies with outward foreign direct investment is actually more intensive than the broadening of the process to those new companies starting directly investing abroad. Companies that started directly investing abroad already at the beginning of the 1990s have been expanding their international affiliate network quite rapidly over the last decade, while the number of 'newcomers' among direct investors abroad is stagnant. It seems that the deepening of internationalization of existing internationalized firms is stronger than is the widening of the process to include newcomers. Many Slovenian exporters plan to upgrade foreign operations from traditional exports to a direct presence in a foreign market, but the lack of knowledge and experience makes them unable to carry out such plans let alone to intensify them further. Necessary knowledge about foreign markets and operations can be acquired mainly through learning by doing such operations abroad. Considering internationalization as an accumulation of knowledge, the geographical concentration of Slovenia's outward FDI of recent times in countries emerging from former Yugoslavia, and the foreign entry mode sequence seeing outward FDI only following export operations, is not surprising.

When a firm is capable of internationalization through outward FDI it is also able to integrate into the wider economic area or, ultimately, into the global economy. Internationalization through outward FDI demonstrates both the increased capabilities of investing firms and a way to improve efficiency by attaining economies of scale and scope. International competition thus motivates the parent company to develop a firm's specific advantages with outward FDI, combine them with local specific advantages and speed up the process of catching up with the rivals.

At the firm level, these positive effects have already proved to be quite important for a number of companies. Direct investments abroad have mainly resulted in higher sales and exports of parent companies, reflecting the prevailing market-seeking type of investments in the case of Slovenia. The learning effect has also proved significant, although knowledge spillover so far occurs only at the level of products, and not yet in the production process.

Acquiring foreign (created) assets also in relation to the production process and technology may still be expected.

Regarding the importance of companies investing abroad in the total Slovenian corporate sector, these companies are clearly more successful than companies not participating in internationalization through outward FDI. They are a vital part of the Slovenian economy and are leading the process of restructuring. The modest level of OFDI (in terms of the companies involved) explains why more important development implications as a result of their activities have not yet been achieved at the macro-economic level. However, Slovenian OFDI is relatively more advanced compared to other CEECs and compared to the level of inward FDI (the volume of OFDI amounts to one-fifth of inward FDI). The main explanations for this are the early start of such undertakings (this type of internationalization) and a stronger tradition in the development of trade relations with Western countries.

Notes

1 This research was undertaken with support from the European Union's Phare ACE Program 1997. The content of the publication is the sole responsibility of the authors and in no way represents the views of the Commission of its services.
2 See, Buckley & Castro, 1998, 1999, Simoes, 2000.
3 See, Luostarinen, 1979 and 1994.
4 Stock and flows were consistently monitored only since 1993.
5 A postal survey was carried out from June 1999 to October 1999. Managers of companies directly investing abroad were addressed. As a sample framework for companies with DIA, we used all of the companies investing abroad as registered at the Bank of Slovenia in 1997. The sample included 32 companies (7.7% of companies with DIA) and represented 15.9% of Slovenian DIA by value and 17.4% of Slovenian DIA by number. Excluding bank capital, this sample represented 22.7% of the DIA of the corporate sector. The survey was prepared within the ACE project 'Outward internationalization facilitating transformation and EU Accession; the case of the Czech Republic, Hungary and Slovenia'.
6 For more, see Svetličič, Rojec, and Lebar, 1994; Svetličič, 1994.
7 Sometimes or initially, it was the only source of finance.

8 See, Rojec, 1998.
9 The only comparable country in transition in this regard would be the Czech Republic with its 'inherited' investment in Slovakia.
10 This second survey was also undertaken with support from the European Union's Phare ACE Program 1997. The content of the publication is the sole responsibility of the authors and in no way represents the views of the Commission or its services.
11 In many cases they are limited mostly to the knowledge of markets of penetration, either they are a former Yugoslav market or markets of former socialist countries.
12 As a measure of transnationality, the network spread index of a country reflects the number of host countries in which foreign affiliates are established (N). The index is derived as a percentage of N^*, the number of foreign countries in which the companies could have potentially located affiliates. N^* is chosen to be the number of countries in the world that have inward FDI minus 1 (to exclude the home country of the companies). On the basis of WIR 1997 N^*=178 (WIR 1998).
13 Croatia has proved itself as the market most frequently used for the first entry to foreign markets through FDI.
14 The Scandinavian countries, i.e., Finland (Luostarinen, 1979, 1994), Sweden (Johanson J., and Wiedersheim-Paul F., 1975), Portugal (Buckley and Castro, 1998, 1999; Simoes, 2000).
15 This is in line with the equity shares of Slovenian firms in foreign affiliates that are usually totally or mostly owned by Slovenian investors.

References

Buckley, P. and Castro, B. (1998), 'A Time Series Analysis of the Locational Determinants of Outward Foreign Direct Investment in Portugal', Academy of International Business, 25th Annual Conference, Vienna, Austria, October 8-11, 1998.

Buckley, P. and Castro, B. (1999), 'Outward Foreign Direct Investment in Manufacturing from Portugal: Internationalization Strategies from a New Foreign Investor', Annual Conference, European International Business Academy, Manchester, UK, December 12-14, 1999.

Buckley, P. and Castro, F. (1998), 'The investment development path: the case of Portugal' *Transnational Corporations*, vol. 1, no. 7, pp. 1-16.

Cantwell, J. (1994), *Transnational Corporations and Innovatory Activities*, London: Routledge.

Chesnais, F. (1995), 'Some Relationship between Foreign Direct Investment, Technology, Trade, and Competitiveness', in J. Hagedoorn (ed.)*Technical Change and the World Economy: Convergence and Divergence in Technology Strategies*, Cheltenham: Edward Elgar.

Dunning, J. (1993), *Multinational Enterprises and the Global Economy*, Workingham: Addison Wesley.

Dunning, J. and Narula, R. (1996), *Foreign Direct Investment and Governments: Catalysts for Economic Restructuring*, London and New York: Routledge.

Johanson, J. and Wiedersheim-Paul, F., (1975), 'The Internationalisation of the Firm - Four Swedish Cases', *Journal of Management Studies*, October, pp. 305-322.

Johanson, J. and Vahlne, J.-E. (1977), 'The Internationalisation Process of the Firm - A Model of Knowledge Development and Increasing Market Commitments'. *Journal of International Business Studies*, vol. 8, no. 1, pp. 23-32.

Kim, J.-D. (1997), 'Outward FDI and Exports: The Case of South Korea and Japan', *Journal of Asian Economics*, Spring, vol. 8, no. 1, p. 12.

Krašovec, T. s sodelavci (1996), *Internacionalizacija Sovenskega Gospodarstva*, Ljubljana: Združenje Manager, Februar.

Luostarinen, R. (1994), 'Internationalisation of Finish Firms and Their Response to Global Challenges', UNU World Institute for Development Economic Research (UNU/WIDER).

Luostarinen, R. (1979), *The Internationalization of the Firm*, Helsinki: Helsinki Scholl of Economics and Business Administration, Ph.D. Thesis.

Ozawa, T. (1992), 'Foreign Direct Investment and Economic Development', *Transnational Corporations,* vol. 1, no. 1, pp. 36-75.

Rojec, M., (1998), 'Foreign Direct Investment's Effect on Restructuring and Efficiency Upgrading in Slovenia's Manufactoring Sector', *Journal of International Relations and Development.* vol. 1, no. 1-2, pp. 46-64.

Simoes, V. (2000), 'The Internationalization of Portuguese Firms: History, Policy and Behaviour', CEDE/ISEG, Technical University of Lisbon.

Svetličič, M. (1994), 'Foreign direct investment and transformation, public expectations and results – The case of Slovenia', in K. Fatemi (ed.), *The Globalisation of Business in the 1990s: Implications for Trade and Investment*, Dallas: Texas International University Press.

Svetličič, M., Rojec, M., and Lebar, S. (1994), 'Internationalization Strategies of Slovenian Firms: The German Market Case', in K. Obloj (ed.) *High Speed Competition in Europe*, Proceedings of the 20th Annual Conference of European International Business Association, Warsaw: International Management Center, University of Warsaw, pp. 361-385.

Tolentino, P. (1993), *Technological Innovation and Third World Multinationals*, London: Routledge.

Vernon, R. (1966), 'International Investment and International Trade in the Product Cycle', *Quarterly Journal of Economics*, vol. 80, pp. 190-207.

Welch, L. and Luostarinen, R. (1988), 'Internationalisation: Evolution of Concept', *Journal of General Management*, vol. 14, no. 2, pp. 36-64.

World Investment Report (1998), *Trends and Determinants*, United Nations Conference on Trade and Development, Division on Transnational Corporations and Investment, Geneva: United Nations Publications.

3 Internationalization of a Post-Communist Economy – Opportunities and Threats: The Case of Poland

MARIAN GORYNIA

Introduction

Until 1990 when the transition towards market orientation began, the Polish economy had been to a large extent closed as regards to its ties with the external environment. Development processes occurring in Poland after World War II bore many signs of autarchy. Economic cooperation with foreign countries outside the Council for Mutual Economic Assistance (CMEA) was very limited and unsatisfactorily used to accelerate the economic growth and increase economic effectiveness. Potential advantages from the international division of labor were not used properly. Poland's share in the world exports and imports was very low. The structure of foreign trade was distorted. The exports of Poland and other Central and Eastern European (CEE) countries to the OECD were much below the level determined by economic factors, while the exports to the CMEA countries were much higher.

One of the characteristic features of the market transformations of the Polish economy is the fact that it is becoming more and more open, i.e., the economic ties with foreign partners are being developed very quickly. There are many forms of internationalization of the Polish economy. Two of them deserve particular attention: trade exchange and foreign direct investment (FDI). Their dynamic development offers many advantages to the Polish economy. At the same time, however, there exist certain threats that, in extreme case, may undermine or destroy the advantages coming from the open economy.

In the post-communist countries the processes of internationalization are of specific nature as they occur in the conditions of very deep restructuring of the internal system of regulation from the administrative-bureaucratic to market oriented. The following problems are touched upon in this chapter:

- Premises for deeper internationalization of competitive relations.
- Most important problems of the development of Polish foreign trade in the period of market transformation of the economy.
- Main aspects of FDI in Poland.

Internationalization of Competition versus Transformation of a Post-Communist Economy

Internationalization of competition is not a new process. One can say that it begins when enterprises traditionally functioning on the internal markets in their home countries start economic operations (trade, production) abroad. These processes began to appear on a larger scale in this century. Internationalization of competition also embraced, although for obvious reasons to a limited extent, the Polish enterprises operating in the whole post-war period when foreign trade was a state monopoly. From the viewpoint of the Polish enterprises the beginning of market transformation of the Polish economy resulted in much wider and more extensive processes of internationalization of competition. In the above-mentioned context one may ask a question – what kind of premises influence the range and acceleration of internationalization of competitive behavior of Polish enterprises. It seems that these premises belong to two categories: the premises of specific character for Poland and other post-communist countries, and non-specific premises, generally pertaining to the evolution of international economic relations on a global scale. Specific premises of internationalization are as follows: opening of the post-communist economies, liquidation of the CMEA, and tendencies towards economic integration with Western industrialized countries. The second group of premises covers various aspects of the progressive globalization of economic activities and attempts of a more liberal organization of economic relations between all the countries in the world.

The concept of opening of the economy is being implemented in most post-communist countries. The programs of fiscal and monetary stabilization are carried out along with liberalization of a broadly defined foreign policy. The main measures in this field include: introduction of (limited) convertibility of the national currency, introduction of relatively liberal customs tariffs, abolishment (to a considerable extent) of non-tariff instruments of exports and imports regulation, demonopolization of foreign trade, implementation of the principle of economic freedom in the sphere of economic relations across national borders (Gorynia and Otta, 1995a; Gorynia and Otta, 1995b).

Abandoning the instruments of central regulation, a typical characteristic of command economies, resulted in the fact that home exporters and importers 'got closer' to the foreign markets. For the exporters this meant above all full self-financing with no possibility of subsidies. On the other hand, imports became a real threat for the home producers who frequently lost their share in the home market because of the free access to convertible currencies for financing imports.

Moreover, the liquidation of CMEA contributed to the internationalization of competition of formerly existing and new businesses. CMEA can be defined as an enclave of non-market behaviors of supranational scale. On the one hand, CMEA brought to member countries among other benefits access to massive, secure markets, and access to 'cheap' raw materials. On the other hand, there was no motivation to introduce innovation, to develop new products, and improve their quality. At the same time the binding principles of exchange (procedure of determining the lists of commodities, yearly protocols, way of establishing prices, exchange rates, etc.) led to a completely blurred calculation of effectiveness of the economic ties between member countries. Thus, one can state that the liquidation of CMEA facilitated the transition to market orientation and the introduction of competitive economic relations by firms in the former communist countries.

A very significant premise for the internationalization of competition of post-communist enterprises is the attempt for economic integration with the European Union (EU). This integration means a quicker and more complete opening of the national CEE economies towards EU partners. It creates both great opportunities and immense threats for the enterprises in the countries that strive for this integration. Some of these opportunities are already experienced by Polish enterprises. Hypothetically, the access to the immense EU market should be easy. However, the abolishment of administrative barriers and customs barriers does not necessarily guarantee success. The rest belongs to the enterprises themselves. They have to develop and rely on their competitive advantage. Threats stem from the resignation of the protection of home producers and their exposure to a direct rivalry with EU competitors. The effects of such a procedure will probably be of twofold. The new competitive challenges will enforce some Polish companies to become more competitive. Others will not be able to cope with the strong competitive pressures that will not positively affect their international competitiveness.

As mentioned above, the general non-specific premises for the internationalization of competition are, among others, connected with progressive and more intensive globalization processes. Globalization of markets results from the fact that some firms, operating on an international scale, carry out global strategies the implementation of which is a result of the changing conditions of international competition leading to a fiercer competitive struggle (Gorynia and Otta, 1989). Globalization is basically connected with demand premises. The main premise of this kind is an idea of 'the global product' according to which, at least in economic sectors, we deal with the uniformity of needs on the international scale (Levitt, 1983). The uniformity of needs creates the grounds for the uniformity of product that in turn provides an opportunity to achieve advantages of scale. In this way the demand premises of globalization are linked with the premises of effectiveness. The following factors are most frequently mentioned among those that favor globalization: the possibility of advantages of scale, necessity to allocate large outlays for research and development and low costs of transport (Hout, Porter and Rudden, 1982). The global strategy is defined as a strategy thanks to which a firm operating internationally tries to achieve competitive advantage either through concentrated configuration (distribution, location of particular kinds of the firm's economic activity) or coordination (a way of coordination of similar or related types of the firm activity). Both ways may be applied simultaneously (Porter, 1986).

Internationalization of competition has been and will be favored by the regulations of international economic relations determined by the General Agreement on Tariffs and Trade (GATT) at the Uruguay Round and recently by the World Trade Organization (WTO) (Kaczurba and Kawecka-Wyrzykowska, 1995). Their aim is a full liberalization of the international economic and trade cooperation. Successive lifting of barriers in the turnover will result in a wider range and more intensified processes of the internationalization of competition.

Foreign Trade in the Polish Economy under Transformation

Sphere of Regulation

Until recently Poland's foreign economic policy, and more specifically foreign trade policy, has been linked to the program of stabilization. The main aim of the stabilization program was to curb inflation.

The aim of the changes introduced in the sphere of regulations in the years 1989–1997 was to transform the Polish economy from a basically closed one into an open one.

The foreign trade policy in the above-mentioned period was not uniform. The following stages can be identified (Płowiec, 1997):

- Stage I (from the beginning of 1990 until August 1991) was characterized by liberalization of commodity prices, lifting of subventions (including export subventions), strong devaluation of the zloty, introduction of its external convertibility and a wide liberalization of imports.
- Stage II (from September 1991 until the end of 1993) when adjustment to be associated with the EU was commenced, despite the lack of positive changes in the structure and volume of the existing production capacities.
- Stage III (commenced in 1994) is marked by a clearly more active trade policy and the stimulation of restructuring of production and exports.

In the economic policy carried out in the years 1990–1997 four main trends can be differentiated (Otta and Gorynia, 1993):

- Fiscal and monetary stabilization.
- Liberalization of trade.
- Institutional transformation.
- Restructuring.

The most significant changes in the sphere of foreign trade regulations are enumerated below in chronological order:

- Liberalization of most prices, elimination of subventions (1990).
- Substantial devaluation of the zloty and introduction of its internal convertibility (1990).
- Extreme liberalization of imports (1990).
- Introduction of a new customs tariff based on terminology used by the EU (1991).
- Introduction of the principle of crawling devaluation of the zloty (1991) and simultaneous jumping devaluations (1991–1993).
- Implementation of transition agreement with the EU on the creation of free trade zones concerning industrial goods (1992). This agreement anticipated that the process of reduction of customs rates on industrial goods would last 10 years. The agreement contained an asymmetric schedule of the reduction of customs rates favorable for Poland.
- Implementation of other agreements similar to that with the EU with EFTA and CEFTA countries (1993).
- Replacing the turnover tax imposed, among others, on imported goods with VAT (1993); the basic rate of this tax amounts to 22% and the preferential rate – to 7%.

- From the beginning of 1993, due to difficulties with the balance of payments, temporary introduction of 6% import tax was agreed on with GATT (this tax was lifted at the beginning of 1997).
- In order to facilitate the restructuring of industry, from the year 1993 the suspension of duties and customs quotas (particularly for raw materials) was applied.
- Introduction of incentives for investment – a possibility to deduct part of investment outlays from taxable income (1994).
- Systematic slowdown in the rate of devaluation of the zloty (1994–1998).
- Poland has gained the status of a market economy country and starts participating in the process of reduction of customs and non-customs barriers in trade relations with WTO member countries.
- February 1, 1994 – Implementation (after a two-year period of ratification) of the European Agreement determining the principles of Poland's association with the EU; unilateral protective clauses for Poland as a weaker partner deserve attention. They include: the clause of the restructuring of industry, a protective clause as regards the establishment of EU enterprises in Poland and the clause enabling Poland to apply restrictions in hard currency turnover until the Polish currency is fully convertible.
- Liberalization of the import of goods caused by a simultaneous implementation of the resolutions of the Final Act of the Uruguay Round, European Agreement, agreements with CEFTA and EFTA (in the period 1995–1998).
- Liberalization of hard currency turnover including, among others, the introduction of convertibility of the zloty (June 1995) according to the standard of the article eight of the IMF Statutes and abandoning of the obligatory reselling of hard currency to banks by the exporters (1995) as well as liberalization of the export of capital from Poland.
- Application of export supporting instruments, such as export credits and insurance of export credits (the range of application of these tools is very narrow).
- Flexibility of the exchange rate policy, i.e., replacing the official exchange rate with the central exchange rate that fulfills the function of a preferential rate while determining the limits of fluctuations (1995).
- Poland's membership in the OECD thanks to which the conditions of access of foreign capital to the Polish market were eased (1996).

Generally, the stated changes in the sphere of regulation should be evaluated as positive. These changes created a basis for Poland's larger participation in the international division of labor. Polish economy became more open to international economic cooperation. This creates many opportunities for Polish companies simultaneously posing some threats.

Dynamics of Turnover against the Background of the Economic Situation

Table 3.1 presents the indicators of the dynamics of exports, imports, GDP, industrial production and unemployment in the years 1990–1997. In this period exports (after a considerable initial growth in 1990) declined in the years 1991–1993 by 2.5% annually. However, from the beginning of 1994 the indicators of export dynamics were already positive.

Throughout the whole analyzed period imports grew dynamically. It should also be underlined that in the period 1995–1997 the turnover of the Polish foreign trade increased much quicker than the turnover of the world economy or of the EU.

Geographical Structure of Trade Exchange

Table 3.2 presents the geographical structure of Poland's foreign trade turnover in 1989–1997.

A characteristic feature of the Polish foreign trade in the 1990s was a strong reorientation of trade from East to West. In 1988 exports to CEE countries constituted about 40% of the total exports, and in 1993 – only 13%. From 1994 this share was steadily growing and amounted to 24% in 1997. In 1988 the share of exports to the EU countries amounted to approximately 28% and in 1993 it reached over 63%. In 1995 these exports amounted to as much as 70% and afterwards they started to decline. It is also easy to notice a steady declining tendency in the share of the developing countries in the Polish exports.

As regards imports, there was a visible growth trend in the share of imports from EU countries in the total imports. This tendency broke down in 1996. On the other hand, the share of CEE countries in Polish imports was declining until 1993 and afterwards it began to increase.

Numerous articles referring to the so-called gravitation model indicated the necessity for a strategic turn in the Polish foreign trade (reorientation from East to West). Political factors were responsible for the fact that the volume of Polish trade with CMEA countries before 1990 was too large, while that with the OECD countries was too small as compared with the level determined by economic factors (Winters and Wang, 1994).

Table 3.1   Dynamics of the volume of Polish exports and imports, GDP and industrial production (previous year=100), and unemployment rates (in %)

Specification	1990	1991	1992	1993	1994	1995	1996	1997
Exports	113.7	97.6	97.4	98.9	118.3	116.7	109.7	113.7
Imports	101.5	137.8	113.9	118.5	113.4	120.5	128.0	122.0
GDP	92.9	93.0	102.6	103.8	105.2	107.0	106.1	106.9
Industrial production	76.8	92.0	102.8	106.4	112.1	109.7	108.3	110.8
Unemployment rate	6.5	12.2	14.3	16.4	16.0	14.9	13.2	10.5

Sources: Assessment of social-economic situation in 1997 along with elements of the forecast for 1998, Government Center for Strategic Studies, Warsaw, February 1998; Polish foreign trade in 1997, Annual Report, Foreign Trade Research Institute, Warsaw, 1998.

Table 3.2   **Geographical structure of Poland's foreign trade turnover in the years 1989–1996 (calculated on the basis of current prices expressed in zlotys, shares in %)**

Specification	1989	1990	1991	1992	1993	1994	1995	1996	1997
Total exports	94.7*	100.0	100.0	100.0	100.0	100.0	100.0	100.0	100.0
Highly developed countries:	49.1	67.1	73.8	71.9	75.1	75.4	75.0	71.7	69.0
• EU countries	32.1	45.6	55.7	58.0	60.2	62.7	70.0	66.4	64.0
• EFTA countries	10.9	16.8	14.1	10.3	7.9	8.2	1.6	2.2	1.5
Developing countries	10.3	10.6	9.4	12.7	11.6	10.1	7.7	7.8	6.6
CEE countries and ex-USSR	35.1	22.3	16.8	15.4	13.3	14.5	17.3	20.5	24.4
• including CEFTA	7.1	5.1	5.3	5.1	4.8	4.8	5.4	6.1	6.8
Total imports	92.7*	100.0	100.0	100.0	100.0	100.0	100.0	100.0	100.0
Highly developed countries:	53.0	65.3	68.4	72.4	76.2	75.1	74.3	73.6	73.5
• EU countries	33.8	47.2	49.7	53.2	57.2	57.5	64.6	63.9	63.8
• EFTA countries	14.7	13.8	14.8	12.9	11.2	11.2	3.1	2.5	2.5
Developing countries	6.9	13.3	12.3	11.3	10.3	10.6	10.3	10.9	11.6
CEE countries and ex-USSR	32.7	21.4	19.3	16.3	13.5	14.3	15.4	15.5	14.9
• including CEFTA	7.3	4.5	4.0	4.1	3.6	4.3	5.6	5.8	6.3

* Excluding the former communist countries.

Sources: Perczyński, 1997; Statistical Yearbooks of the Central Statistical Office.

It must be underlined that the gravitation model makes it possible to measure only distortions in the geographical structure of foreign trade. This model, however, gives no suggestions about the extent of the inherited deformations in the commodity structure of trade exchange with foreign countries.

Commodity Structure of Trade Exchange

Table 3.3 presents the structure of Polish exports and imports in terms of economic sectors. However, the data of such a high level of aggregation are difficult to interpret.

More detailed articles on the changes in commodity structure of the Polish foreign trade in the years 1990–1997 indicate two main factors (Płowiec, 1997):

• Primitive character of the commodity structure of exports.
• Growth of import penetration in certain groups of commodities.

The phenomenon of the so-called backwardness of the structure of exports is obvious. It means that the significance of highly processed export goods and the share of added value were lower in comparison to the value of material and energy intensive export products of relatively low technological level (Perczyński, 1997).

According to the most recent data the share of electromechanical goods in Polish total exports declined to 22.4% in 1997. In the same year growth dynamics higher than the average for all Polish exports were reached in the groups of agricultural-food products, furniture, wood and wood products as well as chemical and metallurgical products (Piotrowski, 1998).

Moreover, some attention should be paid to a positive phenomenon in the structure of imports. Recent years have witnessed a high dynamics of growth in investment import. In the structure of imports according to ways of their use the share of investment import went up from 13.0% in 1995 to 15.3% in 1997.

Trade Balance

Table 3.4 presents the development of Polish trade balance and the relations between repayment of debts and revenues from the export of commodities in the period 1990–1997.

Table 3.3   Structure of exports and imports according to branches in current prices in the years 1989-1997

Specification		1989	1990	1993	1994	1995	1996	1997
Fuels and power	I	12.4	20.7	12.6	10.5	9.2	9.2	8.8
	E	9.6	10.1	9.5	8.9	8.0	6.7	6.5
Metallurgical industry	I	8.8	6.9	4.6	4.9	5.8	5.1	5.0
	E	10.5	14.6	14.6	13.8	12.2	10.4	10.9
Electromechanical industry	I	36.3	39.8	34.4	33.8	35.1	38.2	41.6
	E	38.4	29.3	25.8	25.8	27.6	29.6	27.7
Chemical industry	I	15.2	11.6	17.5	19.2	19.2	18.0	18.0
	E	10.5	12.0	9.8	10.0	11.4	11.4	11.6
Extractive industry	I	1.3	1.3	2.1	2.4	2.6	2.5	2.6
	E	1.3	1.7	3.3	3.4	3.2	3.3	3.1
Wood and paper industry	I	1.9	1.6	3.6	3.9	4.7	4.4	4.5
	E	2.9	4.1	8.3	9.9	11.3	11.4	12.1
Light industry	I	7.6	6.1	10.0	10.6	10.0	8.6	7.9
	E	5.5	6.4	15.3	14.8	14.1	14.0	12.9
Food industry	I	9.5	7.8	7.7	7.8	6.8	6.6	6.1
	E	9.6	10.0	9.1	9.7	8.5	9.6	11.3
Other branches of industry	I	1.7	2.1	3.0	3.0	2.7	2.6	2.5
	E	0.6	0.6	0.8	0.8	0.9	1.2	1.2
Agricultural products	I	4.9	2.0	4.2	3.3	3.5	4.2	2.7
	E	4.1	5.4	3.0	2.5	2.5	1.9	1.7

Sources: Statistical Yearbook of Foreign Trade 1997, Warsaw, 1997; Statistical Yearbook of Foreign Trade 1998, Warsaw, 1998.

The trade deficit, worsening from year to year, has been the main factor influencing the balance of current turnover. In 1997 this balance amounted to US$ – 4.3 billion that constituted 3.2% of the GDP. The factor which smoothes the effect of high deficit in the trade exchange is the revenues from the so-called cross-border trade.

Negative trade exchange balance is created mainly through the exchange with the EU countries. According to customs statistics, which register the flow of goods, not the actually made payments, the deficit in trade with the EU increased from US$ – 7.3 billion in 1996 to US$ – 10.5 billion in 1997. It should also be underlined that a significant factor influencing the Polish trade exchange balance is the balance of exchange of FDI in Poland with export activities. In the period 1994–1997 it amounted to US$ – 2.8 billion in 1994, US$ – 3.9 billion in 1995, US$ – 7.4 billion in 1996, and US$ – 10.0 billion in 1997. Substantial import requirements of the firms with foreign capital result from modernization of their production potential (investment import) and a high demand for the import of materials (Durka, 1998).

The high and still worsening deficit in the balance of current turnover is the biggest threat for the further steady economic development of Poland. Official publications show that the countries which opened their economies and joined the European Union (Spain, Portugal, and Greece) also noted aconsiderable worsening of their current trade balance. Similarly, they have also financed the current balance deficit with the surplus of the capital balance (Nowicki 1997). Implementation of an appropriate macroeconomic policy is necessary in such a situation to prevent overheating of the economy and inflation related tensions.

Foreign Direct Investment – Regulations, Inflow, Effects

Evolution of the Legal Institutional Conditions for the Inflow of Foreign Capital

A major feature of the Polish economic transition is the systematic opening of the economy to foreign investment. This is favored by the changes in regulations on this sphere of economic cooperation with foreign countries.

The following factors had the most powerful influence on the opening of the country to inflows of foreign capital in the form of FDI (Kubielas, Monkowski and Jackson, 1996):

- Liberalization of legal regulations concerning the inflow of FDI.

Table 3.4   Commodity payments and relation between debt repayment and export revenues in the years 1990–1997

Specification	1990	1991	1992	1993	1994	1995	1996	1997
Commodity payments in billion USD								
• Exports revenues	10,863	12,760	13,997	13,585	16,950	22,878	24,420	27,233
• Payments for imports	8,649	12,709	13,485	15,878	17,786	24,705	32,574	38,522
• Balance	2,214	51	512	-2,293	-836	-1,827	-8,154	-11,289
Relation between debt repayment and export revenues in %	6.8	10.5	11.0	13.2	8.7	9.0	10.2	8.3

- Liberalization of international trade exchanges and of the principles of currency convertibility.
- Privatization of state-owned enterprises.

Before the beginning of Polish transition to market, there existed a so-called enclave model concerning FDI's preferential treatment vis-à-vis the other types of investment (Samonis, 1992). The legal-institutional changes in the conditions for the inflow of foreign capital meant abandoning this model in favor of treating FDI in the same way as the domestic investments.

The enclave model functioning in Poland had the following characteristics:

- Participation of foreign capital was permitted only for small foreign businesses or in larger joint venture companies with a minority share of foreign capital in the ownership structure.
- Complicated procedure of granting licenses.
- Wide range of sectors where the penetration of foreign capital was forbidden or restricted.
- Obligation to resell foreign currency revenues from exports to hard currency banks.
- Restrictions on foreign profit repatriation.
- Restrictions in the purchase of real estate.
- Tax holidays in terms of income tax.

The 1991 Act on the activities of economic entities with foreign capital created identical treatment of FDI companies and firms with domestic capital. The most important features of the Act regulating foreign investments are as follows:

- No restrictions to the amount of invested capital and the transfer of profit.
- Necessity to obtain licenses from the state when the property of state owned legal entities is made available to companies with FDI. Licenses are granted by the minister of State Treasury in response to the application of an economic entity.
- Abandoning of the principle of automatic three-year tax holidays.
- Full guarantee of compensation in case of expropriation.
- Foreign entities can start their activity in two major forms: limited liability companies and joint stock companies (this is an exception to the principle of national treatment approved by the OECD).
- In the field of lotteries and betting FDI is impossible.
- Other restrictions in observing the national treatment principle refer to the maximum share of foreign capital in the initial capital of the

company, for example in telecommunication services the limit is up to 49%, in other communications – up to 33%, and in radio and television industries – up to 33%.

Volume and Structure of Foreign Direct Investments

The data on the value of FDI in Poland are presented in Table 3.5. These data show that in the first half of the 1990s the volume of investment in Poland was by no means impressive.

Table 3.5   Stock of FDI in Poland in 1989–1997 (in US$ million)

Year	Investment above 1 million US$	Investment below 1 million US$	Joint investment
1989	8	1	9
1990	105	15	120
1991	324	45	369
1992	1,408	197	1,605
1993	2,828	396	3,224
1994	4,321	605	4,926
1995	6,832	956	7,788
1996	12,028	1,999	14,027
1997	17,705	2,882	20,587

Source: Olesiński and Pac-Pomarnacki, 1998.

Recently Poland has become a leader among the countries of Central and Eastern Europe in terms of the FDI inflow and stock, overtaking Hungary (see Table 3.6). However, it must be kept in mind that in the calculation of the value of foreign investment per capita, Hungary, Slovenia and the Czech Republic rank before Poland.

Table 3.6   Inflow of foreign direct investment in the chosen countries of CEE in the years 1993–1996 (in US$ million)

Country	1993	1994	1995	1996
CEE	6,287	5,882	14,317	12,261
Albania	58	53	70	72
Belarus	10	15	7	18
Bulgaria	55	105	90	150
Czech R.	654	878	2,568	1,200
Estonia	162	215	202	138
Lithuania	30	31	73	152
Latvia	45	214	180	152
Moldova	14	12	67	292
Poland	1,715	1,875	3,659	5,196
Russia	700	638	2,017	1,800
Romania	94	341	410	624
Slovakia	199	203	183	150
Ukraine	200	159	267	440
Hungary	2,350	1,144	4,519	1,982

Source: Olesiński and Pac-Pomarnacki, 1998.

Table 3.7   Entities with the share of foreign capital against the total number of entities registered in the REGON system in the years 1991–1997 (the state as of December 31)

Year	Number of entities with foreign capital*	Share in total number of national economy entities (%)
1991	5,583	4.1
1992	10,817	6.9
1993	15,814	8.6
1994	20,324	10.4
1995	24,635	11.7
1996	29,157	12.2
1997	33,459	12.8

*Includes commercial law firms with foreign capital and foreign small businesses.

Source: Chojna, 1998.

According to the data from the end of 1997 in the recording system REGON, there were jointly registered 33,459 entities with FDI, of which 32,941 were commercial law companies and 518 were small foreign businesses (Chojna, 1998). The FDI entities constituted 12.8% of the total number of the registered businesses in the national economy (excluding investments made by individuals and civil associations), against 12.2% in the end of 1996, 10.4% in the end of 1994 and merely 4.1% in the end of 1991 (see Table 3.7). However, it must be underlined that the very fact of registering the company in the REGON system does not mean engaging in a sustained economic activity. A part of the registered entities have not undertaken any economic operations, others have suspended their activities, while some have been liquidated or gone bankrupt. Foreign investors who have put in capital of at least US$ 1 million have been monitored by the State Agency for Foreign Investment (PAIZ). Table 3.8 presents the number of investors originating from a country that has made more than ten investments in Poland. The table shows that the investors from Germany, the USA, France, and Italy occupy the leading positions.

Table 3.8   The number of largest foreign investors in Poland in the years 1993–1997 (the state for the end of the year)

Countries	1993	1994	1995	1996	1997
USA	45	53	62	77	91
Germany	34	53	79	113	134
International concerns	8	11	14	15	15
Italy	3	6	17	29	44
France	19	20	29	42	51
Holland	9	11	13	32	34
Great Britain	12	15	21	21	26
Austria	10	18	23	30	34
Sweden	8	9	16	30	36
Denmark	5	10	13	16	22
Finland	4	5	6	9	11
Belgium	0	11	13	14	15
Canada	12	13	18	19	19

Source: Olesiński and Pac-Pomarnacki, 1998.

When considering the value of the capital invested by the end of 1997, the list of foreign investors with at least US$ 1 million invested capital is dominated by US firms, followed by German and multinational corporations (Table 3.9).

Table 3.9 List of the largest foreign investors in Poland in the period 1993–1997 considering the actual investments made – as of year end status

Countries	1993	1994	1995	1996	1997
USA	1,028.00	1,413.70	1,698.00	2,965.60	3,981.80
Germany	212.00	386.40	683.00	1,524.40	2,104.90
Multinationals concerns	290.00	808.30	1,101.00	1,493.00	1,654.00
Italy	270.00	365.80	495.00	1,223.80	1,636.30
France	177.00	268.10	574.00	899.90	1,616.40
Holland	233.00	240.40	408.00	9,512.70	1,213.60
South Korea	5.00	5.00	69.00	184.50	1,077.80
Great Britain	68.00	112.20	368.00	509.00	1,002.00
Austria	195.00	159.70	248.00	315.30	660.30
Sweden	71.00	86.70	179.00	361.30	565.80
Switzerland	51.00	112.00	196.00	357.70	445.30
Australia	5.00	6.30	298.00	328.10	354.10
Denmark	24.00	60.20	124.00	238.20	306.80
Norway	42.00	46.90	29.00	80.10	240.00
Ireland	7.00	7.00	47.00	105.70	191.20

Source: Olesiński and Pac-Pomarnacki, 1998.

The list of most significant foreign investors is presented in Table 3.10. It must be underlined that from 1994 the first ten most important investors have not changed. FIAT, EBOR, Polish/American Entrepreneurship Fund, IPC, Coca-Cola and ABB are undisputed leaders. The new firms on the list are Daewoo, PepsiCo, ING Group and Philip Morris.

Table 3.10   The largest foreign investors in Poland – actual investments made by the end of 1997

Investor	US$ Million	Branch
FIAT	1,141.9	Car industry
Daewoo	1,011.3	Car industry
EBOR	616.5	Banking
PepsiCo	412.0	Food industry
IPC	370.0	Paper industry
ING Group	350.0	Banking
Coca-Cola	285.0	Food industry
ABB	282.0	Engineering industry
Philip Morris	282.0	Tobacco industry
IFC	277.3	Financial intermediation
Nestle	248.0	Food industry

Source: Raport o inwestycjach zagranicznych w Polsce, "Rzeczpospolita" nr 157, 7 lipca 1997.

In terms of economic sectors the structure of foreign investment in Poland looks interesting. At the end of 1997 there were three dominating sectors: manufacturing, financial intermediaries and services (see Table 3.11).

Significance and Effects of Foreign Direct Investment

The role of foreign direct investment can be defined through:

- The share of these investments in the GDP and the total number of investments.
- Creation of new jobs and labor productivity.
- The share of entities with foreign capital in Polish foreign trade.

Table 3.11   Foreign investment in economic sectors as of the end of 1997 (in US$ million)

Economic sectors	Investments	Investment plans
Manufacturing including:	11,042.0	5,782.6
• Food products, beverages, tobacco	3,276.9	1,109.4
• Means of transport	2,510.5	1,969.5
• Paper, publishing and printing activity	1,158.4	293.3
• Chemicals, chemical products	1,087.4	518.0
• Other non-metallic raw materials	971.4	864.5
• Optical and electrical appliances	667.4	260.8
• Metals and processed metallic products	375.3	184.3
Financial intermediation	3,130.4	422.0
Trade and repairs	1,408.5	2,033.8
Transport, storage and telecommunications	734.5	299.4
Construction	554.9	511.8
Service and municipal activity	354.6	232.0
Hotels and restaurants	305.5	431.0
Electricity, gas and water supply	96.5	1,040.0
Real estate servicing	38.3	24.5
Mining and extraction	16.2	0.0
Agriculture and fisheries	15.0	0.0
Total	17,705.4	10,777.1

Source: Olesiński and Pac-Pomarnacki, 1998.

- Comparison of invested capital in FDI companies with the investment volume in other enterprises.
- Comparison of the financial performance of FDI entities vis-à-vis other entities.
- Contribution of FDI to the privatization of the Polish economy.

The share of foreign direct investments in the GDP and in the total number of investments is presented in Table 3.12. In the period 1994–1996 this share constantly increased and in 1997 started stabilizing.

Table 3.12   Relations between the inflow of FDI[a] in the GDP value and the total investment made in the period 1994–1997 (in %)

Specification	1994	1995	1996	1997[b]	1994-1997 average
FDI/GDP	1.6	2.1	3.9	4.2	3.1
FDI/total investments	10.0	12.9	21.3	20.6	17.2

[a] Include foreign direct investments exceeding the value of 1 million USD.
[b] Estimates.

Source: Chojna, 1998.

The data on employment in the companies with foreign capital (Table 3.13) show that the share of these entities in the overall employment is not high although it is steadily increasing. This may mean a much better utilization of labor resources in the FDI companies.

Firms with FDI have a clear advantage over other companies in terms of labor productivity measured by revenues calculated per one employee. In 1996 labor productivity in the firms with foreign capital was twice as high as the average in the total number of entities in the Polish economy.

It should be stated that the contribution of FDI companies to the revenues from all economic entities in Poland is steadily increasing. In 1996 this share amounted to approximately 20% of the revenues of all the entities that submitted their statistical annual reports. In the period 1994–1995 this index amounted to 12.4% and 16.6% respectively.

FDI companies are more likely to export their produce than firms with domestic capital. In 1996 the share of export revenues of FDI companies amounted to 13.9% from their total revenue, whereas the one for companies with domestic capital was 8.8%. However, it should be mentioned that in the period 1994–1996 the foreign revenue of FDI companies showed a slightly declining trend from 15.6% to 13.9%.

The share of firms with foreign capital in the total Polish exports in 1997 amounted to 43.0%. In terms of import the share was 49.9% (Durka and Chojna, 1998).

Intense international trade activities of FDI companies resulted in a negative trade balance on company level. This negative value was steadily growing from US$ – 2.8 billion in 1994 to US$ – 10.0 billion in 1997.

Table 3.13 Employment in FDI companies in the period 1991-1996 in relation to total employment in the Polish economy[a] as of December 31

Year	Number of employees (in 1000s)	Share in total employment (in percentages)
1991	117.6	1.3
1992	230.0	2.0
1993	310.2	2.8
1994	373.9	3.3
1995	495.3	4.4
1996	525.9	4.6

[a] Excluding individual firms, national defense and internal affairs sectors.

Source: Chojna, 1998.

The share of imported elements of the supply chain (raw materials, parts and components) in the total imports of FDI firms amounted to approximately 60% of all inputs while the same in the firms with Polish capital was approximately 70% in 1997.

Companies with FDI are characterized by high investment activities. The contribution of FDI companies to the overall volume of investment increased from 11.6% in 1994 to 20.1% in 1996.

When considering the financial results of FDI companies, a positive trend can be observed. In the period 1994–1997 profitability rates were considerably improved and from negative indicators in 1994 they became positive. It should be emphasized that in companies with FDI the profitability indicators look particularly good compared with those of domestic companies.

The share of foreign capital in the privatization of the Polish economy also deserves attention. Out of 203 companies that underwent FDI privatization in 1990–1997, 104 strategic investors who purchased their shares were Polish and 83 were foreign investors, whereas in 16 companies the shares were bought by foreign and Polish investors (Włodarczyk, 1998). In the course of direct privatization of small and medium sized enterprises (the so-called selling path) 80 enterprises were sold to foreign investors. Under the Program of the National Investment Funds, out of 93 portfolio companies 32 were sold to foreign entities.

Opportunities and Threats of Internationalization

International trade and the inflow of FDI are considered to be the two most important forms of internationalization of the Polish economy. The extension of both forms of international economic ties offers a number of advantages and creates many opportunities. However, one must not overlook the threats related to the progressive internationalization.

Internationalization opportunities and advantages have been well identified by the theories of international trade and the theories of foreign direct investment. Here, we shall only indicate these factors that are particularly significant in the case of Poland.

The opportunities and advantages resulting from the development of international trade in the period of transformation are as follows:

- Export is one of the significant factors stimulating the economic growth. Achieving a much higher increase of the GDP is a condition for the overcoming of the so-called product gap that separates Poland from highly developed countries.
- Revenues from export are an important source of the financing of foreign purchases.
- Exports make it possible for the enterprises to achieve advantages of scale against limited extent and demand on the domestic market.
- Exports force the producers to improve the quality of production to meet the high quality expectations of foreign markets.
- Thanks to imports the economy has an access to modern machines and equipment as well as to high quality materials. This is particularly important during a period of rapid economic growth which is expressed in the high rate of GDP growth and the high rate of investment.
- Making part of import purchases on credit increases the country's accumulation capacities that are insufficient to finance the high rate of economic growth.
- Import discipline home producers in terms of pricing and quality assurance and is also the means of diffusion of foreign investments in the Polish economy.

- Imports facilitate the maintenance of equilibrium on the home market.

A rapid growth of foreign trade in the period of transformation is also a source of the following threats:

- Persistence and worsening of foreign trade deficit which in the long run may break down the balance of payments.
- 'Backwardness' of the structure of exports – smaller importance of the high-tech products and the smaller share of the so-called added value in favor of material- and energy-intensive products of relatively low technological level.
- There are no good prospects for development of external demand in the economic sectors where Polish export capacities are most important and in which the development is most dynamic, whereas in the economic sectors where growth of foreign demand is expected Poland has limited possibilities to increase supply.
- Trespassing in some economic sectors, particularly the most technologically advanced, the critical threshold of the penetration of imports in relation to the home production that leads to elimination of certain fields from the Polish industry.

The positive effects of FDI inflow into the Polish economy are unquestioned. They provide Poland with an opportunity to bridge the civilization gap separating the country from the highly developed economies relatively quickly. Advantages resulting from the inflow of foreign investments can be listed as follows:

- Increased accumulation of capital and opportunities for new investments.
- Modernizing and restructuring the industry through the transfer of modern technologies, know-how, and management methods.
- Improved quality of products made by FDI and domestic companies – pressure on the local suppliers for new quality standards of products, materials, components and servicing.
- Creating demand for new products.
- Access to organized networks of sales in the foreign markets.
- Acceleration of privatization processes.
- Creating new jobs and increasing employees' qualifications.

Experiences of the countries that receive foreign investments on a wide scale also show some threats:

- Locating environmentally unfriendly production in the host country.

- Use of obsolete production technologies in the host country.
- Transfer of incomes in the form of transfer prices.
- Limitation of investment duration – an attitude to 'skim the cream' in a short period of time, not re-investing the profits followed by a rapid divestment.
- Investments 'blocking' the local competitors in order to increase import penetration on the market of the host country.

In the context of the opportunities and threats connected with a wider opening of the transformed Polish economy to internationalization, a question is raised about the appropriate economic policy that should be adopted.

Maintaining the high rate of economic growth and also the necessity to service a considerable foreign debt are responsible for the fact that rapid development of export is a must for the development of the Polish economy. Therefore, a pro-export policy is a high priority for the national economy. Such a policy should be a part of the overall economic policy, non-contradictory and coherent with all state economic activities. The fact that Polish exports must grow is generally unquestioned. This, however, does not mean that the export sector should be a kind of enclave strongly subsidized by the non-export sector. This kind of solution was frequently tested in the period of communist economy and its results were unsatisfactory.

The pro-export policy should not be of segmental character. The best pro-export policy is a comprehensive economic policy oriented towards the improvement of effectiveness, efficiency, and growth of international competitiveness of the Polish economy. The economic policy, which concentrates on stabilization measures, is not sufficient to achieve this objective. It should be supplemented with the policy of institutional transformation and restructuring.

In the present reality of Poland and its external environment, the growth of competitive production of goods and services marketable both on internal and external markets is the fundamental strategic problem (Płowiec, 1997).

Thus, two general recommendations to economic policy makers can be made (Gorynia, 1996):

- The state's economic policy should support competitiveness of enterprises.
- The economic policy should favor competitiveness in an integral way, i.e., it should not differentiate in an unjust way the instruments that favor competitiveness in two dimensions – competitiveness of

exporters to foreign markets and competitiveness of producers in the home market.

The above-mentioned criteria are fulfilled by the concept of liberal-institutional industrial policy (Gorynia, 1995). The essence of the liberal-institutional industrial policy is in promoting a widely understood growth and entrepreneurship. Four main trends can be distinguished in the liberal-institutional policy:

- The policy promoting development.
- The policy of supporting competition.
- The policy of privatization.
- The policy of promoting economic self-governance.

The following groups of activities can exemplify the policy of promoting development:

- Promotion of investment.
- Promotion of innovation, research and development.
- Supporting education and training.
- Distribution of economic risk.
- Supporting the construction of the systems of information and its diffusion.

The above-mentioned main directions of the impact of economic policy, defined as the liberal-institutional industrial policy, are characterized by a general, universal approach, which basically does not provide for individualization of the policy measures according to particular economic mezzo systems. However, it seems that in some cases selective application of the chosen instruments can be admissible (Gorynia, 1995). Such cases can be listed as follows:

- Market failure.
- Occurrence of the second-best situation.
- Protection of infant industries.

Some concepts of the economic policy identify the pro-export policy with a selective industrial policy. Some economists put forward a concept of deliberate construction of comparative advantages in the chosen fields of advanced technology and strategic integration with the world market, not the integration with the world market based on the current premises which are unreliable while making decisions of strategic character (Hubner, 1994).

In the discussions concerning the borderline of the pro-export policy and the selective industrial policy there appears the concept of the so-called strategic trade policy (Brander and Spencer, 1985). According to this concept export subsidies may seem to be an attractive measure of the policy because they improve a relative position of home producers in non-cooperative competition with foreign firms, thus enabling them to get a bigger share of the market and to increase profits. The subsidies change the initial conditions of competition. The terms of trade in the subsidizing country get worse but their welfare can increase because under imperfect competition the price exceeds extreme costs.

Numerous arguments can be listed against the strategic trade policy understood in the above-mentioned way. The most important arguments are as follows:

- The governments of rival countries may also start subsidizing. 'The war of subsidies' will result in the decline of prices in the international market and may lead to a decline of welfare in the countries using subsidies.
- A target country of the subsidized exports can take up some retaliation measures (customs, compensation charges, quotas, embargoes, etc.).
- Subsidies granted simultaneously in several countries can lead to over-investment in the subsidized economic sectors.
- Low prices of the subsidized goods on the international market can be a false signal for the potential investors from third countries.
- Ensuring means for the subsidies is an essential problem for the countries with an unbalanced budget.
- According to the binding international agreements export subsidies are forbidden. Such is the attitude of the Code on Subsidies of the GATT Tokyo Round. Agreement on Subsidies and Compensative Duties from the Final Act of the Uruguay Round binding under the WTO introduces quite a precise and extended definition of subsidies.

The Polish policy of foreign trade should, therefore, develop in the following directions (Płowiec, 1997):

- Lifting barriers for exports development: barriers related to the quality of production, barriers related to the terms of payment offered (export credits, insurance of export transactions), barriers of infrastructural character.
- Development of non-tariff forms of the protection of producers against dishonest competition or against excessive imports.

The economic policy should also concentrate on creating the economic climate that attracts foreign investors. Foreign direct investments should prove particularly useful in the development of managerial staff and operational personnel; improvement of the professional level of management; transfer of production and marketing technologies as well as management techniques; introduction of energy and material-saving technologies, friendly to the natural environment; further privatization of the economy and in the long run they should also improve the balance of trade.

Those policies to international trade and FDI into Poland will increase the degree of internationalization of the Polish economy and its competitiveness in the international marketplace.

References

Brander, J.A. and Spencer, B.J. (1988), 'Export Subsidies and International Market Share Rivalry', *Journal of International Economics*, no. 2.

Chojna, J. (1998), 'Miejsce podmiotów z udziałem kapitału zagranicznego w gospodarce narodowej Polski', in B. Durka (ed.) *Inwestycje zagraniczne w Polsce*, Warsaw: Foreign Trade Research Institute.

Durka, B. and Chojna, J. (1998), 'Udział podmiotów z kapitałem zagranicznym w polskim handlu zagranicznym', in B. Durka (ed.) *Inwestycje zagraniczne w Polsce*, Warsaw: Foreign Trade Research Institute.

Gorynia, M. (1995), *Teoria i polityka regulacji mezosystemów gospodarczych a transformacja postsocjalistycznej gospodarki polskiej*, Poznań: University of Economics in Poznań.

Gorynia, M. (1996), 'Międzynarodowa konkurencyjność polskiej gospodarki a polityka ekonomiczna', *Ekonomista*, 1996, no. 3.

Gorynia, M. and Otta, W.J. (1989), 'Zamiany jakościowe w konkurowaniu na rynkach międzynarodowych', *Sprawy Międzynarodowe*, 1989, no. 3.

Gorynia, M. and Otta, W.J. (1995a), 'Polityka handlu zagranicznego w okresie przejścia do gospodarki rynkowej', in W. Włodarczyk-Guzek (ed.) *Stosunki ekonomiczne Polski z zagranic w warunkach gospodarki rynkowej*, Łódź: University of Łódź.

Gorynia, M. and Otta, W.J. (1995b), 'A Strategic Shift in Export Trade', in R. Domański (ed.) *European Studies*, Poznań: University of Economics.

Hout, T., Porter, M.E. and Rudden, E. (1982), 'How Global Companies Win Out?', *Harvard Business Review*, 1982, no. 5.

Hubner, D. (1994), 'Międzynarodowa konkurencyjność gospodarki a strategia rozwoju', *Ekonomista*, no. 3.

Kaczurba, J. and Kawecka-Wyrzykowska E., (ed.) (1995), 'Of GATT do WTO'. *Skutki Rundy Urugwajskiej dla Polski*, Warsaw: IKiCHZ.

Kubielas, S., Markowski, S., and Jackson, S. (1996), 'Atrakcyjność Polski dla zagranicznych inwestycji bezpośrednich po pięciu latach transformacji', in M. Okólski and U. Sztanderska (eds) *Studia nad reformowaną gospodarką. Aspekty instytucjonalne*, Warsaw: Wydawnictwo Naukowe PWN.

Levitt, T. (1983), 'The Globalization of Markets', *Harvard Business Review*, no. 3.

Nowicki, M. (1997), 'Bilans płatniczy w warunkach integracji', in *Polskie przedsiębiorstwa a Jednolity Rynek Unii Europejskiej. Korzyści i koszty, praca zbiorcza*, Warsaw: Committee for European Integration.

Olesiński, Z. and Pac-Pomarnacki, R. (1998), 'Działalność dużych inwestorów zagranicznych w Polsce', in B. Durka (ed.) *Inwestycje zagraniczne w Polsce*, Warsaw: Foreign Trade Research Institute.

Otta, W.J. and Gorynia, M. (1993), 'Export Turnaround – Switching from the CMEA to Competitive Markets', in *Proceedings of the 19thEIBA Conference*, Lisbon.

Perczyński, M. (1997), 'Polska na drodze do integracji z Unią Europejską' in M. Belka and W. Trzeciakowski (eds) *Dynamika transformacji polskiej gospodarki*, vol. 2, Warsaw: Poltex.

Piotrowski, J. (ed.) (1998), *Polski handel zagraniczny w 1997 roku*. Annual report, Warsaw.

Płowiec, U. (1997), 'Proeksportowa strategia rozwoju w procesie przemian systemowych w polskim handlu zagranicznym', in M. Belka and W. Trzeciakowski (eds) *Dynamika transformacji polskiej gospodarki*, vol. 2, Warsaw: Poltext.

Samonis, V. (1992), 'Earning or Learning? Western Direct Investment Strategies in Post-Soviet Economies', *MOCT-MOST Economic Journal on Eastern Europe and Russia*, no. 3.

Winters, L.A. and Wang, Z.K. (1994), *Eastern Europe's International Trade*, Manchester–New York: Manchester University Press.

Włodarczyk, W. (1998), 'Kapitał zagraniczny w prywatyzacji polskiej gospodarki', in B. Durka (ed.) *Inwestycje zagraniczne w Polsce*, Warsaw: Foreign Trade Research Institute.

4 Internationalization of the Albanian Economy through Foreign Investments: The Italian Case

DONATA VIANELLI, PATRIZIA DE LUCA and ROLAND KAJCA

Introduction

Foreign direct investments are considered an important opportunity for the economic development of Albania. In spite of the uncertain legal environment and the social and political instability that have characterized the country in recent years, some significant advantages for a foreign company that wants to enter Albania can still be pointed out. First of all, the low labor cost, which is an important factor especially in labor intensive industries. The presence of natural resources can be another important variable for a location decision. The geographical position of the country serves as a bridge between West and East. Finally, the Albanian government has defined favorable fiscal and financial opportunities in order to attract foreign companies and investment (Assonitis, 1995).

Nevertheless, till present the only countries that are operating significantly in Albania are Italy and Greece. The aim of this chapter is to provide better knowledge about the Italian companies currently operating in the country and to find out what are the main reasons related to the choice of Albania as a foreign investment destination. Finally, the opportunities for future development of the activities of Italian investors in Albania will be discussed and evaluated.

A Brief Overview of Albania

The History

Albania is located in the Western part of the Balkan Peninsula. It borders Montenegro in the Northwest, Kosovo in the Northeast, Macedonia in the

East and Greece in the South. The Adriatic and Ionic Seas border Albania to the West and Southwest. The country covers an area of 11,100 square miles (28,748 square km), of which 24% arable, 15% meadow and pastures, 36% forest. It has a maximum length (North-South) of about 210 miles (340 km) and a maximum width of about 153 km. The population is 3.28 million and the main towns are Tirana, which is the capital city, with 250,000 inhabitants, Durres (125,000), Elbasan (101,000), Vlore (88,000) and Shkoder (81,000). Till the 1980s Albania was one of the fastest growing countries in Europe, with an average annual growth rate of 2.1%. Successively the population decreased because of a drastic reduction of the birth rate primarily due to the situation of economic uncertainty. For the same reason, the number of Albanian emigrant workers increased from 110,000 in 1991 to 428,000 in 1996. The population is ethnically homogeneous. The largest minority are Greeks; there is also population of Vlachs and significant numbers of Roma and Slav Macedonians. Outside the country some ethnic Albanians live in Yugoslavia; a consistent number of historic settlements of Albanians can be found also in Greece (the Cams) and in Italy (the Arboresh).

Albanians descend from the ancient Illyrians. They have lived in relative isolation and obscurity throughout the centuries. This is mainly due to the geography of mountains and a complex of historical, cultural and social factors.

Because of its location at the Adriatic and Ionic Sea, Albania has been long considered by various nations and empires such as Romans, Byzantines, Visigoths, Huns, Bulgars and Slavs, as a bridgehead for their conquests. From the 15th century to the beginning of the 20th century the Turks ruled the country completely cutting it off from Western civilization.

Albania was declared independent in 1912. One year later the Great Powers of Europe assigned about half of its territory and people to neighboring countries. Ruled as a monarchy between World War I and World War II, it was successively transformed into a communist state where almost all aspects of life were controlled by the ruling Communist Party. The communist regime collapsed in 1991 when the Democratic Party won the parliamentary election and its leader, Sami Berisha, became President of Albania. In 1997, after the rioting related to the collapse of the pyramid funds into which a large part of the population had deposited their life savings, the elections were won by the Socialist Party of Albania, whose leader was Fatos Nano.

Today the Republic of Albania is a parliamentary democracy. Since June 1997 it has been governed by a left-of-center coalition comprising the Socialist Party of Albania (SPA), the Albanian Democratic Alliance (DA), the Social Democratic Party (SDP), the Alliance for the State (AS), the Agrarian Party (AP), the National Unity Party (NUP) and the Union for Human Rights (UHR). The prime minister is Pandeli Majko (SPA), who succeeded Fatos Nano when he resigned in 1998 after the assassination of an opposition deputy leader.

The Economy

Before 1991, the ruling communist party that aimed at making the country as self-sufficient as possible controlled the entire economy of the country. All means of production were under the control of the State, agriculture was collectivized and industry was nationalized; furthermore, private enterprise, foreign aids, loans and foreign investments were absolutely forbidden (Cungu and Swinen, 1999).

After the collapse of communism, restrictions on private trade have been largely reduced. The government has been trying to encourage the growth of light industries, food processing and agriculture accepting foreign credits and investments, and creating joint ventures with foreign partners. In fact, Albania could possibly be considered an attractive investment location because it is endowed with considerable resources: petroleum, which is mostly exported, natural gas, metallic mineral deposits such as chromium (Albania is the world's third largest producer), copper, iron-nickel, lignite and natural asphalt. It is also rich in rivers and streams with significant hydroelectric potential. Nevertheless, the results of the government development policy is often limited by a failing infrastructure, obsolete machinery and equipment, lack of raw materials, shortages of skilled workers and managers, low productivity, poor organization and labor discipline, and a transport system which is primitive and far below the European standards. Furthermore, if on the one hand it is true that Albania has a well-developed engineering industry, on the other, the economy is unable to meet consumer demand for various consumer goods. This is due mostly to the distorted state investment made predominantly into the heavy industry. As a consequence, comparative economic indicators (Table 4.1) confirm that Albania can be considered one of the less developed Central and Eastern European (CEE) countries.

Furthermore, as shown in Table 4.2, nowadays agriculture still gives the main contribution to the GDP, followed by industry, construction and transport. The most promising sector seems to be garment making. On the contrary, the domestic textile industry, that supplied the garment industry, has been ravaged by imports from Turkey, Greece and Asia.

Carpet making is reviving and also timber, joinery and furniture making are increasing mainly thanks to the ample forest resources of the country.

The construction and the building materials industry can be considered booming sectors, too. In fact, the two waves of rioting have required reconstruction and residential privatization has increased demand for housing.

Table 4.1   Comparative economic indicators in 1998

Indicator	Albania	Romania	Yugoslavia*	Croatia	Bulgaria	Macedonia
GDP (US$ bln)	2.9	41.4	12.8	20.6	11.7	3.2
GDP per capita (US$)	876	1,836	1,199	4,521	1,410	1,579
GDP per head ($ PPP**)	1,636	4,257	3,229	6,670	4,363	3,800
Consumer Price Inflation (average %)	20.7	60.0	30.0	5.7	22.3	1.3
Exports of goods fob (US$ bln)	0.2	8.2	2.8	4.4	4.3	1.3
Imports of goods (US$ bln)	0.9	10.2	4.7	8.9	4.5	1.6

*   Serbia–Montenegro.
**   Purchasing Power Parities.

Source: EIU, 1999.

Transport and communication are undeveloped and need to be modernized or even rebuilt after the severe damages that occurred during the 1997 insurgency.

Finally, services such as banking, insurance, retailing, tourism, business information and security can be considered very inadequate for a developing country.

Table 4.2   Gross domestic product (GDP) by sector

Indicator	1993	1994	1995	1996	1997	1998*
Total GDP (US$ bln)	0.9	1.4	1.6	2.0	2.5	2.9
Industry (% of GDP)	16.9	13.9	12.4	11.5	12.2	24.5
Agriculture (% of GDP)	54.2	54.6	55.1	55.9	51.5	54.4
Construction (% of GDP)	7.6	9.1	9.5	9.8	11.2	n/a
Transport (% of GDP)	3.0	3.1	3.3	3.2	3.2	n/a
Other services (% of GDP)	18.3	19.4	19.6	19.5	21.9	n/a

*   Estimates.

Source: EIU, 1999; World Bank, 1999.

In a context of low development together with a high fiscal deficit and a considerable stock of non-performing loans, the restructuring of the economy depends on inflows of foreign capital. The latter is connected to the maintenance of order, so that the basic security and stability necessary for a normal economic life can be re-established. On the contrary, the level of poverty is high. Before the crisis of 1997 many people sold their homes in order to gain cash for investments in the pyramid schemes. Now they are among the mass of people looking for welfare accommodation. Furthermore, after the commencement of NATO air strikes against Yugoslavia from March to May 1999, the flood of ethnic Albanian refugees pouring across the border from Kosovo has worsened the economic and social conditions.

Table 4.3   Labor force and unemployment rate

Indicator	1992	1993	1994	1995	1996
Labor force (1000)	1,614	1,621	1,642	1,672	1,702
Total unemployment (1000)	394	402	264	233	158
Unemployment rate (%)	27.9	29.0	19.6	16.9	12.4

Source: EIU, 1999.

As Table 4.3 shows the unemployment rate is high, with a level of average wages of US$ 70 in 1999. Controlling inflation is a priority. It rose from an average of 7.8% in 1995 to 12.8% in 1996, and to 42,1% at the time of the collapse. In spite of that, since 1998 a three year economic program is being implemented with the aim of achieving three principal goals: building an efficient private sector, regulating the public finances and restoring investor confidence. Consequently, consumer prices that increased with 20.7% in 1998, have risen with another 3.0% in 1999 and 4.0% in 2000.

Nowadays the legal status for foreign direct investments (FDI) is satisfactory. Profits are freely convertible and transferable and there are no legal obstacles to property and securities ownership by foreigners. This is important because after the collapse in 1997 some foreign investors left and a consistent number of potential foreign investors became wary.

Analyzing import and export activities (Table 4.4), it is possible to point out that in 1992 the amount of export activities was just US$ 70m, while imports, including humanitarian supplies, amounted to US$ 541m. Between 1992 and 1996, imports increased more rapidly than exports, resulting in a widening trade deficit. In 1997 there was a collapse of foreign trade which declined from US$ 244m to US$ 159m for exports, and from US$ 922m to US$ 694m for imports. Nevertheless, after the insurgency of 1997 both imports and exports have demonstrated the potential to revive, as in 1998 exports were US$ 208m while imports came up to US$ 812m (EIU, 1999).

Finally, as shown in Table 4.5, the main trading partners of Albania are EU countries. In 1998 these countries took 92% of exports and supplied 83% of imports. Greece and Italy represent the leading trading partners, absorbing 80% of total exports and providing 74% of total imports.

Italian Companies in Albania

Literature Review and Research Design

There are approximately 57,000 companies operating in Albania in the industry (16%) and service sectors (84%). About 99% of them are private while the remaining 1% are state owned (Instat, 1999).

About half of these companies have been constituted during the period 1993-1994. After this period the number of new companies created each year decreased, with at least 5.9%. In 1998 newly established companies represented 9.2% of the total number of firms. Companies with more than 10 employees represented only 2% but they employed approximately 60% of the labor force of the country (Instat, 1999).

Table 4.4 Exports and imports – main products (% of total; free on board)

Indicator	1992 Exp	1992 Imp	1993 Exp	1993 Imp	1994 Exp	1994 Imp	1995 Exp	1995 Imp	1996 Exp	1996 Imp	1997 Exp	1997 Imp
Food, beverages, tobacco and live animals	13.3	28.3	14.0	20.1	14.3	25.5	7.5	22.3	8.9	32.0	11.7	23.1
Crude materials excluded fuel	80.8	5.6	24.0	0.7	24.3	2.4	24.7	0.9	16.9	1.2	23.8	n/a
Minerals, lubricants, fuels & related materials	n/a	14.6	8.3	3.3	7.0	10.9	2.9	9.7	4.1	2.6	2.8	2.7
Manufactured goods	4.8	11.9	45.7	23.6	53.2	18.9	59.7	37.3	64.9	32.8	58.7	44.5
Machinery and transport equipment	0.0	33.8	3.6	38.1	3.4	31.8	1.4	20.3	1.7	22.5	n/a	15.9
Total (US$ million)	70	541	112	601	141	601	205	680	244	922	159	694

Source: EIU, 1999.

Table 4.5   Main trading partners of Albania (% of total value)

Country	1992		1993		1994		1995		1996		1997		1998	
	Exp	Imp	Exp	Imp	Exp	Imp	Exp	Imp	Exp	Imp	Exp	Imp	Exp	Imp
Italy	13.6	23.8	41.0	31.2	52.1	35.0	51.5	37.9	57.9	41.7	49.1	46	60	45
Greece	8.5	6.7	18.0	18.5	10.4	24.0	9.9	26.8	13.0	21.2	19.2	26.2	19.7	29.1
Germany	7.3	5.1	4.3	12.4	4.8	5.5	6.1	4.6	6.9	4.1	6.6	4.3	5.6	3.9
Turkey	0.0	3.3	1.4	3.0	0.7	4.6	6.2	4.1	3.1	4.4	n/a	4.5	n/a	3.4
Netherlands	0.7	n/a	0.3	n/a	0.1	n/a	2.1	n/a	2.9	n/a	4.6	n/a	n/a	n/a
France	2.3	17.1	1.8	8.7	2.1	1.9	2.3	1.2	2.0	3.1	n/a	n/a	n/a	n/a
Belgium-Luxemburg	0.9	7.9	6.1	1.0	4.3	1.0	5.4	1.6	1.3	2.5	n/a	n/a	n/a	n/a
US	2.7	5.9	3.7	2.5	11.1	0.2	3.4	0.3	1.2	1.3	11.6	n/a	n/a	n/a
Czechoslovakia *	0.2	n/a	0.2	n/a	0.4	n/a	0.3	n/a	0.1	n/a	n/a	n/a	n/a	n/a
Former Yugoslavia	7.9	n/a	13.6	n/a	6.0	n/a	0.0	n/a	0.0	n/a	n/a	n/a	n/a	n/a
Bulgaria	n/a	n/a	n/a	5.7	n/a	8.2	n/a	8.0	n/a	4.0	n/a	n/a	n/a	n/a
Romania	n/a	0.4	n/a	0.5	n/a	0.6	n/a	0.5	n/a	2.4	n/a	n/a	n/a	n/a
Switzerland	n/a	1.5	n/a	1.7	n/a	0.9	n/a	0.7	n/a	1.7	n/a	n/a	n/a	n/a
Austria	n/a	0.8	n/a	0.9	n/a	1.5	n/a	2.0	n/a	1.0	n/a	n/a	n/a	n/a

* Czech Republic and Slovakia from 1993.

Source: EIU, 1999.

The aim of this chapter is to provide better understanding of Italian companies operating in Albania. Based on information provided by the Association of Italian Investors and by the Italian Embassy in Albania, Italian companies amounted to about 500 in 1998. Most of them operated in the textile, clothing, footwear, woodworking and service sectors. Only few studies (Bandini, 1997; Giuriato, 1999; Massa, 1995; Morone, 1999; Rein *et al.*, 1997; Sharma, 1997) have analyzed the presence of Italian companies in Albania and all of them have handled the analysis mainly from macroeconomic perspective. The current chapter analyzes the microeconomic perspective of Italian FDI in Albania.

The relation between Albania and Italy has well based historic roots. The Romans ruled Albania from II century B.C. to IV century A.D. The links between the two countries were strengthened with the Albanian migrations to Italy that started in 1448 and gave origin to the Albanian settlements in the South of Italy. With the exception of the third migration (1468–1492) that was determined by refugees who escaped from the Turkish invasion, the other migrations were by soldiers recruited in order to suppress rebellions and restore order in the Southern Italy. Those Albanians, known as Arboresh, brought with them their wives and families and settled in different Italian regions such as Calabria, Basilicata, Puglia, Campania and Sicilia.

As pointed out before, nowadays Italy is the main Western partner of Albania. Exports and imports between the two countries are consistent in almost all sectors of activities (Table 4.6). More precisely Albania imports from Italy mainly machinery, food, footwear, clothing and chemicals. In some cases imports are related to raw materials that are successively transformed into finished products. On the other side, exports mainly include footwear and clothing.

Basing our research on the entry and expansion decision literature, we have analyzed the presence of Italian companies in Albania from different points of view in order to investigate whether there are possibilities for future development.

In particular, the first issue that has to be analyzed is the reason why some Italian companies have chosen Albania in order to develop their foreign activities (Peev, 1998; Segrè, 1995). Considering that Albania is one of the less developed CEE countries, there can be various motives mainly related to resource utilization: low cost of raw materials, of production, cheap labor and financial stimuli (Keegan, 1999; Bartlett and Ghoshal, 1990; Czinkota Ronkainen and Tarrant, 1995). Furthermore, geographic proximity to third country markets and low level of competition can be other favorable factors influencing the choice of Albania as an investment destination for Italian capital (Cateora, 1985; Buzzell, 1968; Buzzell, 1987).

Table 4.6　Trade between Italy and Albania: exports to Albania
(FOB) and imports from Albania (CIF) - (US$ million)

Economic Sector	1997		1998	
	Exports	Imports	Exports	Imports
Food	5.4	83.7	4.6	57.3
Beverages & tobacco	-	2.8	-	3.6
Mineral fuels	-	6.6	-	3.6
Chemicals	-	23.3	-	21.4
Textile fibers yarn, cloth & manufactures	1.0	22.1	1.0	21.7
Non-metallic mineral manufactures	-	11.2	-	11.5
Metals & manufactures	9.7	21.9	6.3	20.7
Machinery including electric	-	87.4	-	47.3
Transport equipment	-	20.0	-	27.4
Clothing	24.1	26.8	38.9	34.4
Footwear	36.7	50.6	39.6	36.3
Scientific instruments	-	4.9	-	2.4
Total including others	104.0	435.7	124.7	363.6

Source:　EIU, 1999.

Despite the small size of the Albanian market there can be interesting opportunities for the internationalization of small and medium sized Italian companies in that context (Compagno and Nanut, 1988; Nanut, 1994).

A second aspect that has to be evaluated is the type of foreign investment

(Root, 1987; Globerman, 1986; Schooler, Wildt and Jones, 1987; Hibbert, 1990). Since there are various alternatives to invest in a foreign country, it is important to investigate why some alternatives seem to be preferred by the Italian companies. It is possible to identify local subsidiaries (with a parent company in Italy) or local independent companies (without a parent company in Italy). The two types of companies are either wholly or partially owned by an Italian company or entrepreneur.

In order to analyze the specifics of companies' activities in a foreign market, we should also consider the characteristics of the activities developed in Albania (Terpstra and Sarathy, 1991; Schooler, Wildt and Jones, 1987; Onkvisit and Shaw, 1989) and the distribution channels (Stern and El-Ansary, 1988; Bucklin and Carman, 1986; Pellegrini and Reddy, 1986; Filser, 1992). Depending on the planned production cycle, a company can carry out only a manufacturing activity in order to obtain finished and packaged products, finished products or semi-finished products which will be re-exported to Italy. Similarly, a company can manufacture and also directly commercialize its products and services. Finally, a company can carry out only a commercial activity selling the parent company's products or other companies' products. It would be interesting to find out if there are sectors in which a particular typology of company prevails.

Another critical variable that has to be analyzed is the standardization versus adaptation of the marketing mix strategy (Baalbaki and Malhotra, 1993; Cavusgil, Zou and Naidu, 1993; Jain, 1989; Rau and Preble, 1987, Kreutzer, 1986; Vianelli, 1995; Vianelli, 1999). Since in the Albanian context it is possible to identify only product-oriented rather than marketing oriented companies, the standardization concept has to be mainly related to the characteristics of the product and the product price in order to find out if the products commercialized in Italy and Albania are the same.

At the same time, if a product is manufactured in Albania and exported abroad the country-of-origin effect should be investigated (Bilkey, and Nes, 1982; Chao and Rajendran, 1993; Ettenson, Gaeth and Wagner, 1988; Johansson, Douglas and Nonaka, 1985; Papadopoulos and Heslop, 1993).

Finally it will be interesting to understand which are the main advantages and disadvantages of Italian companies operating in Albania compared with Albanian companies operating in the same industry.

Research Method

The research is based on a questionnaire that was personally submitted to a sample of 110 managers of Italian companies operating in Albania. Since the aim of the research is exploratory, the questionnaire is mainly made up of open-ended questions in order to find out personal opinions and attitudes of respondents. Multiple-choice questions have also been included. The economic sectors and businesses covered by the analysis were the following: wood products, clothing, shoemaking, real estate services, import-export services, carpentry, builders' joinery and glaziers work, fresh fish, chemical and oil industries, communication services, radio and television, pharmaceuticals, food, beverages, concrete products, training, telecommunication equipment, building products, marble, potentiometers and power transformers, pipes, information services and software packages, detergent and cleansers, tourist services. Companies have been identified using the database of the Association of Italian Investors in Albania. The questionnaire was firstly pilot tested using a small group of managers from various Italian companies. Furthermore, before conducting the personal interviews the questionnaire was mailed in order to provide the managers with the opportunity to decide if a face-to-face interview was possible. When determining the response rate, 54 firms did not agree to be interviewed. In total, 56 responses were obtained, representing an overall response rate of 51 per cent. However, the number of usable answers was 52. Finally, a response rate of 47% was obtained.

Analysis and Results

The sample   The characteristics of the sample are shown in Tables 4.7 to 4.10. Although the total range of firm size is wide, more than 70% of the sample companies employed fewer than 100 people. More precisely, 50% had less than 60 employees.

Table 4.7   Firm size: number of employees

Number of employees	Number of companies	Per cent
< 5	6	11
6-20	8	15
21-40	8	15
41-60	5	9
60-100	11	21
> 100	6	14
n/a	8	15

Considering turnover, in 1997 44% of the companies had a turnover that was less than US$ 90,000 and only four companies had a turnover of more than US$ 250,000.

Table 4.8   Firm size: turnover in 1997

Firm's turnover (000$)	Number of companies	%
< 30	5	10
31-60	8	16
61-90	9	18
91-120	5	10
121-250	4	8
> 250	4	8
n.a.	17	30

Most of the companies included in the analysis are independent. Some of them informed us that they had a similar company in Italy that was closed before entering Albania. Nevertheless, there is also a consistent number of companies which had a parent company in Italy; 96% of the parent companies were located in Southern Italy and only 8 of them had foreign direct investments in countries different from Albania.

Table 4.9   Year of entry

Year of entry	Number of companies
1991	2
1992	8
1993	5
1994	8
1995	15
1996	5
1997	7
1998	2

Table 4.10 Presence of a parent company in Italy

Presence of a parent company in Italy	Number of companies
No	32
Yes	20

The analysis of the sample reveals that a consistent number of companies have not indicated the turnover and the number of employees, revealing the existence of a hidden economy which has been already pointed out by other researches (e.g., Morone, 1999).

Key variables in the location decisions   The main reason why Italian companies have chosen Albania to develop their foreign activities is related to cost advantages, in particular the low labor costs, followed by financial and fiscal advantages (Table 4.11).

Table 4.11 Key variables in the location decision

Key variables	Percentage of companies
Cost advantages	65
• Low cost of raw materials	13
• Low cost of production services	15
• Low cost of labor	61
Fiscal advantages	20
Business financing	38
Vicinity to other countries of interest	10
Attractiveness of the Albanian market	10
(High consumer demand and low competition)	

This is particularly true for companies with low value-added products. From the personal interviews it also emerged that Albania was chosen because market demand was mainly unsatisfied and competition was low.

Furthermore, the products offered by Albanian companies have been perceived as having low quality. The geographic proximity to other attractive markets can also be considered one of the reasons for entering Albania. Nevertheless, only one of the analyzed companies, operating in the pharmaceutical sector, was exporting its products to Macedonia and Montenegro.

Type of investment　　As far as the type of investment is concerned (see Table 4.12), the Italian companies were mainly represented by local independent companies (n=32). Of these, the number of partially owned firms was higher if compared to the wholly owned ones.

The number of local subsidiaries amounted to 20. Nevertheless, in this case the wholly owned subsidiaries clearly prevailed over the partially owned ones.

Table 4.12　Type of investment

Type of Company	Subsidiary	Independent	Total
Wholly owned	17	13	30
Partially owned	3	19	22
*of them joint ventures	3	7	10
Total	20	32	52

Many Italian managers reported that in wholly owned subsidiaries the decision making and control processes were facilitated and that the subsidiary credibility and strength were higher in comparison to other companies with Italian capital.

The main reasons for deciding on a partially owned company can be found in the possibility of obtaining fiscal and/or financial advantages. Furthermore, with a local partner it was easier for Italian investors to understand the characteristics of the Albanian market.

Approximately half of the partially owned companies were organized as international joint ventures. However, some of the Italian investors had chosen the joint venture mode of market entry only because at the time they entered Albania it was the only feasible alternative. Some managers pointed out that they had negative experience with joint venture activities or that they were not able to find out a reliable partner in Albania.

Characteristics of the activity   Types of activities carried out by the Italian companies considered in the analysis are indicated in Table 4.13. Even though the number of companies that exclusively carry out manufacturing activities was significant, the number of companies with both manufacturing and commercialization activities was higher.

Table 4.13 Type of activity

Type of activity	Number of companies
Manufacturing	13*
• Finished and packaged products	(4)
• Finished products	(2)
• Semi-finished products	(9)
Manufacturing and commercialization	28
Commercialization of the parent company products	0
Commercialization of other companies' products	3
Service company	8

* Some companies have more than one type of manufacturing activity.

Considering the types of activities and prevalent industries four groups of the studied companies have been identified (see Table 4.14).

Group one consisted of companies that imported raw materials from Italy and exported to Italy packaged finished products, finished products or semi-finished products manufactured in Albania.

The second group of companies imported raw materials from Italy in order to produce packaged finished products. A small part of them were marketed in Albania (usually less than 10%); the rest was exported to Italy and commercialized by the parent company or by other companies (if the company in Albania was independent).

Those groups of companies were in clothing and shoe-making industries.

A third group typically utilizes local raw materials in order to produce products sold in the Albanian and/or Italian markets. In this category the typical sectors are wood products, carpentry, builders' joinery and glaziers work, concrete products, food and beverages. More precisely the last two groups of products were realized only in the Albanian market.

Finally, there were service companies that satisfied demand exclusively of the Albanian market. Of them, import-export companies offering products imported from other countries, mainly Italy, represented a significant number.

Table 4.14 Type of activities and prevalent industry

Type of activity	Prevalent Industry
1) Companies that imported raw materials from Italy and exported packaged finished products, finished products or semi-finished products manufactured in Albania.	Clothing and shoe-making.
2) Companies that imported raw materials from Italy to produce packaged finished products some of them marketed in Albania and the rest exported to Italy.	Clothing and shoe-making.
3) Companies that utilized local raw materials to produce products marketed in the Albanian and/or in Italian market.	Wood products, carpentry, builders' joinery and glaziers work, concrete products, food and beverages.
4) Service Companies.	Import-export services, real estate services, training, information services and software packages, tourist services.

Considering the relation between types of activity and types of investment, it should be pointed out that most of the wholly owned subsidiaries carried out only manufacturing activities (see Table 4.15).

Some of the wholly owned subsidiaries operated also in the service market: in this case the service offered in Albania was identical to the one provided in Italy. On the contrary independent companies always had both production and commercialization activities in the manufacturing industry in which they operated, as well as in the service sector.

The relation between the target market and the type of activity carried out in Albania by the Italian companies is presented in Table 4.16. As expected, the manufacturing companies exported all their production to Italy. Those companies did not bother to develop the Albanian market.

Table 4.15   Type of activity and type of investment

	Type of investment			
Type of activity	Subsidiary		Independent company	
	Wholly owned	Partially owned	Wholly owned	Partially owned
Manufacturing	10*	3	-	-
• Finished and packaged products	(4)	-	-	-
• Finished products	(2)	-	-	-
• Semi-finished products	(6)	(3)**	-	-
Manufacturing and commercialization	3	-	10	15
Commercialization of the parent company products	-	-	-	-
Commercialization of other companies' products	-	-	-	3
Service company	4	-	3	1

*   Some companies have more than one type of manufacturing activity.
**   Joint ventures.

Table 4.16 Type of activity and target market

	Target market		
Type of activity	Italy	Albania	Italy & Albania
Manufacturing	13*	-	-
• Finished and packaged products	(4)	-	-
• Finished products	(2)	-	-
• Semi-finished products	(9)	-	-
Manufacturing and commercialization	9	9	10
Commercialization of the parent company products	-	-	-
Commercialization of other companies' products	-	3	-
Service company	-	8	-

* Some companies have more than one type of manufacturing activity.

Table 4.17 Target market and type of investment

	Type of investment			
Target market	Subsidiary		Independent company	
	Wholly owned	Partially owned	Wholly owned	Partially owned
Italy	10	3	5	4
Albania	4	-	7	9
Italy and Albania	3	-	1	6

* Some companies have more than one type of manufacturing activity.
** Joint ventures.

It is also interesting to consider the relation between the target market and the type of investment (Table 4.17). As stated above, most of the wholly owned subsidiaries had Italy as the only export target market. Italian subsidiaries in producing packaged finished products were also marketing them in Albania. However, those companies were not performing distribution activities relying on local wholesalers and retailers and sometimes even expecting the final consumer to buy the product directly from the company. Finally, Italian subsidiaries that had only Albania as a target market predominately or exclusively operated in the service sector.

Independent companies served predominately only the Albanian or Italian market. Partially owned independent companies were preferred to wholly owned subsidiaries by Italian investors, especially when they served exclusively the Albanian market.

Wholly owned independent companies exported the majority of their production to Italy. Those were mostly services companies.

The distribution process as performed by Italian companies in Albania was as follows (see also Figure 4.1):

- 62% of the companies with Italian capital exported all or a part of their production to Italy to their parent company, 38% of them to other client companies.
- 82% of the production that was initially exported to Italy were successively re-exported in other foreign countries, mainly in the CEE region. Only one company was selling its products directly to other foreign countries.
- Companies that sold all or a part of their production in Albania represented 58% of the total sample. They marketed their products through wholesalers (46%), the retailer (19%), directly to the final consumer (15%).

Standardization versus adaptation decision and country of origin effect
The products marketed in Albania were often different from the products realized by the parent companies in the Italian market. The main differences were related to quality, packaging characteristics, and price. In particular the products marketed in Albania had lower quality, production costs, and price.

Advantages/disadvantages of Italian companies in Albania   Finally,   we have tried to find out whether there are advantages or disadvantages of being an Italian company in Albania compared to Albanian companies operating in the same industry.

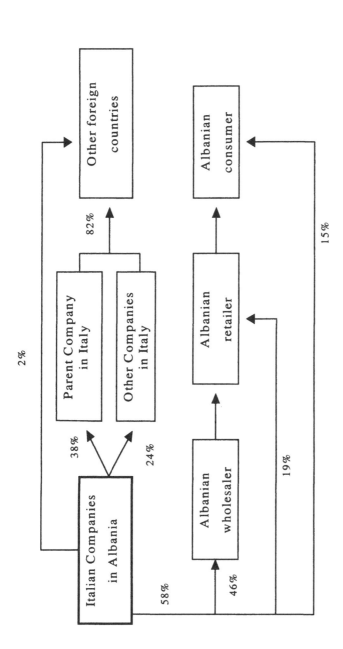

The total of the percentages exceeds 100% because some companies market their products and services both in Italy and Albania.

Figure 4.1   Italian companies in Albania: distribution channels

The interviewees have pointed out that Italian companies are in a more favorable position compared to local companies. Fist of all Italian companies are more competitive because their products are of higher quality if compared with similar products made by Albanian firms. This is mainly due to the professional experience of the management and employees of the former, and their better technologies.

Secondly, Albanian companies find it difficult to re-export their products abroad. One of the reasons is that they have limited international experience, scarce knowledge of foreign markets and restricted resources for foreign market penetration. Furthermore, they have a reputation of low credibility. On the contrary, for Italian companies operating in Albania export sales are granted. Finally, an Italian company operating in Albania can receive loans and funds from the Italian government. That creates very good financial conditions for those investing in Albania. However, one of the main disadvantages of Italian companies, identified by all respondents, are the more stringent controls imposed by the Albanian authorities on foreign investors and their Albanian operations.

Conclusion

Even though the investment risk of operating in Albania is high, Italian companies recognize the existence of significant advantages. This fact emerges not only from the analysis of the key factors in the location decision but also from the reticence in providing information which could be considered useful for the entrance of other foreign companies. One of the reasons for the presence of Italian FDI in Albania is the physical proximity of the two countries and the historic links between them. Hence, the main reason for companies to choose Albania as an FDI location is found in the concept of cultural proximity. The cultural proximity between Albania and Italian companies operating in Southern Italy reduces the perception of risk.

This concept implies an internationalization decision that is not strategic and rationally developed. The fact that only eight Italian companies from those included in this research have FDI in countries different from Albania supports the above. As a consequence, if the Albanian economy will grow in the future and if Albania will be considered a bridge for entering third markets, the advantages gained by the Italian investors will probably disappear with the increase of foreign competition. Actually, if Italian FDI companies in Albania target only the Italian market, without considering the Albanian or third country markets where demand is highly unsatisfied, the cost advantages will gradually disappear. Such Italian companies may well be forced to go out of business. Hence, it is important for them to focus on a long-term strategy for sustaining their competitive advantage in Albania and nearby countries. To be able to do this Italian companies should be facilitated by their better knowledge and experience in the Albanian market and by their cultural proximity. The World Bank has been supporting all efforts of Italy playing an active part in the economic development of Albania.

This research suggests that the main limitation in increasing the contribution of Italian businesses to the overall economic development of Albania lies in the managerial characteristics of the Italian FDI companies in Albania. Being small those firms could support the development of the Albanian economy only through forms of collaboration (de Luca, 1992) such as the development of business networks. The latter have already represented a solution for the development of geographical zones in Italy that had characteristics similar to those of Albania. However, variables such as low management culture, lack of competencies and financial resources, insufficient information and limited communication between different entrepreneurs operating in Albania can actually represent an insurmountable obstacle.

Limitations of the Study and Purpose for Future Research

The first limitation of the study is the reliability of the data. It was difficult to identify Italian Companies in Albania because there is not a reliable source of information. Furthermore, there were serious problems in ensuring the collaboration of Italian entrepreneurs. As a consequence, the sample became a convenient one including only those companies that were willing to contribute to the present research.

The second limitation is related to the fact that the research was exploratory. As a consequence, no generalizations are possible. However, some significant trends have been identified.

Future research of the Italian companies in Albania could be focused mainly on the managerial characteristics of those businesses. It would be also interesting to see how the Italian and Albanian governmental institutions could possibly create the basis for a future growth of the Albanian economy.

References

Assonitis, G. (1995), 'Foreign Investment in Albania: Toward a Liberalization of the Legal Framework?', *Russian and East European Finance and Trade*, vol. 31, no. 3.

Baalbaki, I.B. and Malhotra, N.K. (1993), 'Marketing Management Bases for International Market Segmentation: An Alternate Look at the Standardization/Customization Debate', *International Marketing Review*, vol. 10, no. 1, pp. 19-44.

Bandini, A. (1997), *Albania: Il nostro approccio all'estero vicino*, Limes, no. 1.

Bartlett, C.A. and Ghoshal, S. (1990), *Management Globale*, Milano: Etas Libri.

Bilkey, W.J. and Nes, E. (1982), 'Country-of-Origin Effects on Product Evaluations', *Journal of International Business Studies*, vol. 13, no. 1, pp. 89-99.

Bucklin, L.P. and Carman, J.M. (eds) (1986), *Distribution Channels and Institutions*, 'Research in Marketing', Series, vol. 8, Greenwich, Connecticut: Jai Press Inc.

Buzzell, R. (1968), 'Can You Standardize Multinational Marketing?', *Harvard Business Review*, November/December, pp. 102-113.

Buzzell, R. (1987), 'Designing Multinational Marketing Programs', *Harvard Business School*, Case Number, 9-587-174.

Cateora, P.R. (1985), *Strategic International Marketing*, Dow Jones-Irwin, Inc., Homewood, Illinois, pp. 140, 155-156, 159.

Cavusgil, S.T., Zou, S. and Naidu, G.M. (1993), 'Product and Promotion Adaptation in Export Venture', *Journal of International Business Studies*, vol. 24, no. 3.

Chao, P. and Rajendran, K.N. (1993), 'Consumer Profiles and Perceptions: Country-of-Origin Effects', *International Marketing Review*, vol. 10, no. 2, pp. 22-39.

Compagno, C. and Nanut, V. (1988), *Strutture organizzative e processi gestionali nelle piccole e medie imprese. Il caso del Friuli-Venezia Giulia*, Milano: Franco Angeli.

Cungu, A. and Swinnen, J.F. (1999), 'Albania's Radical Agrarian Reform', *Economic Development and Cultural Change*, vol. 47, no. 3, pp. 605-619.

Czinkota, M.R., Ronkainen, I.A. and Tarrant, J.J. (1995), *The Global Marketing Imperative*, NTC Business Book.

Czinkota, M.R. and Ronkainen, I.A. (1990), *International Marketing*, New York: The Dryden Press.

De Luca, P. (1992), *Il ruolo dei consorzi all'esportazione nel processo di internazionalizzazione delle imprese di minori dimensioni*, Trieste Consult.

EIU (1999), *The Economist Intelligence Unit*, Country Reports/Eastern Europe/Albania.

Ettenson, R., Gaeth, G. and Wagner, J. (1988), 'Evaluating the Effect of Country of Origin and the 'Made in the USA' Campaign: A Conjoint Approach', *Journal of Retailing*, vol.64, no. 1, pp. 85-100.

Filser, M. (1992), *I canali della distribuzione*, Milano: Etas.

Ghoshal, S. (1987), 'Global Strategy: An Organizing Framework', *Strategic Management Journal*, vol. 8.

Giuriato, L. (1999), 'Identità e crisi della transizione al mercato', *Rivista di Politica Economica*, vol. 89, no. 2, pp. 41-86.

Globerman, S. (1986), *Fundamentals of International Business Management*, Englewood Cliffs, New Jersey: Prentice-Hall, pp. 305-309.

Goldstein, M.A. (1997), 'Privatization Success and Failure: Finance Theory and Regulation in the Transitional Economics of Albania and the Czech Republic', *Managerial and Decision Economics*, vol. 18, no. 7&8, pp. 529-544.

Hibbert, E.P., Holt, V., Car P., and Plaidy, J. (1990), *The Principles and Practice of Export Marketing*, New York: Heinemann Professional Publishing.

Hovell, P.J. and Walters, P. (1972), 'International Marketing Presentations: Some Options', *European Journal of Marketing*, vol. 6, no. 2, pp. 69-79.

ICE (1999), http://www.ice.it/balcani/albania.

INSTAT Report (1999), Tirana, Albania.

Jain, S.C. (1989), 'Standardization of International Marketing Strategy: Some Research Hypotheses', *Journal of Marketing*, vol. 53, no. 1, pp. 70-79.

Johansson, J.K., Douglas, S.P. and Nonaka, I. (1985), 'Assessing the Impact of Country of Origin on Product Evaluations: A New Methodological Perspective', *Journal of Marketing Research*, vol. 22, no. 4, pp. 388-394.

Kahler, R. (1983), *International Marketing*, San Francisco: South-Western Publishing Co.

Keegan, W.J. (1999), *Global Marketing Management*, Upper Saddle River, New Jersey: Prentice Hall International.

Kreutzer, R.T. (1986), 'Marketing Mix Standardization: An Integrated Approach in Global Marketing', *European Journal of Marketing*, vol. 22, no. 10.

Levine, N., Manxhari M., and Pitt, D. (1998), 'Albanian Telecommunication Reform: The Road Less Traveled', *Telecommunications Policy*, vol. 22, no. 6, pp. 519-539.

Levitt, T. (1983), 'The Globalization of Markets', *Harvard Business Review*, vol. 61, May-June.

Lieberman, I.W., Nestor, S.S. and Desai, R.M. (eds) (1997), 'Between State and Market: Mass Privatization in Transition Economies', *Studies of Economies in Transformation*, no. 23, Washington, D.C.: World Bank; Paris: Organization for Economic Co-operation and Development.

Massa, S., (1995), 'Gli investimenti stranieri nell'Albania post-comunista', *Rassegna Economica*, vol. 59, no. 1, pp. 173-179.

McGrath, M.E. and Hoole, R.W. (1992), 'Manufacturing's New Economies of Scale', *Harvard Business Review*, May-June, pp. 94-102.

Morone, F. (a cura di) (1999), *Sviluppo umano e sostenibile in Albania*, Milano: Franco Angeli.

Nanut, V. (1994), 'Il ruolo delle aziende commerciali nello sviluppo di nuovi rapporti economici con l'est europeo', *Sinergie*, no. 33.

Onkvisit, S. and Shaw, J.J. (1989), *International Marketing: Analysis and Strategy*, Columbus: Merrill.

Papadopoulos, N. and Heslop, L.A. (1993), *Product-Country Images*, New York: International Business Press.

Peev, E. (1998), 'Ownership and Control in Bulgaria, Romania and Albania', *Economic Systems*, vol. 22, no. 3, pp. 294-298.

Pellegrini, M. and Reddy, S.K. (eds) (1986), *Marketing Channels. Relationship and Performance*, Lexington, Massachusets: Lexington Books.

Perlmutter, H.V., (1969), 'The Tortuous Evolution of the Multinational Corporation', *Columbia Journal of World Business*, January/February.

Prosi, G. (1998), 'Economic Cooperation between Members of the European Union and the Democratic Countries in Europe', *Communist Economies and Economic Transformation*, vol. 10, no. 1.

Quelch, J.A. and Hoff, E.J. (1986), 'Customizing Global Marketing', *Harvard Business Review*, May/June.

Rau, P.A. and Preble, J.F. (1987), 'Standardization of Marketing Strategy by Multinationals', *International Marketing Review*, vol. 4, no. 3, pp. 18-28.

Rein, M., Friedman B.L. and Worgotter, A. (eds) (1997), *Enterprise and Social Benefits after Communism*, Cambridge, New York and Melbourne: Cambridge University Press.

Root, F.R. (1987), *Entry Strategies for International Market*, Lexington, Massachusetts: Lexington Books.

Schooler, R.D., Wildt, A.R. and Jones, J.M. (1987), 'Strategy Development for Manufactured Products of Third World Countries to Developed Countries', *Journal of Global*

Marketing, vol. 1, no. 1&2, pp. 53-67.

Segrè, A. (1995), 'Potenzialità e fattori limitanti dello sviluppo agro-alimentare in Albania', in CNR-Idse, *Albania. Una regione oltre il Mediterraneo*, Milano.

Sharma, S. (ed.), (1997), *Restructuring Eastern Europe: The Microeconomics of the Transition Process*, Cheltenham: Edward Elgar.

Sorenson, R.Z. and Wiechmann, U.E. (1975), 'How Multinationals View Marketing Standardization', *Harvard Business Review*, vol. 53, May/June, pp. 38-56.

Stern, L.W. and El-Ansary, A.I. (1988), *Marketing Channels*, Third Edition, Englewood Cliffs, New Jersey: Prentice Hall.

Terpstra, V. (1987), *International Marketing*, Chicago: The Dryden Press.

Terpstra, V. and Sarathy, R. (1991), *International Marketing*, Chicago: The Dryden Press.

Toyne, B. and Walters, P.G.P. (1993), *Global Marketing Management*, New York: Allyn & Bacon.

Valdani, E. (1991), *Marketing Globale*, Milano: Etas.

Vernon-Wortzel, H. and Wortzel, L.H. (1990), *Global Strategic Management: The Essentials*, Greenbelt, Maryland: John Wiley & Sons.

Vianelli, D. (1995), 'Standardization of the Product Positioning Strategy in International Markets', *Economia Aziendale Review*, no. 3.

Vianelli, D. (1999), 'Standardization/Adaptation of the Product Positioning Strategy in International Markets: An Empirical Study of Some Italian Companies', in *Contemporary Developments in Marketing*, Paris: Editions ESKA.

Vianelli, D., de Luca, P. and Kajca, R. (1999), 'Italian Companies in Albania: An Exploratory Research', in P. Chadraba and R. Springer (eds) *Proceedings of the 7th Annual Conference on Marketing Strategies for Central & Eastern Europe*, December 1-3, 1999, Vienna, Austria.

Yip, G.S., Loewe, P.M. and Yoshino, M.Y. (1988), 'How to Take Your Company to the Global Market', *Columbia Journal of World Business*, Winter.

PART II:

INTERNATIONALIZATION OF ECONOMIC SECTORS

5 Internationalization of the Estonian Economy: Foreign Direct Investment and Banking

MART SÕRG, MAIT MILJAN and HANS KÜNKA

Introduction

The Republic of Estonia lies on the Eastern shore of the Baltic Sea and shares borders with Latvia to the South and Russia to the East.

Estonia's annexation by the Soviet Union in 1940, lead to a forced and radical transformation of its economy. The post-war period was characterized by rapid industrialization, which resulted in aggressive capital formation and forced relocation of labor - from agriculture to industry, and from other parts of the Soviet Union (notably Russia) into Estonia. Today Russian-speaking population make up 30 per cent of the Estonian 1.5 million inhabitants. When in the second half of the 1980s the Soviet authorities started to abandon the central planning, Estonia was the leader, among the former Soviet republics, in implementing the reforms.

The movement for economic and political independence in the three Baltic countries, which gained momentum during the late 1980s, eventually resulted in the approval of a law on economic autonomy by the USSR parliament in 1989. The law opened a way for the initiation of economic reforms in various areas, including price and wage determination, fiscal policy, and financial sector policies. The declaration of independence on August 20, 1991, quickly followed by Soviet and international recognition of Estonian sovereignty, helped Estonia to eliminate all remaining external obstacles for the transformation of its economy (Borner, Kobler and Winiker, 1997).

In transition countries the economic crisis is particularly serious, being expressed by the catastrophic decrease of GDP and by hyperinflation (Table 5.1). The output decline in Estonia was smaller (25.6 per cent) compared to the other Baltic States. The Baltic States have successfully proceeded toward a market economy. During a few years, the countries have achieved considerable results in liberalizing and stabilizing their economies (Alton, 1998).

133

Table 5.1   Estonia's balance of payments 1993-1998 (EEK million)

Indicators	1993	1996	1997	1998
Current account	279.0	-4,806.9	-7,813.2	-6,332.0
Trade and services	-927.9	-6,043.2	-7,423.0	-7,070.3
Trade balance	-1,925.0	-12,288.2	-15,654.9	-15,723.9
Goods: export fob	10,762.7	21,833.4	31,871.4	37,778.5
Goods: import fob	-12,687.7	-34,121.6	-47,526.3	-53,502.4
Services: net	997.1	6,245.0	8,231.9	8,653.6
Services: credit	4,434.3	13,352.8	18,366.7	20,615.2
Services: debit	-3,437.2	-7,107.8	-10,134.8	-11,961.6
Income: net	-185.4	26.2	-2,010.5	-1,342.5
Income: credit	355.5	1,352.5	1,594.1	1,820.0
Income debit:	-540.9	-1,326.3	-3,604.6	-3,162.5
Transfers: net	1,392.3	1,210.1	1,620.3	2,080.8
Transfers: credit	1,434.9	1,406.6	1,877.7	2,422.8
Transfers: debit	-42.6	-196.5	-257.4	-342.0
Capital account	0.0	-7.8	-2.0	25.2
Financial account	2,908.5	6,404.2	10,955.3	6,753.1
Direct investments	2,070.8	1,329,9	1,781.2	7,871.1
Abroad	-82.1	-484.5	-1,912.9	-70.8
Into Estonia	2,152.9	1,814.4	3,694.1	7,941.9
Portfolio investments	-3.0	1,784.4	3,655.1	21.6
Assets	-5.4	-628.4	-2,319.3	1.9
Equity securities	-5.2	-181.0	-1,238.5	619.5
Debt securities	-0.2	-447.4	-1,080.8	-617.6
Liabilities	2.4	2,412.8	5,974.4	19.7
Equity securities	1.3	2,093.8	1,763.6	316.3
Debt securities	1.1	319.0	4,210.8	-296.6
Other investments	840.7	3,289.9	5,519.0	-1,139.6
Assets	-1,909.7	-107.6	-4,635.5	-2,398.1
Long-term	-9.8	-17.5	-1,063.0	-775.5
Short-term	-1,899.9	-90.1	-3,572.5	-1,622.6
Liabilities	2,750.4	3,397.5	10,154.5	1,258.5
Long-term	1,687.5	1,783.0	4,604.9	1,228.4
Short-term	1,062.9	1,614.5	5,549.6	-29.9
Errors and omissions	-611.8	-361.1	-368.8	-319.1
Overall balance	2,575.7	1,228.4	2,771.3	126.4
Reserve assets	-2,575.7	-1,228.4	-2,771.3	-126.4

Source: Eesti Pank, 1999.

Mr. Kalevi Sorsa, a former Prime Minister of Finland, wrote: 'Estonia has become something of a model case for transition, due to its strict commitment to reform policies' (Sorsa, 1994).

A very decisive success factor for Estonia's transition under extremely difficult economic conditions is international support (mainly FDI, i.e., foreign direct investment). FDI inflow into Estonia has been higher than in the other Baltic countries. The FDI inflow into Estonian banking sector has stabilized it quickly and opened new facilities for further capital inflows.

This chapter analyzes the process of attracting FDI into Estonia, particularly into the Estonian banking sector. It focuses both on Estonian accomplishments in attracting FDI and on the mistakes made. The paper is divided into two chapters: Attracting international investments to Estonia, and internationalization of Estonian banking: experience and prospects.

Attracting International Investments to Estonia

Inflow of International Investments into Transition Economies

FDI is one of the most important factors for guaranteeing the economic growth and technological development of fledgling market economies in Central and Eastern Europe (CEE). Transition economies generally have insufficient domestic savings due to their meager incomes. Transition countries find international investments very effective, because they enable the import of new technology, expertise, management skills, and the launch of new business projects, all of which could otherwise be unattainable because of their exorbitant prices.

The 1990s saw an increase in the FDI in transition economies. FDI has become very important, providing economic growth in the countries of CEE. There is a strong competition among transition economies to attract international investments, especially foreign direct investment. In 1990, the total amount of FDI in the countries of CEE was only US$ 2.4 billion, which was equivalent to 1.5 percent of the total GDP of these countries. By the end of 1998 the amount of FDI increased 25 times to reach US$ 61.2 billion. Hungary once held a record of FDI inflow. It received a sizable amount of FDI in early 1990s. The second target country for foreign investors was the Czech Republic. In the 1990s Poland became the main recipient of FDI among all CEE economies and has maintained this position since (Tables 5.2 and 5.3). When comparing the dynamics of FDI in the transition countries, it is more useful to consider the inflows per capita (see Figure 5.1).

Table 5.2 Cumulative stock of FDI in Central Europe, 1990–1998 in US$ million

Region/Country	1990	1991	1992	1993	1994	1995	1996	1997	1998
Central Europe	2,375	5,215	9,180	13,255	18,444	30,476	39,525	46,739	61,243
Hungary	569	2,107	3,435	5,585	7,095	11,926	14,668	15,882	18,255
Czech Republic	72	595	2,889	3,423	4,547	7,350	8,572	9,234	13,457
Slovak Republic	n/a	43	231	453	762	1,066	1,361	1,558	1,888
Poland	353	600	1,125	2,840	4,715	8,374	12,872	17,780	24,780
Estonia	n/a	n/a	82	419	696	955	1,026	1,148	1,882

Source: Hunya, G. and Stankovsky, J., 1999.

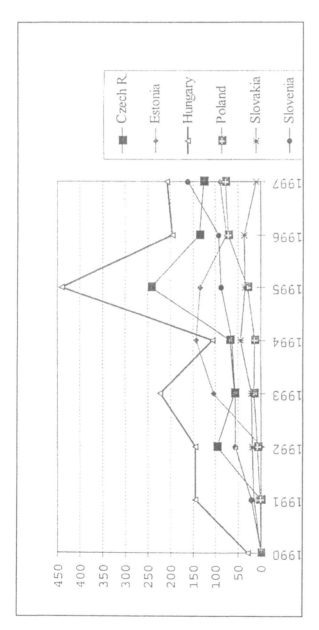

Figure 5.1 **FDI inflow per capita, USD**

Source: EBRD, Transition Report, 1997, 1998.

Table 5.3   Foreign direct investments in some transition economies

Country	Average transition indicator in 1997*	Total FDI 1989–1997 (mln. US$)	FDI inflow 1989–1997 (US$ per capita)	Cumulative FDI stock as a percentage of 1997 GDP	Rise of real GDP in 1995–1997 (average %)
Hungary	3.50	15,466	1,452	34.4	2.4
Czech R.	3.38	8,181	794	15.5	3.2
Estonia	3.38	1,006	689	22.2	5.8
Poland	3.25	17,249	449	13.4	6.7
Slovakia	3.25	0,862	160	4.4	6.6
Slovenia	3.13	1,840	920	9.4	3.4
Lithuania	3.00	0,682	189	7.2	4.3
Bulgaria	2.75	0,980	110	9.8	–5.4
Romania	2.75	2,488	108	7.1	1.5
Russia	2.88	8,790	59	1.9	–2.9

* 4 is advanced.

Source: Calculations by U. Varblane on the basis of EBRD Transition Report, 1997; World Development Report, 1996; and IMF Financial Statistics, 1993–1997; Business Central Europe, 1998.

In terms of attracting FDI, Estonia has been doing quite well. Table 5.3 presents the average transition indicator calculated by EBRD analysts, country risk rating, total and per capita FDI, the ratio of cumulative stock of FDI to GDP, and rise of real GDP in 1995–1997. Table 5.3 shows that Estonia has been relatively successful among transition countries in terms of attracting FDI. The ratio of cumulative stock of FDI to the GDP is a very important indicator as it is measuring the importance of FDI in the countries' economy during the whole transition period. In 1997, the cumulative FDI in Estonia made up 22.2 per cent of country's GDP, placing it second after Hungary whose respective ratio was 34.4 per cent.

Inflow of International Investments into Estonia

By the end of 1998, foreign direct investors made 24.3 billion Estonian kroons EEK (US$ 1.8 billion) worth of investments into Estonia, which placed the country among the leading Central and Eastern European states in terms of per capita FDI (US$ 1,249.3). The direct investment position of Estonian residents abroad accounted for 11 per cent of the first figure, i.e., EEK 2.6 billion. Estonian statistics consider direct investments as foreign investments, made by the companies of other countries, which hold at least 20 per cent of Estonian enterprise assets. For example, statistics indicate that Germany accounts for only 3 per cent of Estonia's total FDI. But the director of the Representative Office of German Industry and Commerce in Estonia, Dr. Ralph-Georg Tischer says that the figure is at least double as much, because there are substantial cover investments, which have been made after the initial investment and which are not officially registered (Maranik, 1998).

Figures 5.2 and 5.3 illustrate direct investments into and from Estonia in terms of countries and spheres of activity.

In 1998 foreign partners invested EEK 7.9 billion into Estonia and resident businessmen invested EEK 0.1 billion into affiliated and associated business ventures abroad (see Figure 5.4). Short-term loan capital was replaced by direct investment capital and the flows of portfolio investment capital were as shown in Figure 5.5.

Mainly due to the attractiveness of the financial sector, the direct investments into Estonia in 1998 increased 2.1 times, compared to 1997. Of the total investments, the direct capital investments into share capital and loan capital accounted for 71 per cent and 17 per cent, respectively. Of the latter, the long-term loans made up 64 per cent.

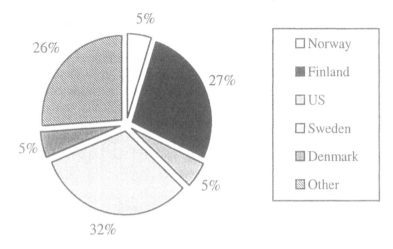

**Figure 5.2 Direct investment in Estonia, by country,
as of 31 December 1998 (% and mln EEK)**

Source: Bank of Estonia.

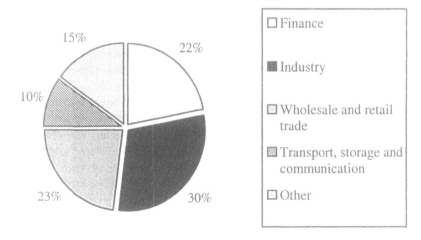

**Figure 5.3 Direct investment of spheres of activities in Estonia,
as of 31 December 1998 (% and mln EEK)**

Source: Bank of Estonia.

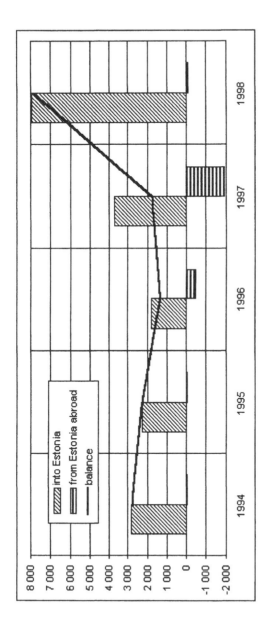

Figure 5.4   Direct investments (EEK mln)

Source: Bank of Estonia, 1999.

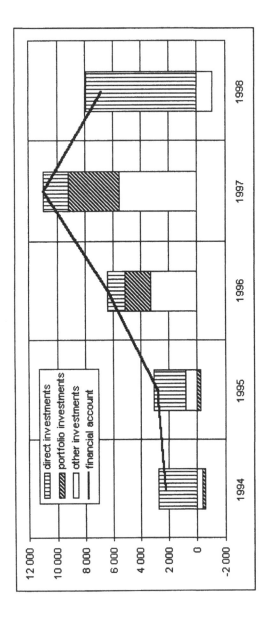

Figure 5.5   **Changes in the structure of foreign capital investment flows (EEK million)**

Source: Bank of Estonia, 1999.

In 1998, the bulk of foreign investments came from Sweden and Finland and was mostly directed into the financial sector and industry. Mostly due to the increase in trade credit claims of industrial companies, direct investments from Russia decreased by more than EEK 189 million (see Table 5.4).

Table 5.4   Structure of direct investments made into Estonia by countries and types of business in 1998

Country	EEK million	Share (%)	Type of business	EEK million	Share (%)
Sweden	4, 623.8	58.2	Finance	4, 268.8	53.8
Finland	1, 694.0	21.3	Industry	1, 508.5	19.0
Denmark	425.5	5.4	Real estate, leasing and services	385.2	4.9
Russia	−189.4	−2.4	Construction	164.9	2.1
Other	1, 388.0	17.5	Other	1, 614.5	20.3
Total	7, 941.9	100.0	Total	7, 941.9	100.0

Source: Bank of Estonia, 1999.

Figures 5.6 and 5.7 give information about portfolio and other investments. The inflow of EEK 3.7 billion portfolio investments made in 1997 was replaced by a relative balance of in- and outflow in 1998.

Incentives for Investment in Estonia

Several surveys have been made on various aspects of FDI in Central and East European countries. Those surveys would discuss investment incentives and problems that foreign investors encounter. They also provide the criteria that prove why some countries in the region were selected for FDI amongst the others, all of which have a similar cost level.

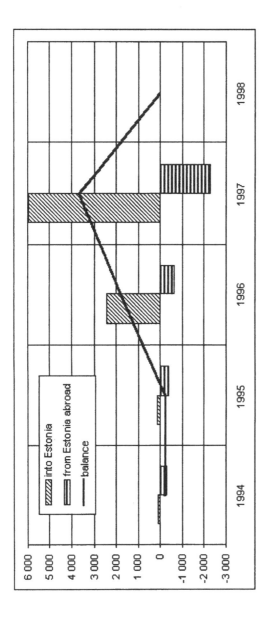

Figure 5.6 **Portfolio investments (EEK mln)**

Source: Bank of Estonia, 1999.

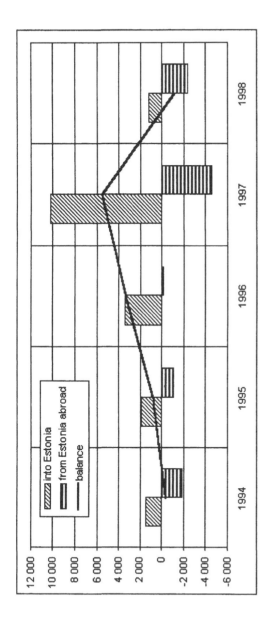

Figure 5.7   Other investments (EEK mln)

Source: Bank of Estonia, 1999.

International surveys have shown that in undertaking FDI investors are primarily motivated by the perspectives of penetrating into new markets and increasing their sales. The situation has been similar in the transition countries of CEE, including Estonia. In transition countries, the political stability and the size of the market have had overriding importance. The incentives consist of the local highly-qualified and reasonably priced labor, favorable and stable business environment, and attractive geographic location.

The results of a study conducted by KPMG (1993) showed that Western investors have considered political and financial security as the main stability actors when making decisions of investment in Eastern Europe (Table 5.5). Other stability factors include the conditions the host country imposes on repatriating profits or investment of capital.

Most of the FDI studies seem to have been concentrated on the general situation with FDI and FDI behavior in the larger investment target countries, e.g., Russia, Poland, Hungary and the Czech Republic. Fortunately some studies have focused also on FDIs in Estonia.

Table 5.5 Factors governing FDI in CEE countries

Ranking	Factor	Points*
1	Political stability	115
2	Important domestic market	71
3	Financial stability	47
4	Skilled labor	40
5	Potential profitability	35
6	Geographic location	33
7	Competitive costs	28
8	Convertible currency	15
9	Transport system/infrastructure	10
10	Company law	6
11	Potential export base	5
12	Beneficial tax system	2

*   Three factors rated at 3, 2 and 1 points.

Source: KPMG, 1993.

The majority of FDI in Estonia has come from Finland. So far the Bank of Finland and ETLA have conducted the most comprehensive surveys about FDI made by Finnish firms in the Baltic States. These studies (Laurila, 1994; Laurila and Hirvensalo, 1996; Hirvensalo and Hazley, 1998) have focused on the FDI made in Estonia because Estonia has clearly been the main target country among the Baltic States and even among all CEE countries for Finnish companies.

One special study on FDI in Estonia, made by C. Claros (Claros, 1996), was focused on investments from US companies and it analyzed both the advantages and disadvantages of investing in Estonia.

The sample size (seventeen firms) of this research is quite small. All the firms were interviewed face-to-face. The results were indicated on a five-point scale where 1 stood for 'very important' and 5 for 'unimportant'. Results indicate that market access is the most important incentive for these firms in Estonia (1.87), followed by the potentials of enterprise expansion (2.14) and of trade expansion (2.29). Protection of existing markets of companies (3.45) and lower cost of production (3.08) were the two least important incentives. The biggest advantages of investing in Estonia included market access, highly educated and skilled labor, and potential for economic growth. Small market size, excessive bureaucracy, and the potential of risk from Russia were the greatest disadvantages.

The study of Larimo *et al.* (1998) concluded that firms of different origin seem to have somewhat different motives for their FDI in Estonia. They divided the countries into three groups, taking into account their investment incentives. Table 5.6 shows that neighboring countries like Finland and Sweden are mainly interested in finding a new market, but other countries use Estonia as a gateway for penetrating the markets of the European Union or Russia. Although these data are not recent, they vividly express the strategic motives of investors.

The most extensive study on FDI in Estonia so far is the project that a group of researchers of the University of Tartu and the Estonian Investment Agency jointly made in 1996–1997. Its results were published (Varblane *et al.*, 1998). Ninety-two foreign firms representing 124 foreign investors, responded to at least one part of the survey. The scope extends beyond incentives and problems.

Participants were asked to rank on a five-point scale (one meant 'none' and five meant 'significant') the impact of each incentive on their investment decision. Market entry is the most important incentive with a score of 3.94 followed by market growth potential (3.77) and the Estonian labor cost (3.69). The relatively lower scores for access to Russia/CIS and EU markets and the small size of the local market indicate that the majority of the firms surveyed are basically interested in the Baltics. Surprisingly, access to the EU markets is the least motivating factor for foreign investors (2.16) followed by availability of raw materials (2.69) and competitors' activities (2.83). Considering the fact that most of the respondents were from Finland (42 per cent) and Sweden (19 per cent), one possible explanation is that these countries, especially Finland, are primarily motivated by Estonia's close geographic proximity (which was not listed as a criterion) and they regard Estonia as a local market (Ziacik, 1998).

Table 5.6   Motives for investing in Estonia, first half of 1995

Groups of countries	Nearest neighboring countries	Countries not members of EU, USA and Canada	EU countries
Strategic interests	• broadening the home market • protecting the home market	• being close to the Russian market	• investing into the hub of North European market • being close to Russia
Advantages when investing into Estonia	• political stability • prospect of Estonia's admission to EU • favorable relation between labor costs and reasonable price of electricity • local natural resources • favorable geographic position		

Source: Larimo *et al*., 1998.

According to the survey, the biggest problem that foreign investors encounter in Estonia is caused by VAT (value-added tax) rebates (3.25). Although firms can be recompensed for the VAT they have paid, it is a slow process, that does not take effect until the firm starts exporting, prior to which it has purchased expensive equipment and driven its costs high. The other serious problems that scored over 3.0 were due to loops in legislation and the quality of labor. The latter one contrasts with those results that listed Estonian labor as one of the main incentives. However, in terms of required skills the labor is quite heterogeneous.

According to the results of FDI studies in Estonia, investors generally have similar incentives for coming to Estonia and they also face similar problems. The most and least important incentives among investors in Estonia and other CEE countries are also closely related. Nevertheless, there are two disadvantages about the surveys done in Estonia: sample sizes were small and the samples were based on one or two investor groups, usually Finnish firms. Therefore the issue of plausibility of the responses still remains.

Building a Favorable FDI Environment in Estonia

The consulting company KPMG has suggested six advantages of investment into Estonia:

- excellent location for economic and business activities at the cross-roads of East-West trade as well as trade from Scandinavia to the South and on the Baltic Sea connecting large markets in Northern, Eastern, Central, and Western Europe;
- one of the most liberal trade regimes in Europe; investors can obtain tariff-free access to the entire European customs area and to the Baltic states with far lower start-up and operating costs than in the EU member states;
- highly educated, western-minded people with excellent command of European languages and Russian;
- a highly developed infrastructure, telecommunication network in particular, compared to the other Baltic states;
- a well developed banking regulatory environment; by the year 2000 the banking system is expected to be fully comparable to European standards;
- developed countries' desire to support economic restructuring in Estonia attracts financial support for projects ventured in Estonia by both national and international sources. Financial support for Estonian reform has been provided by the European Community, EBRD, IMF and several countries (KPMG Estonia, 1998).

According to this KPMG Estonia statement, attractions for investments in Estonia include the country's geographic location and favorable investment climate. Estonian government has been making great efforts in the last ten years to create a favorable setting for investors. Apparently, Estonia's success in its FDI policies is not based merely on facilitating foreign investors to enter into the Estonian market, but also on continuously changing the investment climate according to the market change and investors' desires. That ensures the foreign investors' wish to extend their business in Estonia in the future and turns them into our supporters in promoting the investments in Estonia abroad.

During the mid- to the late-1980s the Estonian economy was dominated by state and cooperative ownership; no private ownership was allowed during that period. The cooperative property, actually, was also controlled by the government. In the Soviet Union, the quota and targets for the government-owned economy were set by the government-owned planning agency, called Gosplan. The Ministers of the Estonian SSR could only approve investments up to the size of one million roubles (Vitsur, 1995).

The essential changes in investment policy took place after Estonia restored its independence in August 1991. It was on September 10, 1991, when the Law on Foreign·Investments was approved. This law stipulated the procedures for making foreign investments and the legal guarantees to investors. Foreign investors have a right to repatriate the proceeds of selling their share of an enterprise. It was important not only to facilitate foreign investors to enter into the market but also to give them legal guarantees.

The Law on Tax Deduction for Companies Operating with Foreign Capital provides the following stipulates the following:

•   If the foreign investor's share in the fixed capital is at least 30 per cent, but not less than US$ 50,000, the enterprise is exempt from income tax for a period of two years. In the subsequent two years, income tax will be decreased by 50 per cent.

•   If the foreign investor's share in the fixed capital of the enterprise is at least 50 per cent, but not less than US$ 1,000,000 the enterprise is exempt from income tax for a period of three years. In the subsequent five years, its income tax will be decreased by 50 per cent.

Table 5.6 shows that for foreign investors the issues of taxation were of least importance. Nevertheless, these tax deductions were very attractive for Estonian entrepreneurs, because they themselves began to seek partners abroad and negotiate with them to invest a small amount of capital into the fledgling Estonian economy. Having arrived in Estonia and familiarized themselves with the local situation, foreign investors would build their confidence and invest bigger amounts in Estonia. They were especially attracted by the possibility to divest in case of any imminent danger.

Statistics also prove the fact that the restoration of independence and the approval of the Law on Foreign Investments lead to the investment boom in Estonia. Though by the beginning of 1991 only 414 enterprises with foreign partnership were registered in Estonia after restoring its independence, about 200 new joint ventures were registered every month. By October 1, 1991 the total figure of such companies was 1,116 and by July 1, 1992 it was 2,759.

Nine months after the restoration of independence (on June 20, 1992) Estonia introduced its own legal tender, the Estonian kroon (EEK). The kroon is pegged to the German Mark with the exchange rate DEM 1 = EEK 8 and the exchange rate is protected by the principles of currency board. Within half a year after the emission of the kroon 1,055 new enterprises with foreign capital participation were registered and the number of such enterprises grew up to 3,814. Table 5.7 shows that almost half of such enterprises were established by Finnish partners and over 10 per cent with the help of Swedish investors. Conclusively, the Estonian businessmen showed initiative: in doing business with Finland the affinity of languages and the neighborhood of the countries were the facilitating factors, while the business links with Sweden were facilitated by their local Estonian community who helped in the brokerage of investments. The share of the countries of the CIS is also implicit, considering the connections that have existed with the East.

In the first stage of investments the main objective was to attract as many Western businesses to Estonia as possible in order to let them discover for themselves the available investment opportunities in the country. It also met Estonian companies' expectation of starting successfully and opening the gateway for penetrating into export markets.

Table 5.7   Active foreign investor countries in Estonia (number of firms)

Country	01.07.1992	01.01.1993	01.01.1994
Finland	1,365	1,999	3,365
Countries of CIS	555	676	953
Sweden	337	446	730
Germany	84	120	231
USA	90	117	203
UK	27	46	88
China	12	34	82
Denmark	19	30	62
Latvia	14	21	46
Norway	20	28	46
Total	2,759	3,814	6,316

Source: Liuhto, 1994.

The risks of transition economy being high due to the continuing economic recession and questionable success of the reforms, it was quite obvious that investors would place their risk capital in Estonia. Thus, Estonia offered foreign investors a possibility to participate in the privatization and cheaply buy its state-owned companies' assets, either partly or entirely. Consequently, in its first stage of FDI policy Estonia attracted a great number of small investments. It was expected that the joint ventures would pick up well, which would attract new investors to the country.

Privatization of small enterprises was quite rapid in Estonia. By the end of 1993, about 100 per cent of the former state-owned small firms had been privatized, mostly by selling their assets on auctions. Quite often the management and employees, supported by foreign investments, bought the assets.

In the course of medium and large-scale privatization, Estonia tried to attract new foreign investors.

Estonia initiated its medium- and large-scale privatization in 1992 (after the tryout privatization phase in 1991). During 1992–1993 three tenders were made, offering the total of 130 companies to both domestic and foreign buyers. The end of 1993 concluded 54 deals. Because foreign investors showed modest interest and participated only in ten purchases, the share of foreign capital accounted for less than 20 per cent of the total investments.

Foreign investors were careful due to two reasons. In 1992–1993 the deep economic crisis continued and the circumstances of privatization conditions were quite difficult. In 1992 and 1993 Estonia's GDP decreased 14.2 per cent and 8.5 per cent, respectively, and it was unclear, whether Estonia would succeed in its economic reforms or whether it would turn back. Enterprises were sold to the Estonian or foreign buyers, provided they would make necessary investments during the following years and keep a requisite number of jobs. Western economic analysts regarded such an approach to privatization as not very promising and believed that it could last for long time (Bergsman and Shen, 1995).

In 1994 the offers of assets were continued, but with the following change: a certain part of the companies' shares was put on public sale. Estonian officials supposed that the most attractive companies had already been offered for privatization. Naturally, there were the first signs of success of all reforms in Estonia and the beginning of rapid economic growth (for example, the rapid growth of the amount of banks' assets and the decrease of loan interests below inflation index). This lead to the first success of reforms in Estonian economy, marking the start of a rapid growth of the banks' assets and the decline of loan interests below the inflation index. Those changes in privatization policy offered new prospects and facilitated the arrival of direct investments (Table 5.8).

Table 5.8   Privatization through prior negotiations in Estonia

Indicators	1993	1994	1995	1996	1997
Number of contracts	54	215	142	43	18
Total revenues, in mln kroons	353	1,340	919	474	1,295
Average sale price, in mln kroons	6.5	6.2	6.4	11	72
Liabilities transferred, in mln kroons	196	691	618	230	416
Guaranteed investments, in mln kroons	237	858	1,003	454	1,714
Number of jobs guaranteed	9,099	25,573	17,297	1,274	2,929

Source: MEARE, 1998.

The commitments to making investments, laid down in the pre-negotiated privatization contracts, guaranteed the necessary funding of the development of companies and helped the arrival of direct investments in Estonia. Only the utilities companies still have to be privatized. The privatization of electricity companies and railroad services will offer new opportunities to foreign investors.

Though during the first and second period of attracting foreign investments into Estonia the initiative was showed by the local business people, who sought foreign investors, and by the Estonian government that provided the investors opportunities for acquisition of assets, now the biggest initiative is taken by foreign investors. There are several reasons for it. First, at present Estonia has reliable industries. Second, the Tallinn Stock Exchange was opened in 1995 that offers everyone an opportunity to make continuous investments into the companies' assets.

By Estonian standards, the direct investment consists of funding the companies' stock and working capital if the investor's foreign direct investment is 20 per cent or more. The rest of FDI is made up of parent company's loans to, or investments in affiliates or subsidiaries. Portfolio investments are made in corporate bonds and commercial papers, with the investor's participation being under 20 per cent.

Table 5.9   Estonian direct investments abroad, EEK mln

Indicators	1995	1996	1997	1998
Share capital	3.6	107.1	539,2	495,1
• of which inflow (resale)	–4.4	–75.3	–251,6	–148,8
• outflow from Estonia	8.0	182.4	790,8	643,9
Reinvested earnings	–	147.2	88,5	–48,4
• of which loss	–	–7.7	–10,9	–129,8
• profit	–	154.9	99,4	81,4
Loan capital (net)	25.5	229.7	1,271,3	–373,5
• of which trade credit	25.5	102.3	318,6	–252,8
• short-term loans	–	2.7	167,2	–79,2
• long-term loans	–	124.7	785,5	–41,5
Other capital	–	0.5	13,9	–2,4
Total direct investments	29.1	484.5	1,912,9	70,8

(-)   designates the resources returned to Estonia.

Source: Bank of Estonia Bulletin, 1999.

Another new indication is the rising capacity of Estonian investments abroad. Table 5.9 shows that, compared with 1995, the growth in 1996 and 1997 was enormous. Greater was the growth of loan capital. This confirms the idea that Western companies use Estonia often as a gateway for going to attractive markets in the East. The first setback was given in 1998 by the financial crisis in the CIS countries. It showed that Estonia's FDI abroad, being oriented only to the East, faced extreme risks.

The continuing intensive FDI inflow into Estonia has several reasons. These reasons are summed up into the concept 'investment climate'. In June 1998 the Estonian Institute of Economic Research (EKI) evaluated the local investment situation as favorable: 5.8 points in June is lower than the 6.0 points in March and the general economic situation in June the same year was marked at 6.7 points. The measuring scale had a range from 1 (bad) to 9 (excellent). Thus 5 is in between, meaning satisfactory. The experts' opinions of the investment situation in June 1998 could be expressed as follows: 32 per cent of the experts thought that the situation was good; 58 per cent thought that it was satisfactory; and 11 per cent felt that the situation was bad (EKI, 1998).

Foreign experts are also considering Estonian economic situation quite acceptable. By the credit risk ratings, Estonia is only preceded by Slovenia and the Czech Republic (Table 5.10).

Table 5.10   Credit risk ratings in transition economies

Country	Standard & Poor's	Moody's	Fitch IBCA
Slovenia	A	A3	A
Czech Republic	A	Baa1	BBB+
Estonia	BBB+	Baa1	BBB
Latvia	BBB	Baa2	–
Hungary	BBB	Baa3	BBB
Poland	BBB-	Baa3	BBB
Croatia	BBB-	Baa3	BBB
Slovakia	BBB	Ba1	BBB
Lithuania	BBB	Ba2	BB+
Russia	BB-	Ba2	BB+
Romania	BB-	Ba3	BB-

Source: Äripäev, April 7, 1998.

Internationalization of Estonian Banking: Experience and Prospects

Goals and Ways of Internationalization of Banking Business

Concept of banking internationalization   The meaning of the concept 'internationalization of banks' has varied from time to time. In the early years of capitalism, the main activity of the banks consisted of offering local companies services for making transactions in domestic currencies. Only very few banks took local risks or ventured some international transactions, made cash remittances or guaranteed loans and payments for imports. It has been alleged that financing of foreign trade led to the formation of the first commercial banks in the cities of Italy, Germany and London (Linnamo and Vanamo, 1980).

Both the world economic crisis in the 1930s and the fiscal policy after WW II significantly restrained the internationalization of banks. However, since the late 1950s the gradual abolition of the restrictions on capital transfers and the liberalization of customs restrictions quickened the internationalization of banks. The internationalization of banks made enormous progress after the oil crisis in 1973, as the international banks tried to solve the deficit in the balance of payments of the oil-importing countries and the surplus in the balance of payments of oil-producing countries by recycling the resources.

Currently most of the companies are already closely connected with the international market. Therefore, the banks have to expand their services abroad and negotiate foreign currencies. Complying with the wide array of international payment facilities (traveler's checks, bank checks, etc.), all banks are somehow involved in international integration. Hence, it can be concluded that currently 'internationalization' primarily means physical presence in the foreign markets. Internationalization of banking is defined as a process of expanding the banks' operations abroad and replacing domestic banking business content by international content (Taeho, 1993). Filip Pettersson defines international banking as the process of building controlled action units within the boundaries of other national banking systems (Pettersson, 1974). These action units can take, for example, the following form: fully-owned foreign subsidiaries, branch offices, cooperation agreements or joint ventures with foreign banks, consortium banks and participation in foreign banks. The new level of the internationalization of banks, as determined here, was necessary until recently concerning the fact that the real presence in the foreign markets enables the banks to offer their clients better services and reduce the bank risks.

One of the factors that is going to change the essence of the internationalization of banks, is the building up of the European Economic and Monetary Union that converts the whole Europe to one big inclusive market.

There is a general agreement that the introduction of the Euro will contribute to intensifying the competition in the European financial sector and speeding up of market integration. These directions will probably accelerate the start of restructuring of the European banking sector (Thomsen, Biltoft and Thuesen, 1999).

In the near future the necessity of the presence of banks in foreign markets will probably decrease owing to the gradual disintegration of barriers between the banking systems of different countries and the introduction of new electronic bank services. Therefore, in the coming years the meaning of the concept 'internationalization of banks' may be deflected toward the one this concept had in the early years of capitalism: the share of international services among the total services provided by the bank.

When discussing the internationalization of banks, we mean their penetration into the banking services of other countries by setting up action units or purchasing and acquiring voting interests in banks abroad.

Reasons for the internationalization of banks   The reasons for the banks' internationalization are primarily due to business needs or restrictions imposed on economic activity (Pauli, 1994). When companies internationalize, the banks will also expand their activity abroad, intending to serve their established clients abroad, to expand their foreign client base, or just to dispel the fear of losing their clients to potential competitors. Better opportunities to earn a profit also lure the banks to the neighboring markets.

First, the banks began to set up their overseas branches, offices and subsidiaries in the old and new financial centers (London, New York, Paris, Frankfurt, Zurich, Tokyo, Luxembourg, and Singapore). That confirms our earlier statement about demands that local companies' managements would impose on a bank for operating the cash flows of their international clients. But very often the Cayman Islands, Bahamas, Bahrain, Panama, Isle of Man, Gibraltar and other well-known offshore countries are chosen for the location of the branches and departments. In this case, the reasons for internationalization are purely related to the companies' thrift, whence the goal is to increase profit by avoiding the high taxes levied in the home country and waive the domestic banking regulations and foreign currency restrictions. The fiscal and monetary policy makers of countries, where banks are forced to use such type of internationalization, can judge whether their tax rates and requirements for the banks' activities are reasonable or unreasonable.

The internationalization of banks has been significantly impacted by structural changes in the world trade, the growth of direct investments into foreign countries, development, military aid programs, etc. The oil crisis in 1973 was one of such macroeconomic factors. Because of the crisis, the monetary resources began to accumulate in the oil-exporting countries without the purpose of exploitation, but the oil-importing countries suffered money scarcity due to the deficit in their balance of payments. The disproportion between the location and demand of money resources gave a powerful boost to the internationalization of banks – the banks began to set up subsidiaries in the oil states. Thus, an opportunity was given to pump money from the oil-producing countries back to the oil-importing countries.

In the last decade, the end of the Cold War and the breakdown of the communist regime became two especially important factors for the internationalization of banks. The Western banks hurried to penetrate the emerging markets, especially the huge Russian market.

Besides the macroeconomic factors that guide the internationalization of banks, an important role is also played by the ambitions of bank managers.

Ways of internationalization of banks   It is rational to carry out the internationalization of banks in two stages:

• To consolidate one's position in a target country, in order to improve one's knowledge of the local market. Mostly, the following ways are being used: setting up of correspondent accounts with local banks, opening of representative offices in the target country or acquisition of a minority stake in some local bank.

• Venturing some form of banking business in a target country, either by setting up affiliates and subsidiaries, buying up a bank, or obtaining a significant stake in a bank through a merger or buying shares.

In the banking markets of different countries, the share of the banking business based on foreign capital varies significantly. In Europe the indicator has been bigger traditionally in Great Britain and Ireland (over 50%) and Belgium (about 35%). Luxembourg with 90% is an exception.

While by the end of 1992 EU members had set up 308 bank branches in other countries of the Union, then in the following three years 179 more branches were added, bringing the increase to 58% (Mäenpää, 1997). This indicates a rapid increase in banking integration in the EU. Table 5.11 shows that in the EU the subsidiaries are preferred to the branches and the share of the EU countries exceeds the share of the banks from outside the Union.

The policy of the EU Economic and Currency Union abolishes barriers between national currencies, which to a certain extent protect local banks against international competition. After the introduction of the European common currency, only geographical location and language differences will protect national banking systems from foreign competitors and slow down the market penetration by foreign banks. Therefore the managing director of the Merita group, Vesa Vainio, forecasts that in relation to the coming euro the competition between banks will become harder and the Finnish banks will be endangered by the more effective Swedish banks (Vainio, 1996). The previously mentioned idea forces the banks of Finland and other countries to manage the banks sparingly and take into account the possibilities of foreign banks invasion of their market in case they may raise their service charges.

Table 5.11 Market share of branches and subsidiaries of foreign credit institutions in euro area as a percentage of the total assets of domestic credit institutions, as of the end of 1997

Country	From EEA countries		From other countries		Total
	Branches	Subsidiaries	Branches	Subsidiaries	
Belgium	9.0	19.2	6.9	1.2	36.3
Germany	0.9	1.4	0.7	1.2	4.3
Spain	4.8	3.4	1.6	1.9	11.7
France	2.5•	.	2.7•	.	9.8•
Ireland	17.7	27.8	1.2	6.9	53.6
Italy	3.6	1.7	1.4	0.1	6.8
Luxembourg	19.4	71.1	1.4	8.1	99.9
Netherlands	2.3	3.0	0.5	1.9	7.7
Austria	0.7	1.6	0.1	1.0	3.3
Portugal	2.5	6.8	0.1	1.0	10.5
Finland	7.1	0	0	0	7.1
Euro area weighted average	3.4	.	1.6	.	12.7

*   1996 figures.

Source: European Central Bank, 1999.

Risks of the internationalization of banks   It cannot be claimed *à priori* that international banking is riskier than domestic banking, provided the steps of internationalization are thoroughly considered and prepared. Still the rosy expectations concerning the internationalization can fail and even prove fatal for the banks involved. As a rule, the risks connected with the internationalization are drawn under a common name 'commercial risk' or 'country risk' (Eiteman *et al.*, 1992). The country risk, first, means that the bank has to work in a market that differs from the domestic market with its legal framework and social, cultural, political and economic environment. Still, it seems to us that the common risk category 'country risk' remains the particular risk factor that is unexplained. Still, the parent bank also functions in a definite country where the risks proceeding from political problems, inadequate banking regulation, crime and other factors can be even greater. In transition countries, for example, the level of internal risks is particularly high due to the economic crisis, setback in reforms, social and political tensions, which will probably bother the banks more than in countries with a stable market economy.

We think that internationalization (for example, entering the Russian market) does not concern a common country risk, which influences all the banks entering the country in the same way. The success of implementing the plans of internationalization depends more on the efficiency of banks in creating the preconditions necessary for a successful entry and efficient operating in the foreign market. When entering a foreign market the bankers must know the conditions well and be accepted for operating there.

Internationalization of Estonian Banking

Goals of the internationalization   In an interview to 'The Baltic Review' on the tendencies in the development of the Estonian banks the former Vice Governor of the Bank of Estonia, Mr. Heldur Meerits, puts the internationalization of banks on the second place after consolidation (Meerits, 1996). But a year later, at the Conference marking the fifth anniversary of the Estonian kroon the Governor of Eesti Pank, Mr. Vahur Kraft, put the internationalization ahead of consolidation. He said: 'Already today we can see the signs of several new processes and trends that could significantly change the face of Estonian banking in the near future: deepening international cooperation, increasing interest in new markets, products and supply channels, continuous consolidation of the financial sector, etc.' (Kraft, 1997).

These statements prove that the central bank well approves the internationalization efforts of Estonian banks. And this is implicit because due to the 1.5 million population and the transition state of the economy in the country the domestic market of Estonian banks is just too small. At the same time, an adequate inter-bank competition has to be maintained on the domestic market, in order to encourage the banks' development and efficiency. The main reason for the internationalization of Estonian banks is due to the saturation of the domestic market, and the banks' desire to earn higher profits on the neighboring markets where competition is weaker (Zirnask, 1997).

Yet, it seems to us that the macroeconomic reasons are more important factors of internationalization than the motives of the bankers and shareholders. Estonia chose the way of an open market economy where all goods and services can cross the frontiers freely. That free movement of goods presumes also that cash flows should cross the frontiers freely as well. This process by itself provides a good ground for the internationalization of banks.

In Estonia the openness of the society has brought along the growth of the economy and the rapid development of international relationships (see Table 5.12). Though the current account of Estonia runs a deficit, it is balanced by the flows of foreign investments.

Foreign banks in Estonia   After Estonia had restored its independence in August 1991, the foreign banks intensively started to enter the Estonian banking market. The Ukrainian Inko Bank was the first to establish a subsidiary in Estonia – Inko Baltic Bank. The establishment of the Baltic American Bank and the entrance of strategic investors into Eesti Innovatsioonipank (Estonian Innovation Bank) and NoWe Bank followed it. But the first ventures were not completely successful. Most of them were closed by the owners either because of losses or inability to find a suitable niche, or because of ignoring the local banking regulations. The branch of the Finnish Merita Bank in Tallinn (license dating from 1994) also developed slowly at first and worked with losses but in 1998 it improved its results sharply and now it is placed among the medium-sized banks in Estonia. The successful stage of the international banks' entry into Estonia started in 1998. In 1998 Hansapank and Eesti Ühispank (Union Bank of Estonia) survived difficult times after they had merged with Hoiupank (Savings Bank of Estonia) and Tallinna Pank (Bank of Tallinn), respectively. The major Swedish banks, Swedbank and SE Banken, that became the major shareholders of the mentioned Hansapank and Union Bank, seized a favorable opportunity for entrance into the Estonian market. Nowadays, the Swedish banks are the strategic investors in the two biggest banks of Estonia and 58 per cent of the shareholders in the Estonian banks are foreign residents (Table 5.13). The share held by the Estonian residents in the two major banks was 21% in Hansapank and 24.2% in Union Bank. It can be concluded that despite current setbacks the foreign banks have been successful in their entry into the Estonian banking market. The major shareholder of the third biggest bank, the Optiva Bank, is the Bank of Estonia. Only the two smallest banks of the five commercial banks in Estonia were more than 50% owned by the Estonian legal entities and natural persons.

Vice Governor of the Bank of Estonia Helo Meigas concluded that with the entry of Swedish banks, the maturity structure in Estonian banking improved, creating sufficient buffers. The share capital of Estonian commercial banks increased and the capital adequacy of banks improved from 12.4 per cent to 17 per cent (Meigas, 1999).

Table 5.12   Inflation, output performance and political credibility in transition economies, 1989–1996

Country	Year in which inflation was highest	Maximum annual inflation	Year in which inflation fell below 50%	Year in which output was lowest	Cumulative output decline (1989=1000)	Cumulative output growth since lowest level	Political credibility (1995)
Belarus	1993	1994.0	–	1996	40.5	–	3.75
Czech Republic	1991	56.3	1992	1993	21.4	10.3	2.50
Hungary	1991	35.0	n/a	1993	18.2	4.5	3.00
Kazakhstan	1994	1900.0	1996	1995	48.3	0.5	4.30
Poland	1989	639.6	1992	1991	18.3	21.1	3.60
Russia	1992	1542.1	1996	1996	49.8	–	3.83
Slovakia	1991	62.0	1992	1993	25.6	15.2	3.88
Ukraine	1993	4735.0	–	1996	63.3	–	3.75
Uzbekistan	1993	1312.0	1996	1996	16.9	–	3.79
Estonia	1992	1069.3	1994	1994	25.6	4.8	3.45
Latvia	1992	951.2	1994	1993	48.3	0.8	4.60
Lithuania	1992	1020.5	1995	1993	55.5	3.4	4.21

Source: Fisher *et al.*, 1996; UBS, 1997.

Table 5.13 **Shareholders of the Estonian credit institutions as of 31 December 1998 (%)**

Banks	Domestic capital			Foreign capital		
	Public sector	Legal entities	Natural persons	Credit institutions	Other legal entities	Natural persons
Eesti Krediidipank	–	2.9	52.7	–	44.4	0.0
Union Bank	0.9	14.4	8.9	68.4	7.0	0.4
Hansapank	1.9	13.2	6.3	64.9	13.1	0.6
Optiva Pank	57.9	30.9	2.6	7.1	1.3	0.2
Tallinna Äripank	0.0	78.9	4.7	–	16.4	–
Total	14.3	19.8	7.8	48.5	9.2	0.4

Source: Eesti Pank, 1999.

Table 5.14 **Baltic banks (US$ million as of June 30, 1999)**

Indicators	Estonia	Latvia	Lithuania
Number of banks	6	26	13
Capital and reserves	450.8	225.1	347.3
Assets	2977.1	2872.6	2789.5
Deposits	1621.9	1809.5	1673.0
• including private deposits	650.8	473.7	950.3
Granted loans	1551.7	1264.0	1361.3

Source: Latvian Banking Association, 1999.

By the end of the second half of 1999, the assets of the banks of the Baltic countries were nearly equal (Table 5.14). The number of Latvian banks is the biggest but their capital adequacy was twice as bad as that of the Estonian banks. The financial troubles of the Baltic states give advantage to foreign banks to come to the Baltic states.

Estonian banks operating abroad   The Estonian banks have used three strategies in their internationalization: setting up of subsidiary banks and branches, buying up local banks, or acquiring a significant stake in some local bank. The first one to succeed was Hansapank, which acquired a

Latvian bank (Deutsche Lettische Bank) in 1996 that had defaulted. The former name of the bank was changed into Hansapank-Latvija, the shares of the former shareholders were exchanged for the shares of Hansapank, and the management of the subsidiary was changed. Because the credibility of Latvian banks had weakened, the Hansapank with its reputation insured that in the second half-year of 1997 Hansapank-Latvija already earned profit. Within the first half of 1999 the Hansapank-Latvija increased its loan portfolio by 85 per cent and today it intends to increase its share of savings on the Latvian banking market from 10 per cent at the beginning to 15 per cent by the end of 1999. Over 600 companies in Latvia are operating on Estonian capital, however not all of them have yet opened their accounts with Hansapank-Latvija. Thus, there is a sizeable growth potential for the bank.

After the success of Hansapank became known, the other commercial banks began to make plans of buying into the banks in the markets of Latvia, Lithuania, Russia and Ukraine. Eesti Hoiupank (Estonian Savings Bank) acquired FABA bank in Moscow for EEK 7.2 million in September 1997. Because in the course of takeover it became evident that the assets of the bank were weaker than expected, Estonian Savings Bank abandoned the bank, for the reason that holding of the bank did not conform to the strategy of the bank's Russian trend. In 1998, Estonian Savings Bank bought 72.4 per cent shares of Zemes Banka in Latvia and later on Hansapank obtained this share due to the merger with Estonian Savings Bank. The activity of Tallinna Pank in acquiring Saules Bankas in Latvia was successful. In 1996 the bank started with the share of 20 per cent and in March 1998, just before Tallinna Pank joined the Union Bank, it already held a controlling block of shares of 79.5 per cent. But the activities of Eesti Forekspank in Pioneer Bank in Moscow lasted only two months. The possible acquisition of 51 per cent of shares was abandoned in June 1998 because the Estonian bank recognized having other development potentials.

As acquisition usually means taking over a poorly functioning bank, which needs restructuring or re-capitalization, and obtaining a controlling stock can meet reluctance of other banks and the central bank, penetrating banks often prefer to start from scratch through greenfield investments. Hansapank reiterated its intentions to establish a subsidiary in Lithuania although its first two attempts failed. On July 7, 1999 Hansabankas opened the doors to the clients in Vilnius, the nation's capital. By the end of 1999 the subsidiary had only 200 clients but it expected to seize 5 per cent of the Lithuanian banking sector in the next three years.

The Union Bank has also announced its desire to set up a subsidiary in St. Petersburg, Russia. According to the announcements made in September 1997, the subsidiary will be called Union Bank of Russia and its average total assets would be about EEK 1.5 billion. The Union Bank has announced its plans to penetrate to the markets in Moscow and Helsinki. Those strategic decisions were made public in 1998, but still there have been no real actions undertaken by the end of 1999. It may be due to changes in the market situation and the new strategic priorities of the Union Bank.

The course of the internationalization of the Estonian banks so far has proved that they have tried to enter the banking market of the Baltic countries and Russia. It proves that the Estonian banks are more competitive, compared to the local banks of those countries, but they are not strong enough to enter the Western European markets.

The internationalization of the Estonian banks has resulted in both positive and negative experiences. We can make two general conclusions, which can apply to the majority of the Estonian banks. The internationalization has been directed toward East. This will raise the risk level of Estonian banking and its sensitivity to crises, due to the higher risks and one-way character of internationalization. The second conclusion is that the realization of internationalization plans is often dragging. Thus, it will not be so successful as expected. Conclusively, it indicates that either the banks are not able to foresee the risks of internationalization or they use the announcement of their internationalization plans to the public as the means of advertising and improving their image.

Conclusions

The objectives of our paper have been to point out the main aspects of Estonian success in attracting significant amount of FDI, and to forecast the country's prospects for continuously attracting FDI.

On the one hand, Estonia attracts foreign investors with its investor-friendly business climate that is formed by low risks, low costs, and low taxes. Those investors' assumptions are supported by the country's consistent free market policies that have, firstly, earned Estonia a reputation of having the most liberal trade and investment laws in Europe and, secondly, have boosted the country's international credibility.

On the other hand, Estonia has been improving its FDI policy in order to keep it efficiency in the changing market situation, in view of Estonia's main peculiarity – its small transitional market.

The first period of Estonian FDI policy was characterized by numerous foreign micro-investments, made in response to Estonian recently born small and medium-sized companies appeal for international business cooperation on the basis of small sums of risk capital. At that time the risk of failure in Estonia was high, but the probability of earning a big profit was also high. The second period was characterized by privatization of medium-sized and large-scale state-owned companies. At that time the foreign capital was attracted by ridiculously low prices of those companies' assets. The third or current period is characterized by making investments into renovated and go-ahead companies which need additional capital to expand their business activity and venture into riskier but more promising markets. Due to the small dimensions of Estonian economy, the local businesses have oriented themselves mainly toward both small and private investors. Both the privatization of infrastructure enterprises and their improvement according to the Western standards have begun to allure foreign large-scale enterprises and well-known international companies.

The recent trends of FDI indicate that the foreign owners in Estonia are increasing their investments by reinvesting the profit and loan capital into the companies' assets. This tendency demonstrates that foreign investors succeed in Estonia and they have made long-term plans for business in this country. Besides, they are making more and more investments through Estonia into the transition markets in the East, using the experience gained in doing business in Estonian emerging markets.

Recently the foreign investors have conducted research that has revealed shortcomings in the investment climate. The quick search for the answers of the problems gives hope that Estonia will keep its good position in attracting FDI.

Internationalization of banks is expanding and intensifying today, due to consolidating of markets' integration and diversifying of the banks' customer base.

The internationalization of the banking sector in Estonia is very intensive and a two way process because foreign banks are trying to penetrate into the Estonian banking market and Estonian banks are attempting to penetrate international banking markets.

For several reasons the perspectives of the Estonian banks for internationalization are promising, primarily in the Central and Eastern European markets of the Baltic Countries, Russia, and Ukraine. However, the scale of active internationalizing of Estonian banks is limited. We think that the Estonian banks have been a bit too optimistic about their plans and paid too little attention to preparing for entering foreign markets. Nevertheless, banks in Estonia have good opportunities to correct their past mistakes and develop successful future strategies by using the experience of foreign banks penetrating the Estonian market.

Acknowledgement

We feel deeply indebted to our colleagues Associate Professors Nadezhda Ivanova and Urmas Varblane, and Mr. Jaan Õmblus, for kindly allowing us to use their research materials.

References

Alton, G. (1998), *Educating Local Businesses to Make Them Competitive: Review of Baltic Business Education*, Lithuania: Vilnius.

Bank of Estonia, (1999), *Bulletins*.

Bergsman, J. and Shen, X. (1995), 'Foreign Direct Investment in Developing Countries: Progress and Problems', *Finance & Development*, December, pp. 6–8.

Borner, S., Kobler, M. and Winiker, C. (1997), 'Institutional Uncertainty and Economic Growth in the Baltics', *Baltic Journal of Economics*, vol. 1, no. 1, Eurofaculty, Tartu-Riga-Vilnius, pp. 27–57.

Claros, C. (1996), *American Investment Survey*. Mimeo, Estonian Investment Agency, July no. 26.

Comments of Eesti Pank on the Significant Developments of the Estonian Balance of Payments of 1997 (1998), *Eesti Pank Bulletin*, no. 2.

EBRD (1995), *Transition Report*, London: European Bank for Reconstruction and Development.

Eesti Pank. (1999), *Annual Report 1998*, Estonia: Tallinn.

Eiteman, D. K., Stonehill, A. I. and Moffet, M. H. (1992), *Multinational Business Finance*, Sixth Edition. New York: Addison-Wesley Publishing Company.

Estonian Economy 1997–1998 (1998), Estonia, Tartu: Ministry of Economic Affairs.

Euromoney (1999), March.

European Central Bank Monthly Bulletin (1999), April.

Geordina, F. (1999), *Communication Basics in International Financial Markets*, Paris: OECD.

Hirvensalo, I. and Hazley, C. (1998), 'Barriers to Foreign Direct Investments in the Baltic Sea Region', *ETLA*, January.

Hunya, G. and Stankovsky, J. (1999), *Foreign Direct Investment in Central and Eastern European Countries and the Former Soviet Union*, Vienna: WIIW-WIFO Database.

Konjunktuur (1998), no. 2, Quarterly Review of the Estonian Economy, August, EKI, Tallinn.

Kraft, V. (1997), 'Estonian Reform Experience and European Developments', *Five Years of the Estonian Kroon*, Tallinn, pp. 7–16.

Lalit, A. (1997), *How to Absorb the Foreign Investment: Handbook for Entrepreneurs Series*, Latvia: Riga.

Larimo, J., Miljan, M., Sepp, J. and Sõrg, M. (1998), Foreign Direct Investments in Estonia. *HWWA- Report*, no. 172, Hamburg.

Laurila, J. (1994), 'Direct Investment from Finland to Russia, Baltic and Central Eastern European Countries: Result of a Survey by the Bank of Finland', *Review of Economics in Transition*, Unit of Eastern European Economies, Bank of Finland.

Laurila, J. and Hirvensalo, I. (1996), 'Direct Investment from Finland to Eastern Europe: Results of the 1995 Bank of Finland Survey', *Review of Economics in Transition*, Unit of Eastern European Economies, Bank of Finland.

Linnamo, J. and Vanamo, I. (1980), 'Kansainvälisesta pankkikilpailusta ja pankkirikistä', *Kansantaloudellinen Aikauskirja*, no. 1, pp. 14–31.

Liuhto, K. (1994), *Ulkomaiset Investoinnit Viroon-Tilastoja ja Totuuksia*, Turku School of Economics and Business Administration.

Maranik, U. (1998), 'German Capital at Home in Estonia', *The Baltic Times*, October, pp. 15–21.

Meerits, H. (1996), 'Banking in Estonia. Trends and Developments', *The Baltic Review*, Autumn, no. 11, pp. 44–45.

Meigas, H. (1999), 'Estonian Banking: an Outline of its Dynamics', *The Baltic Review*, vol. 17, pp. 33–34.

Mäenpää, M. (1997), *Pankkitoiminta sisämarkkinoiden paineissa*, Kanava, no. 9, pp. 514–518.

Pauli, R. (1994), *Pankkitoiminnan rakennemuutos Suomessa*, Helsinki: Suomen Pankki.

Pettersson, F. (1974), 'Will there be a Difference between National and International Banking in 1984?', *Banking in an Integrating World*, The Finnish Bankers' Association, pp. 121–136.

Rugman, A. M. and Kamath, S. J. (1987), 'International Diversification and Multinational Banking', in S.J. Khoyry and A. Ghosh (eds) *Recent Developments in International Banking and Finance*, London: McGraw-Hill.

Sorsa, K. (1994), 'Foreword', in S. Lainela, and P. Sutela (eds) *The Baltic Economies in Transition*, Helsinki: Bank of Finland, pp. 5–6.

Sumben, G. (1999), *Analysing the Regional Image of Eastern Europe*. Toronto: University Press.

Taeho, K. (1993), *International Money and Banking*, London: T.I. Press Ltd.

Thomsen, J., Biltoft, K. and Thuesen, J. U. (1999), 'The Euro and the New Perspectives', *Danmarks Nationalbank Monetary Review*, 1st Quarter, pp. 15–28.

Vainio, V. (1996), 'Banks preparing for tougher competition', *Unitas*, no. 4, pp. 25–26.

Varblane, U. *et al.* (1998), *Otsesed välisinvesteeringud Eesti majanduses*, Tallinn: Estonian Investment Agency and Tartu University.

Varblane, U. (1998), 'The Role of Foreign Direct Investment in the Transformation of Estonian Firms', *Sixth Conference of the ISSEI*.

Vitsur, E. (1995), 'Investment Policy and Development of Foreign Investments', in O.L. Lugus and G. Hachey (eds) *Transition the Estonian Economy*, Tallinn: Institute of Economics, Estonian Academy of Sciences:.

Welfer, S. (1998), *Investment Practice in Eastern Europe*, New York: Addison-Wesley Publishing Company.

Ziacik, T.L. (1998), 'Motivational Factors Behind Foreign Direct Investment in Estonia: A Comparison of Empirical Studies', *Eesti Pank Bulletin*, vol. 4, no. 39.

Zirnask, V. (1997), 'Estonian Banks are Going Global', *ITALIAN, Estonian Air*, Summer, pp. 4–6.

6 The Internationalization of Grocery Retailing in Poland after 1989

JOHN A. DAWSON and JOHN S. HENLEY

Introduction

The chapter assesses and interprets the changes that have taken place in Polish retailing, particularly grocery retailing, over the last ten years. Key issues are the privatization of the existing networks, subsequent restructuring and the opening up of the market to international retail firms. Some implications of these changes for competition and industry structure are indicated. The chapter points to possible ways the sector will develop over the next five years.

Background

Until 1989 retailing in Poland was organized according to centralist planning principles. State firms were managed through central and regional managerial structures applied to the main product classes. Cooperatives were managed regionally but with reference to a central agency. There was a small private sector. Being deemed 'non-productive', retailing was starved of investment. After the Law on Joint Ventures in 1988, there were putative attempts, e.g., Semeco in Gdynia, to inject private capital into retailing but these generally failed (Turban, 1977; Werwicki, 1992; Johnson and Loveman, 1995).

By the late 1980s the retail network comprised about 150,000 shops and seventy seven thousand registered kiosks, itinerant sellers and market stalls. Of this total some forty three thousand were in the private sector. With a few exceptions of department stores the sales outlets were all small. Total floor space of all stores was approximately fifteen million square meters – an average store size of eleven square meters. The system of stores was highly concentrated in its purchasing arrangements with the state organization being responsible for large chains of outlets.

Fundamental changes in retailing followed the change in political system in 1989 (Corporate Intelligence, 1995; Martin, 1997). The centrally planned retail system was subjected to rapid transformation. Legal regulations dismantled previous structures and resulted in:

- the abolition of many controls over the distribution and pricing of goods;
- introduction of free market principles across almost all the retail sector;
- privatization of state trading enterprises;
- low entry barriers for new businesses and a consequent rapid growth of small firms;
- liberalization of many of the regulations governing commercial practices.

The consequences were that by mid 1998 less than one per cent of stores were in state ownership and about six per cent were owned by consumer cooperatives with the remainder being in the private sector.

Some Effects of Privatization

The Law on Private Business became operational on 1 January 1989. This enabled the opening and operation of private business, employment of staff without reference to central agencies and the operation of business bank accounts. There was, for several months, little initial effect on retailing because of the lack of regulations to implement the Law and also the protection afforded to existing occupiers of retail premises by the Property Law. The significant changes came in 1990 with the Small Privatization regulations which allowed termination of current occupancy agreements, transfer of assets from the state to the enterprise (often in effect local government), and sale of commercial property. Local governments were given considerable responsibility in this reallocation of ownership and commonly shops were sold by tender arrangements (Szawlowska, 1990; Tamowicz *et al.*, 1992).

The larger central state chains were privatized through different mechanisms mostly through privatization by liquidation or occasionally through capital privatization. The Law on Privatization of State Enterprises was enacted on 13 July 1990. Regulations based on this law have allowed the transfer of ownership of the total asset base. The rationale was to avoid atomization of the sector but the process of finding buyers for some enterprises has been very slow and convoluted. Ruch, the country's leading press distributor with thirty two thousand sales points, has been locked in a protracted court dispute since the government withdrew a letter of intent declaring it would sell forty per cent of the distributor to the French publishing group Hachette in 1997. D T Centrum, the state-owned department store chain, also became embroiled in complex negotiations before and after privatization in 1998, relating to the alleged under-valuation of the assets.

The effects of privatization in retailing are considerable and complex. It should be remembered that the process of privatization was different through the Central and East European (CEE) countries and the emerging structure of retailing has been closely shaped by the process (Bauer and Carman, 1996; Eurostat, 1998). Some of the key changes in Poland were:

- initial rapid atomization of trade structure;
- emergence of strong price competition;
- massive increase in the number of non-store sales outlets;
- creation of large concentrations of these 'informal' retailers;
- different responses in different local government areas to privatizations of fixed store networks and co-operatives;
- transfer of many small store units to the local management;
- beginnings of a market in small shops and in small businesses, enabling new entrants (in some cases foreign firms);
- slow transfer of large state chains to consortia sometimes involving foreign capital.

Structural Changes

Since 1990 the growth in number of stores and in the total number of retail outlets has been considerable. From Table 6.1 it can be seen that the main growth took place after 1989 with massive growth in stalls, kiosks and mobile retail outlets, such that by 1996 there were over five hundred and twenty thousand of this form of outlet. Even in 1998, a survey revealed that forty four per cent of Polish shoppers still regularly visited markets compared to thirty one per cent of West European shoppers (Healey and Baker, 1999).

Numbers of fixed stores also increased but started to decrease as from 1996. The average size of these fixed shops is small. Table 6.2 shows the size distribution of stores. It is notable that the numbers of small stores began to decrease in 1996. There are now signs that the shop network is starting to rationalize with a reduction in the total number of retail outlets seen also in preliminary results for 1997. The decrease is strongest initially in rural areas (Institute of Home Market and Consumption, 1997). Numbers of larger units are starting to increase and their share of trade is increasing rapidly.

Table 6.1   The retail network in Poland

Year	Total number of sales points (thousands)	Number of stores shops (thousands)
1980	203.7	129.9
1985	219.8	142.1
1988	227.0	150.0
1989	249.5	152.0
1990	469.7	237.4
1991	630.0	311.0
1992	700.0	352.5
1993	785.0	380.6
1994	850.0	415.4
1995	890.0	425.6
1996	927.0	405.6

Source: Central Statistical Office Annual Report on Retail Trade.

Table 6.2   Number of shops by size (thousands)

Year	Retail Floor Space			
	<50 sq.m	201-400 sq.m.	>400 sq.m.	Total
1993	347.7	2.94	1.93	380.6
1994	383.1	2.90	1.99	415.4
1995	391.3	3.24	2.23	425.6
1996	369.9	3.48	2.56	405.6

Source: Central Statistical Office Annual Report on Retail Trade.

Entry of International Firms

A major consequence of privatization has been the opening of the market to foreign capital. Poland has 38.6 million consumers and growth in GDP averaging over five per cent pa since 1994. Foreign retailers, particularly from France and Germany, see big opportunities in Poland. The major developments have been in the grocery sector but there have also been notable entries in non-foods by IKEA, Carli Gry, Bhs, Metro, Stinnes, and others (Domanski, 1996).

The Institute of Home Market and Consumption (1997) estimated that in 1996 there were nine hundred twenty five stores operated by international retailers and emphasized that their number belied their importance. The number more than doubled between 1996 and 1998. Several of the major hypermarket and supermarket companies, for example Ahold, Carrefour, Metro, Casino and Tesco have begun development in Poland and have ambitious opening programs.

There are sequential, structural and spatial dimensions to the development of international retailers in the grocery sector (Dawson and Henley, 1999a,b).

The sequential dimension is seen in three phases so far:

* pioneering;
* colonization;
* consolidation.

Pioneering is represented by the activity of the early entrants who came when the market was unstable, inflation was high, and trading chaotic through to about 1994. GIB, having had sourcing connections, entered in 1991 buying four supermarkets in Warsaw. Dohle, again with previous experience in sourcing, entered the Warsaw market with a hypermarket in February 1994. Billa entered early in the transitional market, in 1990, and developed supermarkets by converting existing stores particularly in Warsaw and Bielsko-Biala. Rema 1000 entered in 1993 through a form of franchise system to target the discount food market. The pioneering phase is characterized by a high level of opportunism in the acquisition of either existing firms or sites for development, and either the existence of prior links into the Polish economy or the use of Polish partners.

Colonization can be dated from about 1995. In 1995 French retailers Leclerc, Auchan and Docks de France opened stores, followed in 1996 by Casino. Jeronimo Martins, from Portugal, entered joint ventures to operate a chain of local discount food stores and a cash and carry chain in 1995 and in the same year Tesco purchased a chain of small supermarkets. Most importantly, perhaps, the German majors Metro and Tengelman entered initially with their discount formats of TIP and Plus in September 1995. These high profile new entrants mark the start of a phase of substantial colonization of the market by foreign firms.

By late 1997 the signs of consolidation were starting to be apparent. This is not consolidation of the traditional type seen in Western Europe, which is related to strong competition and saturated markets. It is consolidation in the 'colonized' market due to changes, often but not always consolidation, in the West European home market of the operating company.

The structural dimension of foreign retailers is seen in their format strategy. In grocery retailing four formats have been introduced: hypermarkets, supermarkets, discount stores and convenience stores (Euromonitor, 1996). Foreign retailers are strong in all cases but dominate the hypermarket sector.

At the end of 1996 there were nine foreign-owned hypermarkets. By the end of 1997 there were twenty-one plus thirteen Makro units that operated, in effect, as hypermarkets. The thirty-four units were operated by nine different international retail companies in Poland. A further thirty stores were announced to be opened by the end of 1998. This trend has continued in 1999. For example, Carrefour, a late entrant, in 1997, had invested US$ 500 million by the end of 1999 with four operational hypermarkets and four under construction.

Table 6.3 shows the position at the end of 1999 with eighty-three stores in operation or about to open. In addition, there were seven Polish-owned hypermarkets operating at the end of the first quarter of 1998. Foreign investors dominate the hypermarket sector owning over ninety per cent of stores and an even larger share of total retail space since foreign-owned hypermarkets tend to be larger than domestically owned stores. Casino-Geant, for example, opened one of the largest hypermarkets in Poland at Janki on the southwest periphery of Warsaw with a sales area of fourteen thousand square meters in August 1999. In addition, there are eighty boutique units as part of the development with a total sales area of a further forty five thousand square meters.

The scale of retail developments would appear to be accelerating. Not to be outdone, Metro opened a retail complex in September 1999, located on a north Warsaw periphery site. This development contains a hypermarket of fourteen thousand square meters, a home supply store with nine thousand square meters, and a computer and audiovisual store of four thousand square meters, all Metro formats, together with sixty-two boutique units available for lease.

Table 6.3   Foreign owned hypermarkets operating in late autumn 1999

Fascia	Year of entry	Number of units	Total Group Polish Investments end 1998 – 1999 (US$ million)	Sales Rank[1]
Hit (Dohle)	1994	7	n/a	3
Makro (Metro)	1994	18	650*	1**
Leclerc	1995	6	n/a	
Jumbo (JM)	1996	4	n/a	2
Auchan	1996	5	n/a	
Geant (Casino)	1996	11	524	5
Real (Metro)	1997	18	650*	1**
Carrefour	1997	7	500	
Allkauf (Ahold)	1997	2	50	
Selgros (Rewe)	1997	1	n/a	4
Tesco	1998	4	160	

(1)   Sales rank based on total Polish sales of different operating fascias in 1998.
*   Total Metro Group investment in Poland.
**   Sales rank in Poland.

Sources: Retail Newsletter, 1998; Eveno, 1998a, 1998b; Corporate Assistance, 1998; Company interviews.

The international retailers have substantial land banks and two hundred or more hypermarkets by 2002 are likely. Even then with ninety-three cities of over fifty thousand population the hypermarket network will still be modest in comparison with Western Europe. The Office for Competition and Consumer Protection (UOKiK) estimated that thirteen per cent of the retail grocery market was foreigner controlled in early 1999 and anticipated further erosion of the market share of Polish-owned grocery stores. Indeed, Poland's inward investment agency, PAIZ, estimated that foreign investment in the retail sector as a whole already amounted to US$ 2.5 billion or more than ten per cent of the stock of foreign direct investment by the end of 1998.

Foreign investment in discount grocery retailing is similarly strong with, in late 1998, more than five hundred units operated by the six foreign retailers in the market. It has been less strong in supermarkets with approximately one hundred and sixty stores owned by eleven foreign firms but there have been signs of renewed interest in 1999. Foreign interest in the convenience store sector is only starting to develop with the creation of stores by the major foreign oil companies. By mid-1999, Statoil, Shell and BP-Amoco were emerging as the dominant foreign players in a fiercely contested sector.

The spatial dimension of foreign ownership is seen in regional concentrations of activity by particular retailers and also in the attraction of the largest cities to the foreign firms. Regional development is related to the logistics platforms of the firms, closeness to the German border and also the historical underdevelopment of Eastern Poland. The city dimension is seen in the strong concentrations of foreign investment in Warsaw, Katowice, Krakow, Gdansk, Poznan, Wroclaw, Lodz and Szczecin.

Unless there is a very severe shock to investor's confidence, the veritable construction boom in hypermarkets looks set to continue. Tesco plans to open new super stores; Metro is planning to spend a further US$ 1.4 billion on stores by 2003; Casino-Geant expects to invest an additional US$ 500 million by 2002; Leclerc has plans for US$ 400 million of expansion by 2002 and Carrefour, the second largest European food retailer, has ambitious plans to open forty new supermarkets by 2002 with a sales area each of two–three thousand m^2.

There are some signs emerging that the direction of expansion and competition is shifting from hypermarket development to discount grocery retailing and supermarkets. By the end of 1998, grocery discount chains were generally restricted to a region and a major conurbation as a result of the under developed state of the Polish logistics and warehousing infrastructure. These are: Edeka (German) centered on Gdansk; Netto (Danish) on Szczecin; Plus-Tengelman on Katowice/Silesia and Sesam-Ahold (Dutch) focused on Silesia/Wielkopolska. The only clearly national discounter is the Biedronka chain of Jeronimo Martins (Portuguese) which had three hundred and forty stores open at the end of 1998, supported by three regional distribution centers which also supply a national network of fifty medium-sized (three thousand square meters) cash and carry outlets. This position was consolidated when Metro sold its fifty-seven TIP stores to Jeronimo Martins early in 1999, and with further store openings had increased the Biedronka network to five hundred forty three units by mid-1999 with plans to reach more than six hundred units by 2002. The basic strategy has been to create a network from re-merchandising existing units bought or leased from existing Polish retail organizations such as co-operatives and local store chains.

The units are typically less than one thousand m^2 in size and have a limited assortment on offer, usually no more than one thousand and five hundred different items. Technology and management systems are relatively simple except that Jeronimo Martins has invested heavily into point of sales scanners and EPOS data-links to regional distribution centers. The efficiency of the warehousing and distribution system is critical in avoiding stock-outs and therefore loss of customer convenience.

While the Biedronka chain is now nearly ubiquitous in towns and cities in Poland, the strategy is simple to emulate once a warehousing and distribution network is in place. The improved buying power and cash flow associated with a limited range of fast moving grocery and non-food household goods that an efficient discount chain produces is likely to be attractive as an expansion strategy to other international hypermarket operators. Ahold, for example, appears to be building up its competitive position by incremental acquisition of small Polish-owned retail chains around its three distribution centers in Southern Poland. By May 1999, it had expanded to one hundred stores including sixty-five discount stores, seventeen supermarkets and three cash-and-carry stores. Although Ahold is one of the world's leading supermarket operators, it is unclear whether it sees its Polish future focused on this format and/or the role of its growing discount chain.

By the end of 1999, there were signs that international interest in the supermarket sector was rising as part of the strategy of capitalizing on the increasingly sophisticated logistics platforms being put in place to support growing hypermarket networks. For example, Carrefour's announced in November 1999, that it was planning to open forty supermarkets under the Stoc fascia by 2002, offering an assortment of eight thousand grocery and non-food lines. Part of this expansion of activity by Carrefour is anticipated to occur as a result of the acquisition of independent Polish regional supermarkets under competitive pressure from the spread of hypermarkets. Perhaps even more challenging to the assumptions of international grocery retailers operating in Poland is Casino's introduction of Leader Price own-brand products into its Geant hypermarkets in 1998 and its plans to launch Leader Price discount grocery stores from 2000. As noted above with respect to other discounters, Leader Price stores will be opened within a one hundred and eighty kilometer radius of the Geant regional distribution center in Lodz. This location also brings the discounter within range of Warsaw. However, the most radical innovation is that Leader Price own-brand products are ninety eight per cent manufactured in Poland.

In order to capitalize on Polish shoppers' expressed preference for 'buying Polish', if there is a choice, (seventy seven per cent of respondents in a 1998 Polish survey by Healey and Baker), packaging has been redesigned to reflect the codes, signs and colors of Poland. The price proposition is also strong to reflect evidence of consumer sensitivity to price and active comparison-shopping. Almost half of Polish shoppers (forty six per cent) still shop every day, only Hungarians shop more often. The West European average is twenty per cent (Healey and Baker, 1999).

If Casino is successful in establishing Leader Price as a real brand, and early evidence is encouraging, and it rolls out its planned chain of hypermarkets and discount supermarkets, it will provide a real challenge to the leadership of Metro and Jeronimo Martins. Of course, the leaders will probably respond to this challenge in novel and unexpected ways as will other domestic and international players and Polish grocery retailing will continue to evolve at a fast rate for the foreseeable future.

Implications of Changes and the Future

Privatization of retailing has been all but completed within ten years. Substantial foreign investment is driving the modernization of the store network particularly in the grocery sector. There are notable implications of these fundamental changes for:

- Consumers: Store and product choice has been increased dramatically; price competition has become strong; retail literacy is still low and consumer culture is under-developed but is developing rapidly. Foreign retailers see this as a major opportunity for them. More complex consumer behavior patterns will emerge.
- Suppliers: Supply chains and logistics systems lag behind the modernization of the store network; retailers may revert to importing if the supplier base cannot meet the needs of a modern retail system. Inter-supplier competition is likely to be on the basis of trade marketing so suppliers of international brands will remain in a strong position.
- Wholesalers: Strong positions in the early 1990s are being eroded by the sourcing policies of foreign retailers so that rationalization and focusing of activity is likely.
- Domestic retailers: Small firm closure will accelerate but also domestic chains will gradually emerge, particularly in more specialist non-food areas; franchise and other forms of organizational co-operation are likely to increase including buying groups in the grocery sector.

- Foreign retailers: Not all existing players will be successful and new entrants, particularly in non-food are likely. Some formats, in addition to hypermarkets, will become dominated by foreign firms. Consolidation in Poland will usually be a consequence of competition and restructuring of retailing in the EU.

- Support services: A potential influx of foreign firms is likely providing support in advertising, marketing, logistics, training and information technology.

- Government: Increased pressure will be felt to limit the activity of foreign retailers but EU entry preparations will inhibit restricting 'freedom of economic activity'. There is a need for initiatives to help domestic food producers increase quality and productivity to EU standards prior to removal of tariff barriers and controls on food imports from EU.

Acknowledgement

The authors gratefully acknowledge the support of the ACE-Phare Program of EU that funded the research on which this paper is based. A program of interviews with retailers, suppliers and support services was undertaken from 1996 to 1998. A version of this paper was presented at the Ninth World Marketing Congress in Malta, June 1999.

References

Bauer, A. and Carman, J.M. (1996), 'Toward Explaining Differences in the Transition of Distribution Sectors in Central European Economies', in *Proceedings of Conference of European Marketing Academy*, May, Hungary.

Corporate Assistance (1998), *Strategic Report on Distribution of FMCG in Poland*. Warsaw: Corporate Assistance.

Corporate Intelligence (1995), *Retailing in Europe: Eastern Europe*. London: Corporate Intelligence on Retailing.

Dawson, J. and Henley, J. (1999a), 'Recent Developments and Opportunities in Retailing in Poland', *Distribucion y Consumo*, Rome, Italy.

Dawson, J. and Henley, J. (1999b), 'Internationalisation of Food Retailing in Poland: The management of scarcity?', *University of Edinburgh Working Paper*, no. 1.

Domanski, T. (1996), *Nowe Formy Dystrybucji w Polsce*, Lodz: University of Lodz.

Euromonitor (1996), 'Polish Food Retailing', *Retail Monitor International*, June, pp. 113-64.

EUROSTAT (1998), *Retailing in the Central European Countries 1997*, Luxembourg: Eurostat.

Eveno, R. (1998a), 'Pologne: le match franco-allemand', *Libre Service Actualite*, 16 Av., pp. 20-23.

Eveno, R. (1998b), 'Tir Groupe de Francais en Pologne', *Libre Service Actualite*, 5 Nov., p. 25.

Healey J. and Baker, M. (1999), *Where People Shop – Poland*, London: Healey and Baker, February.

Institute of Home Market and Consumption (1997) *Poland's Domestic Trade in 1996*, Warsaw: Ministry of Economy.

Johnson, S. and Loveman, G.W. (1995), *Starting Over in Eastern Europe*, Boston: Harvard Business School Press.

Martin, P. (1997), *Retailing in Central and Eastern Europe*, London: FT Publishing.

Retail Newsletter (1998), 'Poland: Foreign retail presence accelerating', *CIES Retail Newsletter*, no. 462, p. 9.

Szawlowska, H. (1990), *Przemiany w Asnosciowe w Handlu*, Warsaw: Institute of Home Market and Consumption.

Tamowicz, P., Aziewicz, T. and Stompor, M. (1992), *Mala Prywatyzacja: Polskie Doswiadczenia 1990-91*, Gdansk: Institute of Market Economy Research.

Turban, J. (1977), 'Some Observations on Retail Distribution in Poland', *Soviet Studies*, no. 29, pp. 128-36.

Werwicki, A. (1992), 'Retailing in Poland', *International Journal of Retail and Distribution Management*, vol. 20, no. 6, pp. 34-38.

PART III:

INTERNATIONALIZATION OF COMPANIES

7 Local Expansion Processes of Dutch Firms in Central and Eastern Europe

RIAN H.J. DROGENDIJK

Introduction

The decisions firms make in their international expansion processes are subject to extended reseàrch rooted in very diverse theoretical approaches. The starting point of this chapter is the internationalization decisions of firms that are dependent upon previous decisions (Aharoni, 1966). Every expansion is seen as a step for further international expansions (see for instance, Kogut, 1983; Wernerfelt, 1984). Firms gather experiences with every step and add to their knowledge base or absorptive capacity. Firms with an increasing absorptive capacity are more prone to recognize and internalize new learning possibilities (Cohen and Levinthal, 1990). Experiential learning is the driving force of the internationalization process according to the evolutionary approach (or Uppsala model) of internationalization (Johanson and Vahlne, 1977; Johanson and Wiedersheim-Paul, 1975; Welch and Luostarinen, 1988). Gathering market knowledge reduces uncertainty and allows the firm to gradually enter an increasing number of foreign countries, using entry modes that are characterized by augmenting resource commitments, at an increasing psychic distance to their home country (Johanson and Vahlne, 1977). With respect to growing resource commitment four stages were distinguished called the 'establishment chain', along which the firm expands in local markets (Johanson and Wiedersheim-Paul, 1975). It has been questioned later, however, whether the steps proposed by the establishment chain are still valid in the current globalizing world (Hedlund and Kverneland, 1983; Nordström, 1991; Turnbull, 1987). Welch and Luostarinen (1988) made a contribution to the evolutionary approach by introducing a framework with six dimensions along which the internationalizing firm is expected to develop. This framework is used as a starting point for this chapter. Its goal is to investigate the patterns Dutch firms have used to enter the newly opened markets of Central and Eastern Europe (CEE). The aim of the chapter is to contribute to the knowledge of the internationalization process of firms within host countries. Sequential steps taken by Dutch firms in the CEE region are investigated and a test for the establishment chain in the context of modern time in a new market is presented (Bridgewater, 1999).

Data are collected both with open interviews held in local subsidiaries and through mail surveys sent to firms' headquarters. This combination of the rich case histories of a small number of subsidiaries with data gathered through a survey on a larger sample offer both deeper insight and better opportunity to test hypotheses using more rigorous methods.

The region of CEE offers excellent opportunities to compare the actual steps of firms with different previous experiences and their local subsidiaries in a new market with about the same starting point in time. It offers a unique context for investigating internationalization processes, because FDI in the CEE region has only been possible in real terms from 1989 onwards (compare Hedlund and Kverneland, 1983 who studied the Swedish multinational corporations market entry into Japan after the opening of the Japanese market in 1973).

The chapter is organized as follows: first attention is paid to the theoretical background of the internationalization process of the firm then empirical contributions are addressed and briefly outlined. Next, hypotheses and research questions following from this background are formulated. In the methodology section, a sample description is given of sixteen cases, as well as an overview of the survey method. Then, results are presented followed by a discussion and finally, conclusions are drawn with respect to learning processes in subsidiaries. Directions for future research are also presented.

Theoretical Background

The Internationalization Process of the Firm

In the internationalization processes of four Swedish firms, Johanson and Wiedersheim-Paul (1975) discovered two patterns: Swedish firms were able to enter foreign countries gradually increasing their resource commitment, entering countries at an increasing 'psychic distance' from Sweden. In this research the focus is only on the first pattern, reflecting the growth of resource commitment in international operations. This pattern was called 'the establishment chain' and consists of four stages with firms proceeding from no investments to exporting through agents to establishing a sales office and finally setting up a production site. Through 'learning-by-doing' firms acquire the necessary market information and capabilities to expand their activities in the host country (Johanson and Vahlne, 1977). Hedlund and Kverneland (1983) raised questions on the slow pace of entry assumed by the early Uppsala model because the international business environment has changed considerably since the model was launched. They state that contemporary multinational companies are global in their orientations and that fast entry into new markets is not impeded by a lack of local market knowledge. According to Nordström (1991) modern means of communication facilitate easy access to several sources of information that firms can tap into in order to learn how to operate in an unknown market. Johanson and Mattsson (1984) have asserted that the evolutionary approach might not be applicable to markets and firms that are highly internationalized. Uncertainty and a lack of market knowledge are probably more important in the early stages of internationalization (Forsgren, 1990; Johanson and Vahlne, 1990).

Turnbull (1987) challenges further the deterministic nature of the sequential stages since many large multinational firms are found to continue exports or sales agent activities next to production facilities depending on the foreign market served. Johanson and Vahlne (1990) bent this point of critique into a motivation to develop the theory and explore differentiated patterns of evolutionary development. Welch and Luostarinen (1988) developed a framework that can be a starting point for this differentiation: internationalization is predicted to occur along six dimensions. Firms may differ in their growth patterns on these dimensions, but are all expected to develop incrementally on each of them. Two of the dimensions are close to the original model and address foreign operation methods and markets. However, instead of predicting a certain order of entry modes used, Welch and Luostarinen (1988) propose that expansion occurs both through deeper commitment and more diverse operation methods. Further, they add the dimension of sales objects, notably physical goods, services and know-how systems, that firms are expected to offer successively at foreign markets. Finally, their framework adds three dimensions that are related to the organizational capacity: personnel, referring to the development of human resources and internationalization skills, finance and the organizational structure. This final dimension refers to the variety of organizational structures that have risen out of the increasing complexity coming with the firm's internationalization. This variety and the differentiation of subsidiaries' expansion patterns are addressed below.

Empirical support for the pattern of growing resource commitment was found in a number of case studies (Buckley, Newbould and Thurwell, 1978; Engwall and Wallenstal, 1988; Hedlund and Kverneland, 1983; Juul and Walters, 1987; Vahlne, Nordström and Torbacke, 1996). The empirical findings of Hedlund and Kverneland (1983) are supportive to the evolutionary model: they found that the eighteen Swedish firms in their sample expanded in Japan in sequential steps but often at a faster pace than expected according to the establishment chain. Interestingly, firms with extensive international experience were found to skip stages and enter through the short route entry strategy more often than less experienced firms. Juul and Walters (1987) achieved similar results in analyzing the investment strategies of twelve Norwegian firms in the UK. Most Norwegian firms started with export activities before setting up sales or manufacturing subsidiaries, though only three firms used an intermediate step. Of the ten firms that started with marketing activities only, five have started production activities as well. Juul and Walters (1987) have also addressed the dimension of sales objects as proposed by Welch and Luostarinen (1988) but they found no support for a progression from physical goods towards offering services or know-how. Vahlne, Nordström and Torbacke (1996) have found that Swedish firms started to invest in CEE with less committing entry modes (e.g., sales) and later extended to more committed modes and activities through establishing local production. Buckley, Newbould and Thurwell (1978) investigated the international behavior of forty-three small UK firms and found that although taking all steps of the establishment chain was not the most popular entry strategy it resulted in the highest possible success rates. Incremental learning through small steps of local commitment was concluded to be 'of great value' for British firms abroad. Turnbull (1987) has rejected the stages model because the organizational forms used by twenty-four UK firms in seventy-two international expansions in three host countries were not related to either firm size or international orientation measured as a proportion of export to total turnover.

The Internationalization Process at Subsidiary Level

A large body of literature focuses on the development of new structural forms of internationalizing firms (see for instance, Bartlett and Ghoshal, 1989; Prahalad and Doz, 1981). The struggle of firms to find a balance between headquarters' need to keep strategic control over foreign subsidiaries and subsidiaries' desire for autonomy is emphasized among others by Prahalad and Doz (1981), Forsgren (1990), and Malnight (1995).

Malnight (1995) investigated expansion processes within the firm and found that subsidiaries' roles, and their scope of activities, autonomy and network linkages, developed depending on the differentiated expansion processes at the functional level. Subsidiaries' roles grow from appendages, to participators, to contributors and finally subsidiaries become integrated parts of the internationalizing firm. In the integration stage, headquarters and subsidiary share responsibility over strategy, resources, technology, etc. Forsgren (1990) recognizes that foreign subsidiaries gain importance and independence from the parent company through local learning processes during the ongoing process of internationalization. Multinational companies are expected to evolve as loosely coupled systems or 'multi-center' firms, in which subsidiaries that have become centers make strategic decisions on resources that other parts of the firm are dependent upon (compare Hedlund's heterarchy, 1986). Subsidiaries that have become a dominant center are characterized by strong network positions vis-à-vis other subsidiaries within the firm and a strong local network (Forsgren, 1990). According to Bartlett and Ghoshal (1989) appropriate lateral linkages within the firm and substantial autonomy for subsidiaries' management teams were further associated with facilitating a good learning environment. Ferdows (1997) has investigated the upgrading of strategic roles of foreign subsidiaries. He has distinguished among six different roles but emphasizes the same development process as Malnight (1995). Several paths lead a venture to a higher strategic role, but this always starts with assuming production responsibilities. From this overview, it can be concluded that the expansion processes at the level of foreign subsidiaries is related to increasing autonomy and starts with assuming increasing decision responsibilities.

Most empirical studies that investigate subsidiary level expansion processes are based on case studies (Ferdows, 1997; Malnight, 1995, 1996; Vahlne, Nordström and Torbacke, 1996) or are basically studying strategic roles of subsidiaries (Birkinshaw and Morrison, 1995; Forsgren, Pedersen and Foss, 1999; Jarillo and Martinez, 1990; Nobel and Birkinshaw, 1998).

Vahlne, Nordström and Torbacke (1996) have concluded from visits to nine case companies in the region of CEE, that although decisions on daily operations are decentralized, Swedish headquarters invest in learning about local operations and affect local decision making seriously. Birkinshaw and Morrison (1995) found that subsidiaries with advanced strategic roles were more autonomous from the firm's headquarters and independent in making strategic decisions. Further, Forsgren, Holm and Johanson (1995) showed that dominant subsidiaries are able to draw division headquarters to a nearby location even if corporate headquarters resist such a move.

Jarillo and Martinez (1990) developed a framework to distinguish among roles of subsidiaries based on the amount of local activities a subsidiary performs and the degree of integration of these activities with the same activities of other subsidiaries. In a test of their framework among fifty subsidiaries of Spanish multinational corporations, they have found support for this framework that differentiates between receptive subsidiaries (performing only a few activities locally that are highly integrated with the firm's corporate activities), active subsidiaries (many local activities, but closely coordinated within the firm) and autonomous subsidiaries (with many local activities, but less integrated, or relatively independent from the parent company). They also tentatively tested for the evolution of subsidiary strategies and found that though receptive subsidiaries changed little, both active and autonomous subsidiaries converged towards more integrated and less localized strategies. Especially autonomous subsidiaries were found to change fast towards active, i.e. more interdependent, strategies.

Research Framework

In this section, propositions based on the literature review are formulated. The starting point for the development of these propositions is the original establishment chain (Johanson and Vahlne, 1977; Johanson and Wiedersheim-Paul, 1975) and the Welch and Luostarinen (1988) framework of internationalization of the firm.

Growing Commitment

According to the original sequential model developed by Johanson and Wiedersheim-Paul (1975) the first steps of firms in an unknown market are through exporting and consequently selling through a local agent. These first stages in the establishment chain are characterized by low levels of local commitment, but also by fewer possibilities for local learning because of the indirect involvement of the firm. Still, the stages of lower commitment enable the firm to gather at least some knowledge about local habits and rules. Little knowledge is the necessary input for decisions on further investments in the host country (Johanson and Vahlne, 1977). Further, initial small investments enable the firm to start working on a local network. The importance of starting with low commitment and small steps are stressed in the literature on market entry into the emerging CEE markets (Peng and Heath, 1996; Shama, 1995; Vahlne Nordström and

Torbacke, 1996). Western firms are therefore expected to use lower commitment entry modes before entering the CEE countries with direct investments.

The establishment chain further suggests that once direct investments are made, in the following stages, learning enables firms to extend their local operations by increasing their local commitment (Johanson & Wiedersheim-Paul, 1975) and by using increasingly diverse operation methods (Welch and Luostarinen, 1988). Carstairs and Welch (1982) emphasize that being physically present in the host country not only facilitates learning by doing but also exposes firms to diverse local opportunities.

This research is based on the following propositions:

P1: Exporting and lower committed market entry modes are used as initial entry modes by Western firms entering CEE countries.

P2: Following initial entry, Western firms increase their commitment and use more diverse operation methods in CEE countries.

Local Activities and Sales Objects

Firms are able to use a shorter entry route and skip stages, especially if they are experienced in international operations (Hedlund and Kverneland, 1983; Nordström, 1991; Turnbull, 1987). But even if firms use direct investment modes at once, without local experiences in less committed entry modes, they might still start to concentrate on a few activities only, for instance marketing and sales, and later extend these activities (Juul and Walters, 1987; Vahlne, Nordström and Torbacke, 1996). Similarly, expansion within certain product lines or extension into product lines that demand more tacit knowledge, like services and know-how, is only possible after learning about local preferences and local culture (Juul and Walters, 1987; Welch and Luostarinen, 1988). In line with the sales objects dimension of Welch and Luostarinen (1988), a third proposition can be formulated as:

P3: Foreign subsidiaries of Western firms in CEE countries expand incrementally with respect to the activities performed and the sales objects offered.

Autonomy of the Local Subsidiary

The structure of the internationalizing firm has to be adapted to the growing complexity the firm faces (Bartlett and Ghoshal, 1989). In the expansion process, subsidiaries can often extend their own responsibilities and decrease company headquarters' involvement with respect to an increasing number of activities or an increasing geographic area (Birkinshaw and Morrison, 1995; Ferdows, 1997; Malnight, 1996). When evolving towards more advanced strategic roles, subsidiaries extend their responsibilities first with respect to daily operations, and eventually, subsidiaries with most advanced strategic roles assume responsibilities over strategic decisions (Malnight, 1995; 1996). Consequently fourth and fifth propositions are formulated as follows:

P4: Subsidiaries of Western firms in CEE countries extend their responsibilities over time, firstly with respect to operational, then strategic decisions.

P5: Subsidiaries of Western firms in CEE countries extend their responsibilities over time, firstly considering local and later regional activities.

Methodology

Data Collection Methods

The presented research is a part of a larger project on market entry processes and organizational learning. Data have been gathered through mail surveys and semi-structured interviews. The analyses presented are based mainly on the qualitative part of the data. Thirteen subsidiaries of Dutch firms in Poland, Hungary, and Russia were contacted and interviews conducted with local general managers and functional managers in order to trace back expansion processes of the local subsidiaries. The quantitative data, gathered through a survey among Dutch firms with subsidiaries in CEE countries, are used to support findings based on the interviews with quantitative data and techniques.

For the quantitative part of data collection, 242 Dutch firms with more than 100 employees have been identified having subsidiaries in one of six selected CEE countries: the Czech Republic, Hungary, Poland, Romania, Russia, and Ukraine. All firms were approached initially by telephone to verify preliminary information and establish contacts with the responsible managers. In total 159 firms have been approached.

In 1998 the questionnaire was mailed to the selected respondents in the telephone interviews accompanied by a personal letter with a short introduction to the research project and the aim of the questionnaire. Out of 159 approached firms, 84 completed and returned the questionnaire (i.e., 53 percent response rate), providing information on 220 entries. Five observations have been excluded because of incompleteness of the data, leaving 215 usable observations.

The qualitative stage of data collection was meant for providing deeper insight in the expansion processes at the subsidiary level and the chosen approach led to a broad set of data on a small number of cases. Thirteen cases have been selected because they are different with respect to the industries, size, the host country, and the activities they perform locally. In 1998, all case subsidiaries were visited at the site and interviews conducted locally. Semi-structured field interviews were chosen because they offer opportunities to discuss the topics of interest, to clarify the meaning of questions and to adapt further questions to the specific situation. The general managers of the thirteen local subsidiaries were approached by telephone or fax, in a few cases after consultation of the Dutch headquarters. None of the contacted general managers refused to cooperate in the research, but because of physical absence during the time of interviews, two of them were conducted with marketing managers and two with financial managers. All respondents had been employed by the subsidiaries for at least two years. Respondents were both expatriate and local managers. Interviews with local managers and non-Dutch expatriates were held in either German or English, depending on the managers' language preferences. A list of topics to be covered in the interviews was mailed to all interviewees in advance. The interviews took between one and four hours. Extended notes were made during the face-to-face interviews. The case descriptions were sent for approval to the respective respondents for comments, agreement, and possible adjustments.

Sample Description

The pull of case studies consists of thirteen subsidiaries of ten Dutch firms in three CEE countries distributed as follows: four in Poland, four in Hungary, and five in Russia, all set up between 1989 and 1995. Table 7.1 summarizes some key features of the case subsidiaries. Four subsidiaries are active in either chemical or electronics: Power, Pharma, and Chemo. Five firms produce food and beverages: Black and Brown who are competitors, Childcare, Sweet and finally Beverage and Bottle that are both owned by the same Dutch parent company. Garden and Greens are horticultural firms. Three subsidiaries are not wholly owned by Dutch firms. Black and Childcare are joint ventures with a local partner, and Bottle is a partial acquisition by a Dutch firm. The case subsidiaries are of very different sizes: seven subsidiaries have more than 100 employees, while the smallest subsidiaries employ less than 10 persons. The starting years of each subsidiary are given in Table 7.1. In most cases, it is the year in which foreign direct investments were made resulting in sales subsidiaries or production sites.

Table 7.1　Key features of the 13 case subsidiaries: country, industry, starting year and size

Type of Industry	Poland	Hungary	Russia
Chemical / Electronic	Chemo Poland (1992)[a]	Power (1989)[b]	Chemo Russia (1991)
			Pharma (1993)
Food & Beverage	Childcare (1993)	Beverage (1991)	Black (1995)
	Bottle (1992)		Brown (1995)
			Sweet (1993)
Horticulture	Greens Poland (1994)	Garden (1993)	
		Greens Hungary (1992)	

[a]　Starting years in brackets.
[b]　Underlined names of subsidiaries refer to those with less than 10 employees.

Results from the Case Studies

From First Contacts to Initial Entry

Generally, entry processes always start sometimes long before the official date of entry is determined and the official entry is made public. All but one subsidiary in the sample were preceded by export activities in the countries of interest (see Table 7.2). Only Childcare started through cooperative marketing activities with a local company.

Table 7.2   Entry mode patterns of Dutch firms in CEE

Internationalization Process (Subsidiaries)	Export	Licensing/ Cooperation	Representative Sales offices	Production Facilities
Complete (Black, Garden, Greens Hungary and Greens Poland)	Yes	Yes	Yes	Yes
Complete (Brown, Chemo Russia)	Yes	Yes	Yes	No
Skipping stages from export to sales office (Chemo Poland, Pharma, Power)	Yes	No	Yes	No
Skipping stages from export through sales office to production (Sweet)	Yes	No	Yes	Yes
Skipping stages from export to production (Beverage, Bottle)	Yes	No	No	Yes
Skipping stages from cooperation to production (Childcare)	No	Yes	No	Yes

Many of the exporting activities were stopped or taken over when direct investments were made and a local subsidiary was established. The early exporting activities were combined with other operation methods, like licensing agreements with local state owned trading companies. This was common in the horticultural firms in the sample and in Power. They have all built their current activities from contacts with the former local state trading companies, the only companies that were allowed to do business with Western companies. These contacts go back many years: the Polish General Manager of Greens even mentioned historical ties dating back from the nineteenth century. All four persons who were responsible for the trade with the Dutch companies before 1989 are now the general managers of the local subsidiaries. Chemo Poland had extensive contacts in Poland before 1989, but these were dependent on the individual contacts of different business units.

Other firms that started their contacts after 1989 have also extended their exporting activities by establishing representative offices or sales offices, mostly in the first half of the nineties. Few firms started cooperation activities with local distributors or producers next to their exporting activities and became physically present with a representative or sales office only after these cooperative activities.

Increasing Resource Commitment and Local Activities

The increase in resource commitments as proposed in P2, appears to be related to two processes. Firstly, an increase of the share of ownership by the Dutch firm is considered. Secondly, an extension of the local activities of the subsidiary is analyzed. The first process took place in both Beverages and Bottle and also in the horticultural subsidiaries. Three subsidiaries were brought under full ownership with the establishment of a sales office. In the case of Greens in Poland, with some steps during the stages of sales office and production facilities resource commitment gradually increased. In Bottle a minority share of 24 percent was extended to a majority stake of 75 percent in several steps between 1996 and 1998. Beverage changed a 50 percent share into full ownership in two steps in 1993 and 1994.

The second process, extending local activities, took place in five cases: the Greens subsidiaries, Garden, Black, and Sweet started out as sales offices and later changed into production subsidiaries. Table 7.3 gives more details on the local activities of the case subsidiaries. There is a tendency to start with marketing activities, in as many as six cases accompanied by sales activities simultaneously. Marketing activities only followed sales activities in Brown, while its competitor Black never performed marketing activities itself.

The local distribution of products is only taken care of by few subsidiaries and is mostly started soon after the initial activities began. In many cases, organizing distribution in-house is judged to be too risky, especially in Russia. Most distribution activities are arranged with local distributors, because of their network ties and knowledge of the local environment.

Table 7.3 Assumption of activities by Dutch subsidiaries by industry

Industry	Marketing	Sales	Distribution	Production	R&D
Chemo Poland	1992	1992	1996		
Chemo Russia	1991	1992	1997		
Pharma	1991	1993			
Power	1990	1990			
Beverage	1991	1991	1991	1991	
Bottle	1993	1993	1993	1993	1993
Brown	1996	1995			
Black		1995		1996	
Childcare	1991	1993		1993	1993
Sweet	1993	1997		1998 Only packaging	
Garden	1989	1989	1992–98	1989 Restarted 1992	1993
Greens Hungary	1989	1989 Restarted 1991	1991	1989 Restarted 1991	1997
Greens Poland	1985	1994	1991–94		1994

Production activities are performed in half of the subsidiaries and, interestingly, none of the chemical and industrial product firms in the sample have started to produce locally. The same has been true for food and beverage subsidiaries that lacked local partners. Firms in this industry that have a local partner or started with one, in acquisitions as well as in greenfield subsidiaries, are all active in local production. In the acquired subsidiaries, production often had taken place before the acquisition and the production process was only adapted to Western quality standards and sometimes changed to producing the acquirer's brands. These production sites are often set up at the same time as the marketing and sales offices, see for instance Beverage and Bottle, or very soon after that, Black and Childcare. Only Sweet has set up a production site without a local partner, but has only installed packaging lines. All production activities of these food and beverage subsidiaries are for the local market.

The horticultural firms in Hungary are also active in local production, in all cases seed breeding, and later expanded these activities through establishing local cleaning and processing factories. The Hungarian subsidiaries were both producing and developing products for global market, while the Polish subsidiary only breeds for the local market.

R&D activities are done in the Polish subsidiary of Greens, and in Childcare and Bottle. They are performed with a special attention on the local market. Only in the two Hungarian horticultural subsidiaries R&D activities are pursued for global market purposes.

Sales Objects

P3 not only mentioned the expansion of local activities, but also expected subsidiaries to expand through the sales objects they offer. It turned out that the most obvious way in which all subsidiaries expanded their sales objects was by broadening the product range offered at the local market. In some subsidiaries this was the only way to grow, especially in smaller subsidiaries, such as Black in Russia. Some larger and more experienced companies, however, also introduced new products stepwise in their CEE subsidiaries, for instance Childcare and Sweet. In five cases, the two Greens subsidiaries, Power, Garden, and Chemo Russia, the expansion of the product range was the consequence of a company merger. In many food and beverages subsidiaries, but also in Greens in Poland, products have been adapted specifically to local market tastes and sometimes to legal requirements. A pattern of expanding sales objects from products to services and know-how is not found in any of the thirteen cases.

Division of Responsibilities among Headquarters and Local Subsidiaries

According to P4, subsidiaries will extend their responsibilities over time, firstly with respect to daily operations and later with respect to strategic decisions. The extension of local responsibilities is visible in the formal structure in only three cases. In Greens subsidiaries in Hungary, 'permission had to be asked for almost anything' while direct responsibility for the daily operations was still in the hands of a regional exports director. When a new export manager arrived, autonomy was felt to increase, because 'he let go of decision power and asked for monthly reports only'. With the promotion of the local deputy manager to local managing director this subsidiary gained even more autonomy. In Chemo Poland, the promotion of the local manager to General Manager also increased local autonomy: the General Manager stated that since his promotion he is 'free in using budgets as long as the results are good'. In Childcare the establishment of a regional office resulted in looser ties with headquarters in the Netherlands, illustrating the subsidiary's 'growth towards adulthood' according to the General Manager.

In five cases, growing autonomy was experienced by the respondents illustrated by a decrease in the number of visits by Dutch headquarters representatives. Generally, these subsidiaries have been able to make decisions on daily operations themselves, but they still needed approval of Dutch headquarters for strategic matters. However, most of the subsidiaries in the sample are (still) controlled also with respect to operational decisions by Dutch headquarters. This means that all their plans have to be sent to the headquarters for approval and several respondents in these subsidiaries added further that they were financially very dependent on parent company resources.

Geographic Area Responsibilities

P5 predicted an increase in responsibilities with respect to regional activities. Although we have seen that production is meant for selling at the local market in almost all cases, many subsidiaries report that they have extended their responsibilities across borders. Though none of the subsidiaries in Russia are responsible for activities in countries outside the former Soviet Union, most Russian subsidiaries experienced stepwise geographical expansion, from Moscow and St. Petersburg regions to other large cities in Russia and sometimes even beyond. For instance, Brown in Russia is responsible for activities in Belarus, while the responsibilities of Chemo and Sweet extend over the whole territory of the former Soviet Union, to Kazakhstan, Azerbaijan, and even Mongolia, in case of Sweet. The larger subsidiaries in Hungary and Poland, except for Beverage and Bottle, have also extended their regional responsibilities in neighboring countries. Greens in Poland, for instance, was made responsible for activities in the Baltic States and Belarus, while its larger Hungarian subsidiary expanded its responsibilities firstly to the Czech Republic and

Slovakia, and later to Romania, all former Yugoslav countries, Moldova, and Ukraine.

Results from Survey Data

In this section, the results from the survey among 84 Dutch firms with 215 subsidiaries in six countries in CEE are presented.

Table 7.4 presents initial operation methods and 1998 operation methods. Exporting activities were used as initial entry mode in more than half of the 215 entries. Less popular were low commitment modes, as licensing and cooperative agreements. More than 60 percent of all first operation methods were through direct investments of which 71 cases were wholly owned subsidiaries. Exporting was often used next to other operation methods: in ten entries exporting was combined with low commitment modes, and in fifteen entries with direct investments. Low commitment modes were used together with direct investments in 21 entries. In fourteen cases, all three types of operation methods, i.e., exporting, low commitment modes and direct investments, were used in combination.

Table 7.4   Operation methods used initially and in operation modes in 1998 in 215 Dutch subsidiaries in CEE

	Export	Licensing, cooperation	Minority and 50/50 IJV	Majority IJV	WOS
Initial entry mode	113	40	16	17	71
Operation mode - 1998	40	23	18	21	130
Difference	-73	-17	+2	+4	+59

In 1998 less than 20 percent of all cases were still active in exporting and in almost all entries exports were combined with low commitment entry modes (in 6 cases) or direct investments (in 22 cases). Low commitment modes are also used less in 1998 (and in only four cases it is the sole method of local operations), while numbers of minority and majority participations slightly increased over time. The number of wholly owned subsidiaries has increased most to reach 60 percent of the 215 entries. In total 78 percent of the activities in 1998 were through direct investments. Only eight observations have been found to combine the three types of operation methods.

In Table 7.5 initial entry modes are compared to 1998 operation methods in more detail. The table shows that in many entries more committed operation methods have followed less committed modes. In eight cases low commitment methods are preceded by exporting activities. In 85 of the 169 cases that invested directly in the host countries by 1998, exporting was used as an initial entry mode. Thirty-seven out of 169 cases used low commitment entry modes before entering through direct investments. Only in 10 cases, subsidiaries were able to enlarge their share from minority to majority or full ownership, or from majority to full ownership. In three of the 215 observations, firms initially used operation methods characterized by more commitment than they had in 1998. Two entries were direct investments that were taken back to low commitment modes and in one entry a firm started its activities by combining cooperative agreements with exporting, but then decided to cut the cooperation and continued only its exporting activities.

Table 7.5   Change of operation methods over time in 215 subsidiaries

Initial entry modes	Exporting 1998	Licensing and cooperation 1998	Minority & 50/50 IJV 1998	Majority IJV 1998	WOS 1998
Exporting	34	8	5	12	68
Licensing & cooperation	11	15	7	12	18
Minority & 50/50 IJV	-	1	13	2	1
Majority IJV	4	5	-	10	7
WOS	7	7	-	-	67

Note: Different operation methods have been used next to each other in various subsidiaries.

Conclusions

Expansion processes of Dutch firms in CEE markets have been investigated in this chapter. These newly opened markets are an excellent context to test the validity of the Uppsala stages model of internationalization. The globalized business environment was thought to have speeded up internationalization processes and firms were not expected to take all steps predicted in the establishment chain (Hedlund and Kverneland, 1983; Nordström, 1990; Turnbull, 1987). It has also been expected that the underlying mechanism of market knowledge increase would allow firms to expand in foreign markets and shed light on the explanation of contemporary internationalization processes. Therefore, propositions have been formulated with regard to different dimensions along which firms and their local subsidiaries grow without presupposing a certain order of stages (Welch and Luostarinen, 1988).

It has been found that the first steps Dutch firms undertook in CEE were characterized by low local commitment. Most firms started local activities through exporting, licensing or other cooperative agreements, supporting P1.

With P2, it has been expected that Dutch firms would increase their local commitment in the CEE host markets following their initial entry. This proposition is largely supported by the entry processes of the thirteen cases as well as the survey data on 215 entries of Dutch firms. The extension of local commitment was done through using operation methods demanding more commitment, especially direct investments, as well as through extending the ownership share in local participations. Patterns with respect to expanding local activities are less obvious. In most cases, marketing and sales activities were started, followed by production activities on a later stage. In subsidiaries where distribution activities were organized locally, this followed with sales and marketing activities. Only few subsidiaries have been active in R&D and these activities often started in the same year as production activities. With respect to sales objects, sixteen cases expanded stepwise, but only by adding new products.

Finally, it has been expected that local subsidiaries would expand by increasing local autonomy (P4). Several respondents confirmed that their local subsidiaries extended their responsibilities. In most cases, however, respondents referred to decisions made in subsidiaries on local operations and not on strategic matters. Even with respect to operational matters, the majority of subsidiaries needed approval of the Dutch company headquarters. P4, therefore, received little support from the thirteen cases.

The expansion of geographical responsibility (P5) has been mostly confirmed. Several subsidiaries adopted responsibilities stepwise over neighboring markets within the CEE region.

To summarize, P1, P2 and P3 considering the most visible dimensions of expansion, received enough support to conclude that the learning model of the internationalizing firm did not loose its validity for explaining entry processes of firms in new markets, even in the current globalized environment. The thirteen cases do support the expectations that firms are able to enter new markets via short routes (Hedlund and Kverneland, 1983). The fact that P4 received only little support can be due to the time consuming character of extending responsibilities. The subsidiaries in all case studied are still young and in the early stages of their development.

The data support Johanson and Vahlne's (1990) plea for differentiation of the internationalization patterns of firms. Future research should explore further the dimensions along which firms expand internationally. The autonomy of the local subsidiary and the geographic expansion of its responsibilities are only partial operationalizations of the aspects of changing structure in internationalizing firms and the expansion processes at the level of subsidiaries. Future research can benefit from combining the literature on subsidiary's strategic roles, network approaches and learning theory.

References

Aharoni, Y. (1966), *The Foreign Direct Investment Decision Process*, Boston: Harvard University.

Bartlett, C.A. and Ghoshal, S. (1989), *Managing Across Borders: The Transnational Solution*. London: Hutchinson Business Books.

Birkinshaw, J., Hood, N. and Jonsson, S. (1998), 'Building Firm-Specific Advantages in Multinational Corporations: The Role of Subsidiary Initiative', *Strategic Management Journal*, vol. 19, pp. 221-241.

Birkinshaw, J.M. and Morrison, A.J. (1995), 'Configurations of Strategy and Structure in Subsidiaries of Multinational Corporations', *Journal of International Business Studies*, vol. 26, pp. 729-753.

Birkinshaw, J. (1997), 'Entrepreneurship in Multinational Corporations: The Characteristics of Subsidiary Initiatives', *Strategic Management Journal*, vol. 18, pp. 207-229.

Bridgewater, S. (1999), 'Networks and Internationalisation: The Case of Multinational Corporations Entering Ukraine', *International Business Review*, vol. 8, pp. 99-118.

Buckley, P.J., Newbould, G.D. and Thurwell, J. (1978), *Going International: The Experience of Smaller Companies Overseas*. London: Associated Business Press.

Carstairs, R.T. and Welch, L.S. (1982), 'Licensing and the Internationalization of Smaller Companies: Some Australian Evidence', *Management International Review*, vol. 22, no. 3, pp. 33-44.

Chang, S.J. (1995), 'International Expansion Strategy of Japanese Firms: Capability Building through Sequential Entry', *Academy of Management Journal*, vol. 38, pp. 383-407.

Cohen, W. M. and Levinthal, D.A. (1990), 'Absorptive Capacity: A New Perspective on Learning and Innovation', *Administrative Science Quarterly*, vol. 35, pp. 128-152.

Engwall, L. and Wallenstål, M. (1988), 'Tit for Tat in Small Steps: The Internationalization of Swedish Banks', *Scandinavian Journal of Management*, vol. 4, pp. 147-155.

Ferdows, K. (1997), 'Making the Most of Foreign Factories', *Harvard Business Review*, March-April, pp. 73-88.

Forsgren, M. (1990), 'Managing the International Multi-Center Firm: Case Studies from Sweden', *European Management Journal*, vol. 8, pp. 261-267.

Forsgren, M., Holm, U. and Johanson, J. (1995), 'Division Headquarters Go Abroad - A Step in the Internationalization of the Multinational Corporation', *Journal of Management Studies*, vol. 32, pp. 475-491.

Forsgren, M., Pedersen, T. and Foss, N. (1999), 'Accounting for the Strengths of MNC Subsidiaries: The Case of Foreign-Owned Firms in Denmark', *International Business Review*, vol. 8, pp. 181-196.

Hedlund, G. (1986), 'The Hypermodern MNC - A Heterarchy?', *Human Resource Management*, vol. 25, pp. 9-35.

Hedlund, G. and Kverneland, A. (1983), 'Are Entry Strategies for Foreign Markets Changing? The Case of Swedish Investment in Japan', Reprinted in P.J. Buckley and P.N. Ghauri (eds) (1993), *The Internationalization of the Firm, A Reader*, London: Academic Press Limited, pp. 106-123.

Jarillo, J.C. and Martínez, J.I. (1990), 'Different Roles for Subsidiaries: The Case of Multinational Corporations in Spain', *Strategic Management Journal*, vol. 11, pp. 501-512.

Johanson, J. and Mattsson, L.G. (1988), 'Internationalization in Industrial Systems - A Network Approach', in N. Hood and J.-E. Vahlne (eds) *Strategies in Global Competition*, New York: Croom Helm.

Johanson, J. and Vahlne, J.-E. (1977), 'The Internationalization Process of the Firm - A Model of Knowledge Development and Increasing Foreign Market Commitments', *Journal of International Business Studies*, vol. 8, pp. 23-32.

Johanson, J. and Vahlne, J.-E. (1990), 'The Mechanism of Internationalization', *International Management Review*, vol. 7, pp. 11-24.

Johanson, J. and Wiedersheim-Paul, F. (1975), 'The Internationalization of Firms - Four Swedish Cases', *Journal of Management Studies*, vol. 12, pp. 305-322.

Juul, M. and Walters, P.G.P. (1987), 'The Internationalization of Norwegian Firms – A Study of the U.K. Experience', *Management International Review*, vol. 27, pp. 58-66.

Kogut, B. (1983), 'Foreign Direct Investment as a Sequential Process', in C.P. Kindleberger and D. Audretsch (eds) *The Multinational Corporation in the 80s*, Cambridge, MA: MIT Press.

Malnight, T.W. (1995), 'Globalization of an Ethnocentric Firm: An Evolutionary Perspective', *Strategic Management Journal*, vol. 16, pp. 119-141.

Malnight, T.W. (1996), 'The Transition From a Decentralized to Network-Based MNC Structures: An Evolutionary Perspective', *Journal of International Business Studies*, pp. 43-65.

Nobel, R. and Birkinshaw, J. (1998), 'Innovation in Multinational Corporations: Control and Communication Patterns in International R&D Operations', *Strategic Management Journal*, vol. 19, pp. 479-496.

Nordström, K.A. (1991), *The Internationalization Process of the Firm. Searching for New Patterns and Explanations*, Stockholm, Sweden: Institute of International Business, Stockholm School of Economics.

Peng, M.W. and Heath, P.S. (1996), 'The Growth of the Firm in Planned Economies in Transition: Institutions, Organizations, and Strategic Choice', *Academy of Management Review*, vol. 21, pp. 492-528.

Prahalad, C.K. and Doz, Y.L (1981), 'An Approach to Strategic Control in Multi National Corporations', *Sloan Management Review*, vol. 22, pp. 5-13.

Shama, A. (1995), 'Entry Strategies of US Firms to the Newly Independent States, Baltic States and Eastern European Countries', *California Management Review*, vol. 37, no. 3, pp. 90-109.

Turnbull. P.W. (1987), 'A Challenge to the Stages Theory of the Internationalization Process', in P.J. Rosson, and S.D. Reed (eds) *Managing Export Entry and Expansion,* New York: Praeger.

Vahlne, J.E., Nordström, K.A. and Torbacke, S. (1996), 'Swedish Multinationals in Central and Eastern Europe - Entry and Subsequent Development', *Journal of East-West Business*, vol. 1, pp. 1-16.

Welch, L.S. and Luostarinen, R. (1988), 'Internationalization: Evolution of a Concept', *Journal of General Management*, vol. 14, pp. 36-64.

Wernerfelt, B. (1984), 'A Resource-Based View of the Firm', *Strategic Management Journal*, vol. 5, pp. 171-180.

8 Internationalization of Interbrew in Eastern Europe: A Case Study

MARIN ALEXANDROV MARINOV and SVETLA TRIFONOVA MARINOVA

'Do your job properly in the first time and even better every time after.'
Michel Naquet-Radiguet
Vice President of Interbrew for Eastern Europe

Introduction

The management of Interbrew, the largest Belgian brewery, is currently facing market challenges in the implementation of their global investment strategy. The management are determined to build on the company's well-established value system. Interbrew has always considered the customer of primary importance. The high quality of products, professionalism, innovation and willingness for communication set the cornerstones of the internationalizing strategy pursued by the company.

In the world market place Interbrew has to meet the ever increasing pressure of the world-wide competition and the challenges of intensified industry consolidation. In spite of the economic instability in Asia, Africa and Latin America, their regional beer markets have been growing fast while the European and North American markets have been saturated and shrinking. The company, world market leader, Anheuser-Busch has an almost unbeatable position, far ahead from Heineken of the Netherlands and Miller of the US Interbrew is amongst the market followers where volume differences are small and ranking can easily change. New international players as South African Breweries (South Africa), Brahma (Brazil) and Coors (US) have been growing fast, aggressively expanding their international operations and attempting to kick out long established world recognized brewers as Interbrew and Guinness (Ireland).

The members of the management team of Interbrew are sitting in the spacious headquarters Conference Room to reflect on and discuss the internationalization strategy of the brewery in Eastern Europe. In the period 1991-1997 Interbrew has become the biggest investor in the brewing industry of Eastern Europe with controlling stakes in nine companies. The management team has to evaluate Interbrew's experience in the region and the prospects for their operations.

Interbrew: The Company and Its Internationalization

Interbrew is a wholly privately owned international company with headquarters (HQ) in Belgium. It produces and bottles beer, soft drinks and mineral water. The company has strong market positions in 80 countries worldwide. Its beer production is more than 80 per cent in volume. In 1997 beer sales were 34.721 million hectoliters, amounting to a turnover of more than BEF106 billion. If Interbrew minority participations are included the companies annual output in 1997 was 42.1 million hectoliters.

The Interbrew Group was created in the 1980s with the merger between the two leading Belgian breweries: Piedboeuf, founded in 1853 and Artois, founded in 1366. The merger took place because of the increased international pressure, constantly decreasing consumption on the Belgian market and the drive for the company to increase its presence abroad. After the merger, the new company became strongly internationally competitive. In its international expansion Interbrew has mostly applied the acquisition foreign direct investment mode of entry in international markets. In any acquisition transaction it has aimed at full decision control over the acquired firm, excluding the possibility for other companies to buy into its subsidiary.

Interbrew's mission is to develop existing and new markets with strong and reliable partners, aiming at building sizable and profitable, premium priced, famous branded positions with long term growth potential. To achieve this mission Interbrew offers leading local beers alongside with the most successful and best selling Belgian beers: the premium lager beer Stella Artois, the original white beer of Hoegaarden and its specialties, the Abbey beers of Leffe and the spontaneously fermented Lanbic beers of Belle-Vue. It also produces and markets the highly successful range of Labatt beers, as well as the premium US beer Rolling Rock.

Over the years Interbrew managed to develop and enhance a consistent and coherent company philosophy, laying the foundations for the company's internationalization strategy. The management believes in: decentralized operations of subsidiaries, relying on local management expertise and commitment; concentration on local brands; focusing on a limited number of key international brands; offering consumers the largest possible choice of specialty beers; putting quality as a key to market success.

Interbrew's strategy is very much focused on value growth in beer, divesting of non-strategic assets worldwide. They sold their Italian beer operations, the UK brewing and retailing interests, US dairy operations and stakes in the Canadian entertainment industry, Coca-Cola interests in Belgium and the Netherlands. The most significant strategic priority is to develop new segments with higher value added in specialties and premium lagers. The company also aims at long term productivity gains in its core European and North American markets. Another major priority of Interbrew's strategy is to enter beer markets with long term development potentials and high growth rate in volume in countries such as China and Mexico. Interbrew believes that in the future there will be mostly value potential for Eastern European beer market development. Interbrew shows strong willingness to enter into strategic partnerships to enhance its world market position.

In line with the consolidation throughout the brewing industry, Interbrew strives to consolidate and even improve its presence in four key European markets: Belgium, France, the Netherlands, and Hungary. In North America the major attention is drawn on Canada, Mexico, and the US. Via partnerships Interbrew wants to develop presence in the growth markets of Latin America and Asia Pacific. Although the Group has presence in markets around the world and is open to evaluating and grasping new opportunities in the global marketplace, its strategic priority remains Europe.

In 1997 Interbrew marketed 34.721 million hectoliters of beer, waters, and soft drinks, with sales of this operation amounting to BEF106,644 million (excluding excise duties). Interbrew performance results for the period 1988-1997 are given in Table 8.1. From 1996 Interbrew reports the financial results of the company on the basis of the 12-month calendar year. The 1994-95 financial results cover a period of 15 months. Therefore, the results from this period are not directly comparable.

Interbrew focuses on strong product image building and extended use of brand portfolio. In the blonde-beer segment of the market, Interbrew offers the customer a broad range of local beer brands, together with the Belgian market leader Jupiler and the international brand Stella Artois. Interbrew has acquired a strong reputation in specialty beers. Each brand produced by Interbrew is a leader in their respective segment: Hoegaarden - in the white beers segment, Leffe - in the Abbey beers segment, and Belle-Vue - in the spontaneously fermented beers segment. In its world markets Interbrew is now aggressively pursuing growth of premiums and specialty beers, forming their international brand portfolio, including: Stella Artois, Rolling Rock, Leffe, Hoegaarden, Belle-Vue, and Labatt Blue.

Table 8.1   Interbrew performance figures

Indicators	1988-89	1989-90	1990-91	1991-92	1992-93	1993-94	1994-95	1996	1997	Increase 1997/1996
Total Sale (000 HL) (1)	18,288	18,420	18,765	21,957	20,584	17,599	28,854	32,857	34,721	5.7%
Turnover (BEF million) (2)	46,011	47.841	53,279	59,112	57,661	48,683	81,395	96,596	106,644	10.4%
Cash Flow (BEF million) (3)	7,905	6,108	6,795	7,812	8,771	10,083	14,161	15,268	18,302	19.9%
Net Profit (BEF million)	2,000	1,949	2,139	1,545	2,059	2,684	3,462	4,068	5,336	31.2%
Capital and Reserves (BEF million) (4)	29,195	30,438	33,502	34,503	35,031	33,602	38,823	42,425	49,209	16.0%
Investment (BEF million) (5)	6,178	7,283	9,150	11,031	9,599	5,187	7,103	6,045	6,745	11.6%

Source: Interbrew Information Service.

(1) Volumes do not include minority participations.
(2) The turnover does not include excise duties.
(3) Cash flow includes net profit of the consolidated companies after deduction of undistributed earnings of companies accounted for under the equity method, increased by the addition (+) and subtraction (-) of depreciations, write-offs and provisions of liabilities and charges, as well as deferred taxes; reduced by capital subsidies taken into the profit and loss account but without the exceptional capital gains during the respective fiscal year.
(4) Minority interests included.
(5) Tangible fixed assets.

The company has also developed a strong portfolio concentrated on key domestic lager brands. Major American local brands are: Wild Cat, Kakanee, Labatt 50 (all in Canada); Alexander Keith's (Atlantic Region); Tecate and Sol in Mexico. Some of the main domestic lager brands in Europe are: Jupiler (Belgium), Dommelsch and Oranjeboom (the Netherlands). In Eastern Europe Interbrew relies heavily on the acquired local brands as Kamenitza, Burgasko Pivo, and Astika (in Bulgaria); Borsodi Világos, Rákóczi, and Borsodi Kinizsi (in Hungary); Ozujsko Pivo and Bansko Pivo (Croatia); Bergenbier and Hopfenkönig (Romania); Chernigiv (Ukraine).

At the end of 1997 Interbrew had production operations in several western European countries: Belgium (where it has been an acknowledged market leader with more than 50 per cent market share), France, the Netherlands, and Luxembourg. Its presence in North America has been in the form of owned production facilities in Canada and the US. The company has held 22 per cent stake in a large Mexican brewery and has formed a strategic joint venture with a Venezuelan brewery for a long term pan-South American expansion. Interbrew has also joint ventures in China, the Philippines, and the Dominican Republic. In March 1998 Interbrew established a 50/50 per cent international joint venture beer company with Oriental Brewery Co., the largest South Korean brewery owned by Doosan Group.

The major focus of Interbrew's international expansion in the last seven years has been the Eastern European region making the Group the largest investor in the brewing industry in that region. By the end of 1997 the company owned three breweries in Bulgaria (merged into one entity in July 1997), two in Romania, one in each Hungary, Croatia, Montenegro, and the Ukraine.

Parallel to its numerous acquisitions in Eastern Europe in the 1990s, in 1995 Interbrew made a US$ 2 billion investment through buying 100 per cent of the shares of John Labatt Brewing Ltd. in Canada, the second largest brewery in the country after Molson. Since the acquisition Labatt has been continuously gaining market share from Molson.

Interbrew's international investments, operations, and market positions by company and country are shown in Tables 8.2 and 8.3.

Seeking corporate growth outside the saturated Belgian market, Interbrew has attempted to gain international presence through brewery acquisitions, equity stakes and licensing agreements. The specific market entry mode has been influenced by the macro- and micro-economic characteristics of the target country.

**Table 8.2   Interbrew's international investments:
January 1988-March 1998**

Company	Country	Type of Company	Year
Borsodi	Hungary	Subsidiary	1991
Zagrebacka	Croatia	Subsidiary	1994
Bianca Bergenbier	Romania	Subsidiary	1994
Proberco	Romania	Subsidiary	1994
Zhu Jiang	China	Joint Venture	1994
Oranjeboom	Netherlands	Subsidiary	1995
Kamenitza	Bulgaria	Subsidiary	1995
Burgasko Pivo	Bulgaria	Subsidiary	1995
John Labatt	Canada	Subsidiary	1995
Astika	Bulgaria	Joint Venture	1996
Blue Sword	China	Joint Venture	1996
Vegana	Dominican Republic	Joint Venture	1996
Desna	Ukraine	Subsidiary	1996
Jinling	China	Subsidiary	1997
Trebjesa	Montenegro	Subsidiary	1997
Cisneros	Venezuela	Joint Venture	1997
Nanjing	China	Subsidiary	1998
Doosan Group	South Korea	Joint Venture	1998

Source: Interbrew Information Service.

Table 8.3   Interbrew - market position in various countries in 1998

Country	Market Position	No. of Breweries	Number of Employees	Main Brands
Belgium	Leader	4	3,400	Jupiler, Stella Artois, Hoegaarden, Leffe, Belle-Vue
Bulgaria	Leader	3	880	Astika, Kamenitza, Burgasko Pivo
Canada	Leader	1	3,450	Labatt Blue, Kokanee, LGD, Blue Light, Budweiser
Croatia	Leader	1	800	Ozujsko, Stella Artois, Tomislav, Bansko
Romania	Leader	2	1,690	Bergenbier, Hopenkönig
Hungary	Second	1	1,260	Borsodi Világos, Rákóczi, Holsten, Spaten
Mexico (22% interest)	Second	1	15,000	Dos Equis, Tecate, Sol, Carta Blanca, Indio, Bohemia
The Netherlands	Second	3	1,270	Dommelsch, Oranjeboom, Hertog-Jan, Leffe, Hoegaarden
USA	Second	n/a	420	Rolling Rock, Labatt Blue, Tecate, Dos Equis
France	Third	n/a	890	Leffe, Hoegaarden, Stella Artois, La Bécasse
Luxembourg	Third	n/a	n/a	Stella Artois, Hoegaarden, Belle-Vue
Ukraine	Third	1	780	Chernigiv, Vienna

Source: Interbrew Information Service.

The World Brewing Industry

Key Trends and Developments

Beer is the largest volume alcoholic drink in the world. In the major world markets it accounts for more than 80 per cent of all alcoholic drinks consumed in Germany, 78 per cent in the United Kingdom, 63 per cent in the United States of America. It is outshone by wine in other countries, for instance France and Italy. Alcohol consumption preferences are dependent upon country specifics such as culture, history, climate, etc.

Lately the worldwide beer sales have been hit by healthier diets and life styles, and the shift from hard to soft drinks. There is a clear trend of drinking habits becoming more cosmopolitan encouraging wider variety of products and brands in every market. This poses an increasing threat to domestic brewers who are having a fight to maintain market share in an increasingly competitive marketplace.

There is no such thing as a typical beer consumer in world terms. Patterns of beer consumption vary widely on a national and regional basis. The common patterns are: beer consumption does tend to be heaviest amongst males and in relatively young age groups.

New product development in world brewing has tended to be based around traditional brewing methods and is generally based on a process of 'rediscovery' of old types of beer, the adding of new ingredients, or the use of a new type of packaging. Branding is of supreme importance in the beer market. Brands like Miller, Heineken, Stella Artois and many others have gained world recognition.

The multinational brewing companies are better positioned than domestic brewers to respond to the growing internationalization and globalization of world beer industry. In a severe competition of establishing global brands and gaining more market share, the key issues in the world brewing industry are consolidation and globalization of production and sales. Therefore, the multinationals expand via acquisitions, joint venture formation, and local licensing agreements.

While the top five beer producing countries in the world account for more than 50 per cent of the total world beer production, the ten largest breweries in the world account for approximately one third of the world beer production (see Tables 8.4 and 8.5A & B). While the beer producing companies in the US and Germany serve saturating domestic markets and search for global growth opportunities, the beer production in Brazil and especially in China serves high growth national markets of enormous size.

Table 8.4   Top five beer producing countries in the world in 1994

Rank	Country	Production in 1994 in million hectoliters	Percentage Change 1994/1993	Percentage of Word Output
1.	US	238.1	+ 5.0%	19.5%
2.	China	123.6	+ 19.5%	10.1%
3.	Germany	117.5	+ 0.3%	9.6%
4.	Japan	72.7	+ 2.0%	5.9%
5.	Brazil	65.2	+ 9.1%	5.3%

Source: NTC Publications, 1997.

Table 8.5 A   The largest breweries in the world in 1995

Rank	Company and Country	Output (in million hectoliters)	World Market Share	Regional Market Share
1.	Anheuser-Busch (US)	105	8.6%	23.2% of N&S American market
2.	Heineken (Holland)	56	4.6%	13.4% of European market
3.	Miller (US)	52	4.2%	11.4% of N&S American market
4.	Interbrew (Belgium)	36	2.9%	8.8% of European market
5.	Kirin (Japan)	34	2.8%	11.7% of Asian & Pacific market
6.	Foster's (Australia)	31	2.5%	10.1% of Asian & Pacific market
7.	Danone (France)	28	2.3%	6.3% of European market
8.	Carlsberg (Denmark)	27	2.2%	6.1% of European market
9.	Brahma (Brazil)	25	1.9%	5.3% of N&S American market
10.	Guinness (Ireland)	24	1.8%	5.6% of European market

Source: The World Beer Report 1996, The Confederation of Belgian Brewers.

Table 8.5 B   The largest breweries in the world in 1996

Rank	Company and Country	Output (in million hectoliters)	World Market Share	Regional Market Share
1.	Anheuser-Busch (US)	106.9	8.6%	24.6% of N&S American market
2.	Heineken (Holland)	64.3	5.1%	14.7% of European market
3.	Miller (US)	54.2	4.3%	12.9% of N&S American market
4.	South African Breweries (SA)	36.9	3.0%	42.6% of African market
5.	Brahma (Brazil)	36.4	2.9%	7.3% of N&S American market
6.	Interbrew (Belgium)	32.8	2.6%	7.6% of European market
7.	Kirin (Japan)	32.7	2.6%	12.1% of Asian & Pacific market
8.	Carlsberg (Denmark)	31.8	2.5%	7.2% of European market
9.	Foster's (Australia)	28.9	2.3%	9.6% of Asian & Pacific market
10.	Coors (US)	27.3	2.2%	6.4% of N&S American market

Source: The European newspaper, 1997.

The world beer consumption presented by regions is given in Figure 8.1.

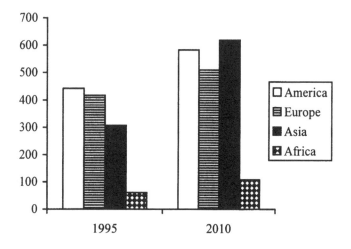

Figure 8.1   World beer consumption in 1995 and 2010

Source: The World Beer Report 1996.

The European Beer Market

The European beer market is presently the second largest in the world in volume terms. In the early 1990s it was surpassed by the North and South American beer market that became regional market leader. The European beer market was worth over US$ 93 billion in 1997. Lager accounts for over 74 per cent of volume share, followed by ales and stouts.

The beer market in Europe is very highly fragmented and nationally focused. The biggest brewer in Europe, Heineken of the Netherlands, has 13.4 per cent of the European market share, while Anheuser-Busch the biggest brewing company in the USA and the world, has a share of 23.2 per cent of the North and South American market (the largest regional beer market in the world) and around 45 per cent of the US beer market. Although Germany produces more than one fourth of the European beer, its domestic market is so fragmented that the three largest German breweries have each slightly more than 2 per cent of the European beer market. The average output per plant in Europe is less than 0.1 million hectoliters. This is very low in comparison with the average output of US breweries (3.8 million hectoliters). This means that there is a good precondition for consolidation and globalization of the European beer market. Beer production by country and company in the top ten European countries and companies is given in Tables 8.6 and 8.7.

Although it is not dynamic, industry sources remain optimistic about the long-term future of the European beer market. The West European beer market as a whole has experienced a sluggish rate of growth compared to the rest of the world, in both value and volume terms. Unsurprisingly, the much-publicized alcoholic soft drinks category experienced the highest rate of growth over the last five years, volumes having risen by over 70 per cent every year since 1993.

Table 8.6   The top ten largest beer producing countries in Europe in 1994

Rank	Country	Output (in million hectoliters)	Percentage of the European Output	Percentage of the World Output
1.	Germany	117.5	27.3	9.6
2.	UK	56.8	13.2	4.6
3.	Spain	25.4	5.9	2.1
4.	Holland	23.2	5.4	1.9
5.	France	20.7	4.8	1.6
6.	Russia	20.4	4.7	1.6
7.	Czech R.	18.7	4.3	1.5
8.	Poland	16.4	3.8	1.4
9.	Belgium	14.5	3.5	1.2
10.	Ukraine	12.8	2.9	1.1

Sources: CBMC 1995; National Statistics of Poland, Russia, and Ukraine.

Table 8.7   The ten largest breweries in Europe in 1994

Rank	Company and Country	Output (in million hectoliters)	World Market Share	European Market Share
1.	Heineken (Holland)	56.0	4.6%	13.4%
2.	Interbrew (Belgium)	36.0	2.9%	8.8%
3.	Danone (France)	28.0	2.3%	6.3%
4.	Carlsberg (Denmark)	27.0	2.2%	6.1%
5.	Guinness (Ireland)	24.0	1.8%	5.6%
6.	Bass (UK)	19.4	1.6%	4.7%
7.	Courage (UK)	12.2	1.0%	2.9%
8.	Oetker (Germany)	9.6	0.8%	2.3%
9.	Brau und Brunnen (Germany)	9.4	0.8%	2.2%
10.	Maerz (Germany)	9.3	0.8%	2.2%

Source: The World Beer Report 1995, The Confederation of Belgian Brewers.

The low growth rate of West European beer market has led to a flood of new product innovations. Flavored specialty brews are the latest trait of an industry seeking to exploit the increasingly adventurous beer drinking population.

The industry will be encouraged by the trends witnessed not only in the beer trade but also in other European markets, where consumer expenditure has grown. Consumers now seem willing to pay extra for better quality products. This can only benefit the manufacturers of premium brands and result in higher margins.

Price is not the only value measure that is important. The need to stand out from the crowd has made brand image more vital than ever. Dominant brand loyalty is the goal that all manufacturers strive for and they are now seeking new methods to enhance the way their brands are perceived. Packaging, advertising, image and taste now hold increasing importance for consumers.

As the market continues to change, only the strongest brands will survive. It is believed that the main threat to the industry is the "over-spill" of brands. The ten most popular brands in Europe are given in Table 8.8. Too many brands could exceed demand. Although the highly fragmented beer market in Western Europe offers huge opportunities for the large manufacturers willing to exploit the potential, the brand proliferation in recent years could lead to consumers seeking the popular "tried and tested" brands they know. Heineken has two of the top five brands (Heineken and Amstel), Carlsberg has two of the top ten - Carlsberg and Tuborg, while Interbrew has one of the top ten - Stella Artois.

Table 8.8   The ten most popular beer brands in Europe in the early 1990s

Rank	Beer Brand	Rank	Beer Brand
1.	Heineken	6.	Aquila Pils
2.	Carlsberg	7.	Skol
3.	Kronenbourg	8.	Stella Artois
4.	Guinness	9.	San Miguel
5.	Amstel	10.	Tuborg

Source: Jacobs and Steel, 1997.

This will lead to product life cycles shortening, as manufacturers and retailers withdraw products that under-perform. The end result is that smaller, lesser-known brands fall by the wayside as the dominant brands avoid the clear out and compete for the ever important customer loyalty.

Until the late 1980s the only European companies that had a truly worldwide approach to globalization were Heineken and Carlsberg. Lately companies such as Bass, Guinness, and Interbrew have been actively applying their internationalization strategies. The most significant internationalization activities in the Eastern European region have been made by Interbrew (the largest investor in the region), Heineken, Bass, and South African Breweries.

The prospects of the European brewing industry are somewhat different in terms of individual country markets, but the overall trend is one of static demand. The largest markets of Germany and the UK are expected to stagnate or perhaps contract over the next five years. Markets such as the Italian one are expected to grow. Same trends are foreseen for some of the Central and Eastern European countries and the region as a whole. This is more probable in the medium to long term perspective than in the short run.

The Belgian Brewing Industry

The Belgian beer market is one of the largest in the world. There are more than 400 different beer brands. Until the late 1990s Belgian breweries concentrated on winning more market share on the home market. In the beginning of the 20th century there were more than 3,300 breweries in Belgium, in 1994 there were only 115 left. The larger breweries bought up smaller family owned ones. Despite the fact that consumption has almost halved per person, from 221 liters in 1900 to 106 liters in 1994, beer production lay around the same level in 1994 as it did in 1900.

According to the figures released by the Central Economics Board in Belgium the brewing sector realized a turnover of more than BEF 69 billion in 1994. This has brought the sector to the fifth place in the food and drinks industry with a share of 8.5 per cent. Major export markets for Belgian beer in 1994 were: France - with 2.3 million hectoliters, the Netherlands - 0.9 million hectoliters, Germany - 0.25 million hectoliters, Italy - 0.2 million hectoliters, Japan - 0.25 million hectoliters, United Kingdom - 0.18 million hectoliters and Russia - with 0.12 million hectoliters.

Consumer preferences for a certain type or brand of beer usually tie in with regional traditions or market protectionism.

The Beer Market in Eastern Europe

There have been positive economic indicators in Eastern Europe lately. Its combined gross domestic product (GDP) reached US$1.1 trillion in 1997. Detailed information of how it changed by country during 1993-1997 is presented in Table 8.9. The regional GDP grew almost three times faster than the average regional consumer income and the consumer expenditure in the period 1993-1997. The citizens of the Czech Republic have benefited from the highest average income in the region, closely followed by the Hungarians. Low average personal income has been recorded in Albania, Bulgaria, Romania, Ukraine, and Russia.

All Eastern European country markets have had positive market growth during 1993-1997 except for the Bulgarian, Hungarian, and Romanian. While the severe market decline in Bulgaria was due to economic and financial crisis, the Hungarian market suffered mostly from over-maturity and high taxation.

Table 8.9   Changes in GDP in per cent in East European countries

Country	1993	1994	1995	1996	1997	1989=100% 1997=?%
Bulgaria	- 1.5	+ 1.8	+ 2.1	- 11.9	- 7.5	62
Croatia	- 0.9	+ 0.6	+ 1.7	+ 4.2	+ 5.0	72
Czech Republic	+ 0.6	+ 2.7	+ 5.9	+ 4.1	+ 1.3	99
Hungary	- 0.6	+ 2.9	+ 1.5	+ 1.3	+ 4.2	96
Poland	+ 3.8	+ 5.2	+ 7.9	+ 6.1	+ 6.9	112
Romania	+ 1.5	+ 3.9	+ 7.1	+ 5.1	- 6.6	84
Russia	- 8.7	-12.7	- 4.1	- 4.9	+ 0.4	59
Slovakia	- 3.7	+ 4.9	+ 6.9	+ 6.9	+ 6.0	98
Slovenia	+ 2.8	+ 5.3	+ 4.1	+ 3.1	+ 3.5	99
Ukraine	- 14.2	-23.0	- 11.8	- 10.0	- 3.2	38

Source: Bank of Austria Economics Department.

Values of sales in the beer market have risen from US$5.5 billion in 1993 to US$7.8 billion in 1997. The increase of 42 per cent in value of sales corresponds to less than 10 per cent increase in volume of sales that reached 160 million hectoliters in 1997 for the whole of Eastern Europe with per capita annual consumption of approximately 30 liters. Beer has been always viewed as a traditional drink in the Czech Republic, Slovakia and Hungary. For additional information on beer consumption patterns in Eastern Europe see Table 8.10.

For many years the Czech beer drinkers have consumed more per capita than any other country in the world. This along with the low price has driven the high consumption rate even higher in the past years. The price point of beer has been a major factor in the whole Eastern European market. In the majority of on-trade establishments across the region, mineral water has been the only beverage cheaper than beer. This has made beer a popular drink for the mass market, affordable to almost all levels of the population. With the increase of the purchasing power the consumers are beginning to trade up to more expensive premium quality branded products. As a result of this, per capita beer consumption shows slower increase. Another reason for this fact can partly be attributed to beer consumers seeking alternative alcoholic drinks.

Table 8.10 Eastern Europe: per capita beer consumption in liters (1993-1997)

Country	1993	1994	1995	1996	1997	Change 1993 - 1997
Czech Republic	151	150	153	157	160	+ 1.8%
Hungary	75	79	74	73	72	- 1.1%
Poland	33	35	38	43	46	+ 8.9%
Romania	41	41	41	42	43	+ 0.9%
Russia	12	12	14	15	18	+ 12.6%
Slovakia	91	91	92	92	94	+ 0.7%
Average	29	30	32	34	36	+ 5.8%

Source: Datamonitor, Drinks Database.

As the trade barriers have been disappearing and competition constantly increasing, the beer market in Eastern Europe is changing. It is one of the most prominent examples for prosperity, particularly in the Czech Republic. Such progress has brought about many transformations in the regional domestic markets and will continue to do so in the future. National beer brands have been the most popular for many years, but are now facing increasing competition from imported beers and from the changing market dynamics.

The large domestic companies have been consolidating their positions, however many smaller local breweries will suffer in the near future. In the past, brewers were assigned geographical regions in their countries and were guaranteed an absolute monopoly on production and distribution. Competition was a foreign concept in the market. Regional brewers now have no protectionism from other domestic and international competitors. In order to survive, they have either to develop a niche for their beers or seek partnerships with leading foreign companies. The overcapacity in the beer market of Eastern Europe will continue to lead to greater market concentration.

Table 8.11 Beer consumption in some Eastern European countries

Country	Per capita consumption in 1996 in liters	Total in 1996 in million liters	Expected total in 2002 in million liters	Expected increase in total consumption in per cent
Bulgaria	26	229	245	6.7
Czech R.	157	1,754	1,950	11.2
Hungary	73	874	982	12.5
Poland	43	1,764	2,194	24.4
Romania	42	951	995	4.9
Russia	15	2,240	2,784	23.9
Slovakia	92	500	541	8.2

Source: Datamonitor.

The major features of the Eastern European beer market and the prospects for its development have encouraged foreign brewers to tap into the regional market in a bid to gain a significant share of it. Competition among local breweries has been intensifying with the removal of state subsidies and the advancing privatization processes. Foreign brewers have already found success through various agreements with local producers. These partnerships have mostly proved to be beneficial to both parties involved in them. To satisfy the increasing demand for high-quality beer in Eastern Europe, in 1996 the European Bank for Reconstruction and Development provided ECU 52 million loans to two breweries in Croatia and Romania, helping them to expand their production of internationally recognized brands.

Measured by volume potentials and growth rate expectations, Russia and Poland are the most promising beer markets in Eastern Europe. The beer consumption in 1996 and expected increase in volume for year 2002 is presented in Table 8.11.

Major Foreign Investors in the Eastern European Brewing Industry

Czech Republic

Brewing has been a part of the Czech national identity since the Middle Ages. The country has a long lasting reputation for producing and consuming high quality beer. Currently, the Czech Republic has the highest per capita annual beer consumption rate in the world. International sales of Czech beer brands have been constantly growing since 1993.

Bass Breweries PLC (UK) was the first foreign brewer to enter the Czech beer market in 1993 through buying 34 per cent stake in Prazske Pivovary boosting its share to 55 per cent in 1996. Through merging their three Czech brewing interests into one company in 1997 presently Bass Breweries have almost 16 per cent of the Czech beer market and hope to have one third of it in five years. Bass operations in the Czech Republic have become profitable since 1995. The company believes that the key to greater success lies in export.

In 1996 the Austrian brewer *Brau AG* signed an agreement for strategic alliance with Lobkowickzky Pivovar. They are now producing Austrian beer brand Kaiser and testing both the domestic and export markets for their reactions.

Russia

The Russian beer market is currently very attractive to producers and investors because of its enormous growth potential. Most of Russian beer is low quality, low price with a very short self-life. There are over 600 breweries in Russia with an annual capacity of 22 million hectoliters. Currently the Russian breweries cannot meet the increased domestic demand and are unable to compete with foreign beer producers because of low capacity and outdated equipment.

In 1995 and 1996 India's *Sun Breweries Limited* established joint ventures with 17 breweries in Russia and invested US$ 11.7 million in the improvement of beer quality and taste. The Indian company has majority shares in six Russian breweries. Currently the Sun Breweries Ltd has 5.3 per cent of the Russian beer market and is the largest brewer in the country.

Other Eastern European Countries

South African Breweries investment in Eastern Europe has been made through its branch SAB International Europe BV. Information about the Eastern European companies where South African Breweries have shares is presented in Table 8.12.

Table 8.12   South African Breweries interests in Eastern Europe

Country	Company	Year of Investment	Share in January 1998
Hungary	Kobanya Sörgyâr RT	1992	97%
Poland	Lech Browary Wielkopolski SA	1996	48%
Poland	Browary Tyskie Górny Slask SA	1996	45%
Romania	SC Vulturul SA	1996	99%
Romania	SC Ursus SA	1996	91%
Slovakia	Pivovar Saris AS	1997	98%

Source: South African Breweries Annual Report 1997.

Heineken N. V. Brewery (The Netherlands) has shown some interest in Eastern European beer market. Approximately nine per cent of Heineken's investment abroad is made in Eastern Europe. The countries in which the company has shares in breweries in the region are: Bulgaria, Hungary, Poland, and Slovakia. More detailed information about the Eastern

European companies where Heineken made its investments are given in Table 8.13.

Table 8.13 Heineken's investments in Eastern European breweries

Country	Company	Year of Investment	Share in March 1998
Bulgaria	Ariana	1997	60.2%
Bulgaria	Zagorka	1995	43.2%
Hungary	Komáromi Amstel Sörgyâr	1992	100.0%
Poland	Zywiec	1993	50.0%
Slovakia	Zlaty Bazant	1994	37.5%
Slovakia	Pvovar Karsay Spol.	1997	49.0%

Source: Heineken Annual Report 1997.

Interbrew: Internationalization in Eastern Europe

The Experience in Hungary and Bulgaria

Only three countries from the former Soviet Bloc have been members of the European Brewing Union - Bulgaria, former Czechoslovakia and Hungary. While retail consumption of beer per capita is dominated by the Czech Republic, Hungary leads the per capita consumption of wine in Eastern Europe. Therefore, wine appears to be a major substitute threat for beer consumption in the Hungarian alcoholic drinks market. In Bulgaria there is an old tradition for the consumption of wine in winter, while in summer consumption of beer is dominant. Currently in both Hungary and Bulgaria, as in the whole Eastern European region, the brewing industry is considered to have challenging growth opportunities. In the Hungarian and Bulgarian beer markets these opportunities are not related to quantity, but to quality, where there is significant potential for improvement.

Hungary   The Hungarian beer market is mature with high taxation. It has a relatively high average consumption amounting to ten million hectoliters in 1991. In the transition period it has suffered from the reducing purchasing power of the Hungarian population. Beer production in Hungary has been highly concentrated - with only seven regional breweries; two of them (Kobanya - market leader and Borsodi - market challenger) have had more than 60 per cent of the Hungarian beer market.

Interbrew was among the first movers into the Hungarian brewing sector, parallel with the acquisition made by the German brewer Brau und Brunnen AG. With the acquisition of a majority stake in the Borsodi brewery in 1991, Interbrew investment ranks second in scale on the Hungarian brewing market after the investment made by South African Breweries that acquired Kobanya in 1992. The investment in Hungary was regarded as a test and model case for the future potential investment of the company in Eastern Europe.

Bulgaria   From 1989 until the end of 1993 there was a constant decrease in beer consumption as the purchasing power of the average consumer drastically diminished. The consumption of beer reached its minimum in 1993 when the whole Bulgarian brewing industry produced less than 50 per cent of its capacity. In 1994 and 1995 the beer market was in constant recovery. In 1996 a second decline in beer consumption, related to worsening macroeconomic conditions, started to develop. In 1997 per capita beer consumption in Bulgaria was 27 liters.

The Bulgarian brewing industry has long established traditions and internationally recognized trade marks. Thirteen brewing companies spread over the country have a total annual capacity of 5.5 million hectoliters. About 10 per cent of the beer production, mostly special and de luxe stabilized beer, has been exported. Before the foreign investment acquisitions, Zagorka brewery was the market leader followed by Astika and Kamenitza breweries.

Interbrew made the first investment move by buying majority stakes in two Bulgarian breweries in the first half of 1995 - Kamenitza and Bourgasko Pivo (a small brewery of regional importance). Heineken (The Netherlands) and Coca Cola (US) jointly bought Zagorka in November 1995. In early 1995 the market challenger, Astika brewery, signed an agreement with Interbrew for the transfer of management and technological know-how and Interbrew created a joint venture with the company in 1996.

The Acquisition in Hungary

Hungary was chosen by Interbrew as a country in Eastern Europe with least risk associated characteristics and most promising market potential. Major reasons for this decision were: good market features and perspectives, supportive legislation, stable social climate, opportunities for company reorganization and restructuring, many foreign investors were already in Hungary (e.g., Digital, Opel, Sara Lee, Unilever, etc.), the target company was in good condition. The success of Hungary in attracting foreign investment was a result of the "gradualist" approach to implementing economic and institutional reforms in the country. Hungary had foreign investment legislation in 1991 much better developed than in any of the other Eastern European countries. The drawbacks of the macroeconomic characteristics were: high inflation and negative economic growth in the years before the acquisition. There were some obstacles to foreign investors in Hungary: underdeveloped infrastructure, bureaucratic privatization procedures, lack of experience in dealing with foreign investors, lack of business support structures, companies with high debt rates and inefficient operations.

The Borsodi brewery was selected for acquisition because: it was relatively new - established in 1974; it had a creative and dynamic management; it made profits; it produced a broad range of brands, including the high quality Világos beer (positioned at the lower end of the range), and brewed under license the German premium beer Spaten.

Investments in Bulgaria

The investments in Bulgaria were considered by Interbrew to be very important. The investor acquired two breweries and made a joint venture with a third covering all segments of the Bulgarian beer market. The host companies lacked finance and marketing experience but had always been famous for the professionalism and motivation of their work force.

The then Bulgarian socialist government was trying indirectly to regulate the brewing industry. It had difficulties in creating a market supportive legal system and in improving the overall economic situation, essential for long term investment success. The obstacles for foreign investors in Hungary were to be faced by Interbrew in Bulgaria as well, but in the context of worse political, economic, and social instability and volatility.

In January 1995 Interbrew acquired the oldest brewery in Bulgaria - Kamenitza, in April 1995 - the regional brewery Burgasko Pivo. In February 1996 Interbrew created a joint venture with Astika. In July 1997 Interbrew decided to merge the three companies into one.

Interbrew Investment Strategy and its Implementation

Hungary

The main investment motive of Interbrew in Hungary was to gain access to the local market. Its goal was long term positioning in the Hungarian market. All activities at the acquired brewery were designed by the investor and based on its corporate plan. The objectives were that:

- The Borsodi Világos brand became national.
- The Belgian brand Stella Artois was to be brewed by the Hungarian subsidiary.
- A wide spread national distribution network was to be developed in the first two years post-acquisition.
- Soft drinks were to be used as a cash cow to partly finance the restructuring of the beer production.
- Some changes in the product and packaging were to be implemented.
- The marketing function, which did not previously exist, was to be launched, and a separate marketing department created.
- The sales department, unaware of how to function in a market economy, was to be restructured.
- Strong promotion and forward integration had to be implemented.

Interbrew introduced management, technical, technological, marketing and personnel changes in the Borsodi brewery making it more effective, efficient and profitable. The Belgian headquarters provided assistance, mostly in the introduction of the marketing function, setting up of a marketing department, and the improvement of the managerial approach and teamwork. However, the constant trend of diminishing national beer consumption in Hungary (more than a 25 per cent decrease in 1996 versus 1991), contrary to the anticipation of an increase, negatively influenced the investment plans of Interbrew.

The investor did not bring to Hungary its own brands. Borsodi failed to introduce premium beers and only the existing local brands were used and developed. Although operating under the same market conditions, all other breweries with foreign investment introduced premium beers, both imported and local brands, gaining tight hold of the Hungarian market. Interbrew did not realize in time that it had to be quick and flexible considering the swift changes in the overall business environment in Hungary - massive foreign investment in brewing, intensified competition, radical technological/product/brand changes introduced by other foreign players. Strategic flexibility for adaptation to the changing environment was needed, but as it was mostly reactive, defensive and slow, Interbrew lagged behind the competition.

Latest developments in 1998 and 1999 in Interbrew business strategy for Hungary clearly reveal a process of strategy evaluation and adaptation in the specific country context based on the experience gains from the investments made in the other Eastern European countries, in particular the Bulgarian. The company has decided to move into direct competition in the upper market segments through introducing production of high quality de luxe investor brands, including Interbrew's top brand Stella Artois, in their Hungarian subsidiary. Interbrew is presently trying to shift from a reactive and defensive approach towards its major foreign competitors to a proactive and offensive strategy for competitive positioning in the high quality segments of the Hungarian beer market.

The overall evaluation shows that the strategy designed by the investor for its Hungarian subsidiary was implemented only partially. Adapting its strategy reactively rather than proactively, Interbrew was forced to change its goal from long term positioning in different market segments towards profit maximization in a single mass market segment. The company put a priority on the short term return on investment by aiming at high volume sales with low margins. The investor was too slow and inflexible in reacting to the market developments that had not been anticipated at the time of strategy development.

Bulgaria

Interbrew's major motive for investing in Bulgaria was gaining access to the local and export markets through acquisition of existing assets. The goal was to establish itself in all segments of the domestic beer market with a long term intention which had to be achieved through a series of acquisitions. The objectives were:

- To have strong national brands.
- To have good Bulgarian brands for export.
- To have geographically spread regional brands.
- A national distribution network to be developed using the distribution networks of the acquired companies.
- Changes in the existing products and packaging were to be made.
- The marketing function, not existent previously, was to be launched and separate marketing departments created.
- Strong promotion, adapted to the Bulgarian market context, was to be launched.

To achieve these objectives, Interbrew decided to buy well established breweries producing brands for different market segments. Through the acquisition of three companies, the investor became market leader in Bulgaria. It guaranteed its leadership position with total market share of about 27 per cent. While the first two privatization deals allowed the investor to tap into the local market mostly of ordinary, original and special beer, the acquisition of the third brewery - Astika, positioned Interbrew in the deluxe beer segment. That last acquisition provided opportunities for increasing the export of beer to adjacent and other export markets which could secure more stability for the investment in the volatile Bulgarian economy. Interbrew set up the objective of Kamenitza brand becoming national. An integrated national distribution network started to develop using the experience and existing networks of Astika and Kamenitza breweries. The products and their image were improved and new forms of packaging were introduced. The marketing strategy was developed with the assistance of the local management and closely tied to the strategy of the investor. Marketing departments were set up and the marketing function was introduced in the three acquired companies. The planning and strategic management of all marketing actions - product enhancement, promotional campaigns, beer festivals, flexible pricing policy, was done with the active direct involvement, close direction and supervision of the expatriate marketing managers. The investor started also to improve the technological and management level of its Bulgarian subsidiaries.

The strategy designed for Bulgaria was gradually implemented with certain tactical adaptations. Faced with problems created by the Bulgarian government which was attempting to regulate the structure of the brewing industry, Interbrew found itself unable initially to acquire the brewery Astika. However, it managed to buy a minor stake in it and to sign a contract for transfer of management and technological know-how. In the meantime, it established strong presence in Bulgaria through the acquisitions of Kamenitza and Burgasko Pivo. Adopting a proactive approach to the strategic opportunities Interbrew guaranteed its presence and signaled strong commitment to becoming a major player in the Bulgarian brewing industry. Being the first mover and using the lessons from Hungary, the investor managed quickly to move, adapt and establish itself in Bulgaria. When Interbrew sensed the chance to acquire Astika, it stepped in using its company and country specific knowledge and experience gained by that time. Strategic vision, speed, strong desire for success, local networking, and experience gained from Hungary were considered of crucial importance. The strategies for the Bulgarian subsidiaries were designed by the investor with input from the management of the three acquired companies. Strategy implementation was done by the Bulgarian managers backed and assisted by expatriates. Short term trade-offs and options for strategy adaptation were analyzed and envisaged by the Belgian HQ from the very start of the investment moves. In spite of the deteriorating macroenvironmental conditions in Bulgaria in 1996 and 1997, Interbrew adopted a long term perspective for achieving its strategic goal and objectives, and for satisfying its investment motives.

Interbrew's Strategic Positioning in Hungary and Bulgaria

Hungary

Despite being an early mover in the Hungarian brewing market, Interbrew lost momentum in competition with other strong foreign competitors, such as Heineken (The Netherlands), South African Breweries (South Africa), Brau Union (Austria).

In the beginning of 1992 six of the seven Hungarian breweries were owned by foreign investors with excellent financial and management capabilities. By that time the market structure was largely established. South African Breweries became market leader, followed by Interbrew.

The competition in the Hungarian beer market proved to be much stronger than initially anticipated by Interbrew. The company did not grasp the opportunities for proactive strategy evaluation and adaptation to the rapidly changing environment. Gradually positioning the acquired company in the low end of the market, in profit terms the Borsodi investment results were positive.

Bulgaria

The Bulgarian brewing market was regionally divided before 1989. By early-1996 four of the thirteen brewing companies in Bulgaria were privatized with foreign investment. Owning three breweries Interbrew became market leader with 27 per cent share of the Bulgarian beer market. The former market leader, Zagorka brewery, enjoying 21 per cent of the market share, was bought by Coca Cola (USA) and Heineken (The Netherlands). The remaining nine companies, sharing 52 per cent of the market, were owned by the state which allowed some degree of government control over the market structure and pricing in the industry. The situation changed when in 1997 Heineken bought a majority stake in Ariana brewery. Thus the two foreign brewers - Interbrew and Heineken controlled approximately the same shares of the beer market in the country. Consequently, Bulgarian brewing industry became dominant by a foreign duopoly.

Interbrew - Strategic Challenges

The investments of Interbrew in Hungary and Bulgaria neither followed the sequencing approach of internationalization nor were there consequences of incremental adjustment to changing conditions. While in the case of Hungary before the investment, there had been some import of Interbrew beer meeting the requirements of the high end of the market, in Bulgaria the investor lacked any experience in the local market. Yet, it saw an open strategic window and grasped the challenge. Despite some pre-acquisition knowledge and experience in Hungary, no prior production and first hand market experience was in place to help Interbrew build a successful strategy for the Hungarian growing premium beer market segment.

The strategy for Hungary underwent considerable change as the investor could not realize the significance of the rapidly changing characteristics of the Hungarian brewing market. The main goal of Interbrew gradually became profit maximization through selling cheap lower end of the market beer in large quantities. Thus, the Hungarian subsidiary of Interbrew found itself serving a constantly declining market segment. This strategic approach resembles "cherry picking". In creating, implementing and developing its strategy for the Hungarian beer market, Interbrew failed to foresee the trends and the dynamics in the changes of the society, the consumer needs and wants, as well as the more appropriate and aggressive strategies of its foreign competitors. Although Borsodi was left with second market share its position did not seem guaranteed.

Interbrew invested in Bulgaria with a similar motive to the one in Hungary. However, spreading investment risk and seriously considering export opportunities, it gained access to all market segments of the Bulgarian beer market and to the export of premium beer. Through buying companies with distribution networks and bottling facilities the main focus of post-acquisition investment became quality improvement and promotional activities. Thus, the investor strategy in Bulgaria can be evaluated as gaining market share through attacking various market segments and developing new segments with long term intention of dominating the Bulgarian beer market, and constantly increase export to adjacent markets. To date this strategic approach has proved to be successful and profitable, although its scale was negatively influenced by the unstable economic and political conditions in the host country.

In both countries the investor adopted product strategy of preserving and developing well established local brands which reflected the spurring nationalist characteristics of Eastern European consumers. While in

Hungary the emphasis was on cash cow brands, in Bulgaria a widespread product portfolio was designed and implemented.

Interbrew had similar investment characteristics in Hungary and Bulgaria. Although the first mover in those markets it did not buy the host company market leader leaving this opportunity to its major competitors. Instead, the investor followed its tradition in foreign acquisitions buying the host country market challenger and in some cases other smaller companies trying to turn the market challenger into market leader post-acquisition.

The strategy development, implementation and adaptation in Bulgaria greatly benefited from the experience gained by the company in Hungary. In Bulgaria Interbrew adopted a process of continuous improvement through implementing a proactive strategy evaluation and adaptation based on previous knowledge and created intelligence.

Name Index

Aaker, D. 5
Aharoni, Y. 183
Alton, G. 133
Andersen, O. 3
Assonitis, G. 105
Auerbach, P. 2

Baalbaki, I. 115
Baker, M. 171
Bandini, A. 113
Bartlett, C. 2, 113, 187, 188, 190
Bauer, A. 171
Beamish, P. 2
Bebler, A. 20
Bederly, J. 44
Bergsman, J. 152
Bilkey, W. 2, 115
Biltoft, K. 156
Birkinshaw, J. 187, 190
Borner, S. 113
Bridgewater, S. 184
Brinar, I. 44
Buckley, P. 2, 3, 73, 74, 186
Bucklin, L. 115
Buzzell, R. 113

Cantwell, J. 48
Carman, J. 115, 171
Carstairs, R. 189
Casson, M. 2, 3
Castro, B. 74
Cateora, P. 4, 113
Cavusgil, S. 3, 115
Chao, P. 115
Chojna, J. 91, 92, 96, 97
Claros, C. 147

Coase, R. 2
Cohen, W. 183
Compagno, C. 114
Cungu, A. 107
Czinkota, M. 3, 113

Daniels, J. 5
Dawson, G. 173
Day, G. 5
De Luca, P. 127
Dimovski, V. 27
Domanski, R. 173
Douglas, S. 115
Doz, Y. 186
Dunning, J. 3, 4, 48, 49, 53, 54, 63, 65, 69
Durka, B. 87, 97

Eiteman, D. 159
El-Ansary, A. 115
Engwal, L. 186
Ettenson, R. 115
Eveno, R. 175

Fayerweather, J. 4
Ferdows, K. 187, 190
Filser, M. 115
Fink-Hafner, D. 44
Forsgren, M. 185, 187

Gaeth, G. 115
Ghoshal, S. 113, 187, 189
Giuriato, L. 113
Globerman, S. 115
Gorynia, M. 77, 79, 80
Graham, J. 4

Green, D. 5

Hamel, G. 2
Hazley, C. 147
Healey, J. 171
Heath, P. 188
Hedlund, G. 2, 183, 184, 185,
    186, 187, 189, 200, 201
Henley, J. 173
Heslop, L. 115
Hibbert, E. 115
Hill, C. W. L. 6
Hirvensalo, I. 147
Holm, U. 187
Hout, T. 79
Hubner, D. 101
Hunya, G. 136
Hymer, S. 4

Ikeda, T. 44

Jackson, S. 87
Jain, S. 115
Jarillo, J. 187
Johanson, J. 2, 3, 58, 169, 183,
    184, 185, 188, 189
Johansson, J. 115
Jones, J. 115
Joynt, P. 2
Juul, M. 186

Kaczurba, 79
Kawecka-Wyrzykowska, E. 79
Keegan, W. 113
Kim, J.-D. 69
Kindleberger, E. 2
Kobler, M. 133
Kogut, B. 3, 183
Kornai, J. 28
Koyama, Y. 44
Kraft, E. 44
Kraft, V. 160

Krašovec, T. 55
Kreutzer, R. 115
Kubielas, 87
Kumar, A. 31
Kverneland, A. 2, 183, 184, 185,
    186, 189, 200

Larimo, J. 147, 148
Laurila, J. 147
Lebar, S. 50
Levinthal, D. 183
Levitt, T., 79
Linnamo, J. 155
Liuhto, K. 151
Lovelock, C. 6
Loveman, G. 169
Luostarinen, R. 2, 3, 47, 49, 73,
    74, 183, 185, 186, 188, 189,
    200

Mäenpää, M. 158
Malhotra, N. 115
Malnight, T. 187, 190
Maranik, U. 139
Marin, D. 4
Martin, P. 170
Martínez, J. 187
Massa, S. 113
Mattsson, L.-G. 3, 185
Meerits, H. 160
Meigas, H. 161
Melin, L. 2
Mencinger, J. 27, 28, 29, 30, 32,
    34, 43, 44
Monkowski, S. 87
Morone, F. 113, 118

Naidu, G. 115
Nakamura, Y. 44
Nanut, V. 114
Narula, R. 69
Nes, E. 115

Newbould, G. 186
Nobel, R. 187
Nonaka, I. 115
Nordström, K. 3, 183, 185, 186,
    187, 188, 189, 200
Nowicki, M. 87

Ohmae, K. 1, 16
Olesiński, Z. 91, 92, 93, 95
Olleros, F. 5
Onkvisit, S. 115
Otta, W. 77, 79, 80
Ozawa, T. 48, 49, 53, 54, 64

Pac-Pomarnacki, R. 90, 91, 92,
    93, 95
Papadopoulos, N. 115
Patterson, W. 5
Pauli, R. 157
Peev, E. 113
Pellegrini, M. 115
Peng, M. 188
Penrose, E. 2
Perczyński, M. 84, 85
Pettersson, F. 156
Piotrowski, J. 85
Płowiec, U. 79, 85, 102
Porter, M. 79
Prahalad, C. 2, 186
Preble, J. 115
Prunk, J. 44

Rajendran, K, 115
Rau, P. 115
Reddy, S. 115
Rein, M. 113
Robbins, J. 44
Rojec, M. 50, 73
Ronkainen, I. 113
Root, F. 115
Rudden, E. 79
Ryans, S. 5

Samonis, V. 89
Sarathy, R. 115
Sassen, S. 1
Schnaars, S. 5
Schooler, R. 115
Segrè, A. 113
Senjur, M. 44
Shama, A. 1188
Sharma, S. 113
Shaw, J. 115
Shen, X. 152
Simoes, V. 73, 74
Sorsa, K. 135
Stern, L. 115
Svetličič, M. 21, 22, 23, 24, 25,
    26, 27, 44, 50, 52, 73
Svetlik, I. 29
Swinnen, J. 107
Szawlowska, H. 170

Taeho, K. 156
Tamowicz, P. 170
Tarrant, J. 113
Terpstra, V. 115
Tesar, G. 2
Thomsen, J. 156
Thuesen, J. 156
Thurwell, J. 186
Tolentino, P. 70
Torbacke, S. 186, 187, 189
Turban, J. 169
Turnbull, P. 2, 183, 185, 186,
    189, 200

Vahlne, J.-E. 2, 3, 58, 183, 185,
    186, 187, 188, 189, 201
Vainio, V. 158
Vanamo, I. 155
Varblane, U. 138
Vernon, R. 3
Vianelli, D. 115
Vitsur, E. 150

Wagner, J. 115
Walters, P. 186, 189
Wang, Z. 82
Welch, L. 2, 3, 47, 49, 185, 186, 188, 189, 200
Wernerfelt, B. 183
Werwicki, A. 169
Wiedersheim-Paul, F. 183, 184, 188, 189
Wildt, A. 115

Williamson, O. 2
Winiker, C. 133
Winters, L. 82
Włodarczyk, W. 98

Yip, G. 6

Ziacik, T. 148
Zirnask, V. 160
Zou, S. 115

Subject Index

ABB, 94
Abbey beers, 205, 206
Acquis Communautaire, 21, 44
acquisition, 8, 13, 58, 153, 158,
    164, 173, 177, 191, 195, 196,
    205, 208, 211, 225, 226, 227,
    228, 229, 231, 232
acquisition of securities, 36
activities, 1, 2, 4, 5, 6, 7, 8, 13,
    14
adaptation, 115
Africa, 204
Agency for Privatization, 33
Ahold, 173, 175, 176, 177
Albania, 7, 14, 105, 106, 107,
    108, 110, 112, 113, 114, 115,
    116, 118, 119, 120, 121, 122,
    123, 124, 125, 126, 127, 129,
    130, 219
Albanian economy, 126, 127
Albanian market, 114, 118, 119,
    121, 122, 124, 127
Alexander Keith, 208
Amstel, 217, 224
Anheuser-Busch, 204, 212, 213,
    214
approach to globalization, 217
Ariana, 224, 230
Artois, 205, 206, 210, 211, 217,
    227, 228
Asia, 6, 107, 204, 206
Association of Italian Investors in
    Albania, 116
Astika, 208, 209, 210, 225, 226,
    229
Auchan, 173, 175

Australia, 212, 213
Austria, 11, 19, 20, 30, 51, 60,
    74, 112, 159
Azerbaijan, 197

Bahamas, 157
Bahrain, 157
balance deficit, 87
balance of payments, 81, 99, 134,
    156, 157
Balkan Peninsula, 19, 105
Baltic American Bank, 161
Baltic countries, 7, 9, 133, 135,
    163, 164
Baltic Sea, 133, 149, 167
Baltic states, 133, 147, 149, 163,
    197
Bank of Estonia, 161
Bank of Slovenia, 49
Bank Rehabilitation Agency
    (BRA), 39
banking markets, 158
banking regulations, 157, 161
banking systems, 156, 158
bankruptcy, 33, 35, 38
Bansko Pivo, 208
Bass, 216, 217, 222
beer markets, 204, 206, 222, 224
Belarus, 162, 197
Belgium, 112, 158, 159, 205,
    206, 208, 210, 212, 213, 215,
    216, 218
Belle-Vue, 205, 206, 210
Bergenbier, 208, 209, 210
Berlin Wall, 8
Bhs, 173

Billa, 173
Blue Light, 210
Blue Sword, 209
BMW, 30
born global, 55
born multinational, 55
Borsodi, 208, 209, 210, 224, 225,
    226, 227, 230, 231
Borsodi Kinizsi, 208
Borsodi Világos, 208, 210, 227
Bosnia and Herzegovina, 22, 51,
    53, 56, 60, 61
BP-Amoco, 176
Brahma, 204, 212, 213
brand image, 216
brand loyalty, 216
brand proliferation, 217
Brau AG, 222
Brau und Brunnen, 216, 225
Brazil, 204, 211, 212, 213
brewing industry, 205, 206, 208,
    211, 217, 224, 225, 226, 229,
    230
Browary Tyskie Górny Slask SA,
    223
Budweiser, 210
Bulgaria, 7, 9, 10, 12, 108, 112,
    129, 138, 208, 209, 210, 219,
    221, 223, 224, 225, 226, 228,
    229, 230, 231, 232
Burgasko Pivo, 208, 209, 210,
    226, 229
business environment, 146
business ventures, 139

Canada, 148, 206, 208, 209, 210
capital inflows, 135
Carli Gry, 173
Carlsberg, 212, 213, 216, 217
Carrefour, 173, 174, 175, 176,
    177

Casino, 173, 174, 175, 176, 177,
    178
Cayman Islands, 157
Central and Eastern Europe
    (CEE), 6, 7, 8, 9, 10, 12, 13,
    14, 20, 36, 107, 113, 124, 135,
    146, 147, 149, 171, 184, 186,
    188, 189, 196, 198, 200, 201
Central and Eastern European
    countries (CEECs), 47, 48, 54,
    60, 73, 218
Central Europe, 136
Central European Free Trade
    Agreement (CEFTA), 9, 11,
    21, 31, 80, 84
Central European economies, 7
central regulation, 78
centrally planned economies, 31
Chernigiv, 208, 210
China, 151, 206, 208, 209, 211,
    212
Cisneros, 209
Coca Cola, 7, 94, 206
Cold War, 20, 157
command economies, 78
commitment, 183, 184, 185, 186,
    188, 189, 194, 198, 199, 200,
    205, 229
commercial privatization, 32
Common Agricultural Policy, 41
Commonwealth of Independent
    States (CIS), 147, 152, 154
competition, 5, 16, 47, 48, 62, 64,
    66, 69, 72, 77, 78, 79, 101,
    102, 103 135, 156, 158, 160,
    164, 170, 171, 174, 176, 178,
    179, 204, 211, 220, 227, 230
competitive advantage, 24, 78, 79
competitive positioning, 228
competitiveness, 22, 23, 27, 48,
    53, 58, 65, 70, 72

consolidation, 173, 174, 204, 206, 211, 215
consortia, 5
consumer expenditure, 216, 218
consumer products, 6
convenience stores, 174
cooperative agreements, 198, 199, 200
Coors, 204, 213
core competences, 2
Council for Mutual Economic Assistance (CMEA), 8, 9, 76, 77, 78, 85, 104
country-of-origin effect, 115
Courage, 216
Croatia, 10, 19, 31, 51, 53, 56, 60, 155, 208, 209, 210, 219, 222
cumulative stock of FDI, 139
customer loyalty, 217
customs tariffs, 77
Czech Republic, 7, 9, 10, 11, 12, 13, 14, 21, 23, 42, 45, 53, 60, 90, 136, 137, 138, 146, 155, 162, 190, 197, 213, 218, 219, 220, 221, 222, 224

D T Centrum, 171
Daewoo, 94
Danone, 212, 216
decentralized operations, 205
decentralized self-managed socialism, 19, 21
demand conditions, 24
Denmark, 143, 151, 212, 213, 216
Desna, 209
Deutsche Lettische Bank, 164
devaluation, 80, 81
diffusion of foreign investments, 99
Digital, 225

direct exporting, 3, 4, 5, 13
discount stores, 174, 177
distribution, 6, 170, 171, 176, 177
distribution channels, 6
distribution network, 227, 228, 229
divestment, 52
Docks de France, 173
Dohle, 173, 175
domestic banking, 156, 157, 159
domestic brewers, 211
domestic investment, 48
Dominican Republic, 208, 209
Dommelsch, 208, 210
Doosan Group, 208, 209
duopoly, 230
Dutch firms, 183, 184, 190, 191, 193, 198, 200

early mover advantage, 5
Eastern Europe, 204, 208, 218, 219, 220, 221, 222, 223, 224, 225
eclectic paradigm, 3, 69
internalization, 2, 3
location, 3, 5
ownership, 3, 6, 8
economic crisis, 38, 44, 152, 155, 160
economic development strategy, 22
economic deregulation, 6
economic growth, 22, 26, 31, 76, 98, 99, 100, 135, 147, 152, 226
economic integration, 1
economic liberalism, 20
economic performance, 5, 27, 31
economic recession, 152
economic reforms, 28
economic relationships, 9
economic restructuring, 6, 8

Edeka, 176
Eesti Innovatsioonipank
  (Estonian Innovation Bank),
  161
Eesti Krediidipank, 163
Eesti Ühispank (Union Bank of
  Estonia), 161
entrepreneurship, 23
environmental factors, 5
equity capital, 34
equity stakes, 208
establishment chain, 183, 184,
  186, 188, 189, 200
Estonia, 7, 10, 12, 13, 14, 37,
  133, 134, 135, 136, 137, 138,
  139, 140, 141, 142, 143, 144,
  145, 146, 147, 148, 149, 150,
  151, 152, 153, 154, 155, 160,
  161, 162, 163, 165, 166, 167,
  168
Estonian banking sector, 135
Estonian banks, 160, 161, 163,
  165, 166, 167
Estonian economy, 150, 152, 166
Estonian Institute of Economic
  Research (EKI), 154
Estonian Investment Agency,
  147, 167, 168
Estonian investments, 154
Estonian kroon, 151, 160
Euro, 156, 159, 168
Europe, 20, 21, 22, 28, 30, 31,
  43, 45, 46, 135, 146, 149, 156,
  162, 170, 172, 173, 205, 206,
  208, 214, 215, 216, 217, 223
European Bank for
  Reconstruction and
  Development (EBRD), 222
European Brewing Union, 224
European Economic and
  Monetary Union, 156

European Free Trade Association
  (EFTA), 21, 30, 81, 84
European integration, 22
European Union (EU), 7, 9, 11,
  20, 21, 22, 23, 29, 30, 31, 36,
  41, 43, 44, 45, 46, 54, 59, 60,
  61, 66, 72, 78, 80, 81, 84, 87,
  147, 148, 149, 158
exchange rate policy, 81
export, 19, 28, 29, 30, 31, 41, 47,
  48, 50, 58, 59, 66, 69, 70, 72,
  73, 76, 77, 79, 80, 82, 83, 84,
  85, 89, 97, 99, 102, 103, 110,
  116, 121, 124, 128, 218, 222,
  228, 229, 231
exporting, 184, 188, 193, 194,
  198, 199, 200
export penetration, 31
export performance, 4
export quota, 28

FABA bank, 164
FDI inflow, 135
FIAT, 94
financial sector, 133, 139, 143,
  156, 160
Finland, 47, 74, 135, 142, 143,
  147, 151, 158, 159, 168
first-mover advantage, 60
fiscal and monetary stabilization,
  77
foreign affiliate, 59, 61, 62
foreign currency restrictions, 157
foreign debt, 100
foreign direct investment (FDI),
  3, 6, 7, 8, 10, 12, 13, 26, 36,
  47, 48, 49, 50, 51, 52, 53, 54,
  55, 56, 58, 59, 62, 64, 65, 70,
  72, 73, 74, 75, 76, 77, 87, 89,
  90, 91, 95, 96, 97, 98, 99, 103,
  110, 113, 126, 127, 135, 136,
  137, 138, 139, 143, 146, 147,

148, 149, 152, 153, 154, 165, 166, 184
foreign investment, 6, 8, 47, 52, 66, 72, 105, 114, 139, 143, 150, 152, 153, 161, 225, 227, 230
foreign investors, 35, 36, 38, 92, 93, 94, 99, 103, 110, 126, 135, 143, 147, 148, 149, 150, 152, 157, 169, 170, 225, 226, 230
foreign market, 2, 5
foreign market penetration, 126
foreign policy, 77
foreign profit repatriation, 89
foreign subsidiaries, 187
foreign trade, 155
Foster's, 212, 213
France, 11, 112, 159, 173, 206, 207, 210, 211, 212, 215, 216, 218
franchising, 4

Geant, 174, 175, 176, 177
General Agreement on Tariffs and Trade (GATT), 79
General Motors, 7
geographic proximity, 113, 116
geographical concentration, 49, 59, 72
Germany, 9, 11, 19, 27, 30, 60, 112, 139, 151, 155, 159, 173, 211, 212, 214, 215, 216, 218
Gibraltar, 157
global brands, 211
global channels, 6
global investment strategy, 204
global strategy, 79
globalization, 23, 24, 26, 43, 47, 48, 62, 70
globalization of economic activities, 77
globalization of production, 211

globalization processes, 79
globalized economy, 24, 47, 48
Goodyear Tire & Rubber joint venture, 36
government foreign policies, 4
Greece, 87, 105, 106, 107, 110, 112
greenfield investments, 13, 65, 164
greenfield subsidiaries, 196
grocery retailing, 169, 174, 176, 178
Gross Domestic Product (GDP), 19, 27, 29, 30, 35, 37, 39, 40, 41, 42, 54, 55, 82, 83, 87, 94, 96, 98, 107, 108, 173, 218, 219
Guinness, 204, 212, 216, 217

Hachette, 171
Hansapank, 161, 163, 164
Hansapank-Latvija, 164
Heineken, 7, 204, 211, 212, 213, 214, 216, 217, 223, 224, 225, 230
Hoegaarden, 205, 206, 210
Hoiupank (Savings Bank of Estonia), 161
Holland, 212, 213, 215, 216
Holsten, 210
Hopenkönig, 210
Hopfenkönig, 208
host country, 231, 232
host country determinants, 62, 63
Hungary, 7, 9, 10, 11, 12, 13, 14, 19, 21, 23, 31, 37, 42, 45, 51, 53, 60, 74, 90, 91, 135, 136, 138, 139, 146, 155, 162, 190, 191, 192, 193, 195, 196, 197, 206, 208, 209, 210, 219, 220, 221, 223, 224, 225, 226, 227, 229, 230, 231, 232

hypermarkets, 174, 175, 176, 177, 178, 179

IBM, 7
IKEA, 173
imperfect competition, 102
import penetration, 85, 100
importing, 5
imports, 29, 30, 41, 47, 60, 66, 76, 77, 78, 80, 82, 83, 84, 85, 86, 89, 97, 98, 99, 103, 110, 116, 121, 134, 135
industrial production, 82, 83
industrial products, 7
inflation, 152, 162
inflows of foreign capital, 89
information technology, 6, 27
ING Group, 94
institutional industrial policy, 101
institutional owners, 34, 35
institutional reforms, 225
intangible knowledge, 47
Interbrew, 7, 204, 205, 206, 207, 208, 209, 210, 212, 213, 216, 217, 224, 225, 226, 227, 228, 229, 230, 231, 232
internal market, 2
internalizing, 2
international banking, 156, 159, 166
international brands, 205
international business, 1, 5, 7, 8
international business operations, 47, 56
international competitiveness, 14, 78, 100
international economic relations, 77, 79
international expansion, 183, 205, 208
international integration, 24

international investments, 208, 209
international involvement, 2, 3
international joint ventures, 5, 119, 208
international operations, 51, 58, 184, 189
international production theory, 4
international relations, 24, 25, 26
international retail firms, 169
international trade, 4, 6, 9, 12, 50, 89, 97, 98, 103
internationalization activities, 3, 7
internationalization approach, 49, 59
internationalization capabilities, 52
internationalization decision, 126, 183
internationalization model, 49
internationalization of banks, 155, 156, 157, 158, 160
internationalization of Estonian banks, 160
internationalization of firms, 47
internationalization of competitive behavior, 77
internationalization opportunities, 98
internationalization plans, 165
internationalization process, 1, 2, 4, 6, 7, 14, 48, 56, 58, 64, 65, 66, 183, 184
internationalization skills, 185
internationalization strategy, 204, 205, 217
internationalization theory, 2, 4
investment barriers, 56
investment climate, 149, 154, 166
investment decisions, 4

investment development path, 48, 49, 50, 53, 54, 74
investment impediments, 56
investment locations, 62
investment modes, 4, 5
investment motives, 230
investment opportunities, 7
inward FDI, 48, 49, 52, 54, 73
inward foreign investments, 27
Ireland, 158, 159, 204, 212, 216
Isle of Man, 157
Italian investors, 105, 119, 124, 126
Italy, 11, 19, 20, 22, 51, 60, 105, 106, 110, 112, 113, 114, 115, 117, 120, 121, 122, 123, 124, 125, 126, 127, 155, 159

Japan, 23, 30, 59, 61, 184, 186, 202, 212, 213, 218
Jeronimo Martins, 173, 176, 177, 178
Jinling, 209
joint stock companies, 90
joint venture, 208, 211, 225, 226
Jumbo, 175
Jupiler, 206, 208, 210

Kaiser, 222
Kakanee, 208
Kamenitza, 208, 209, 210, 225, 226, 229
Kazakhstan, 162, 197
Kirin, 212, 213
know-how, 225, 229
knowledge creation, 2
Kobanya, 223, 224, 225
Kobanya Sörgyâr RT, 223
Komercialna Banka Nova Gorica (KBNG), 38
KPMG, 146, 149

Kredina Banka Maribor (KBM), 38

Labatt, 205, 206, 208, 209, 210
labor productivity, 94, 96
Lanbic beers, 205
late entrants, 5
Latin America, 6, 204, 206
Latvia, 10, 12, 133, 151, 155, 162, 163, 164
Lech Browary Wielkopolski SA, 223
Leclerc, 173, 175, 176
Leffe, 205, 206, 208
liberalization, 77, 79, 80, 81
licensing, 3, 4, 193, 198, 220, 228, 211
Lithuania, 10, 12, 138, 155, 162, 163, 164, 167
Ljubljanska Banka (LB), 38
Ljubljanska Banka Group, 39
lobbying group, 36
Lobkowickzky Pivovar, 222
local factor conditions, 24, 25
location decision, 62, 105, 119, 126
logistics, 6
London Club, 38
Luxemburg, 112, 157, 158, 159, 208, 210

Macedonia, 105, 108, 119
majority stake, 225, 230
Malaysia, 61
management culture, 127
manufacturing industry, 121
market challenger, 224, 225, 232
market challenges, 204
market commitment, 2
market economy, 133, 160
market entry, 3, 4, 5, 13, 119
market entry mode, 59, 189

market experience, 231
market failure, 2, 101
market follower, 204
market information, 185
market knowledge, 183, 185, 200
market leader, 204, 206, 208,
    214, 225, 228, 230, 232
market orientation, 76, 78
market potential, 224, 225
market recognition, 62
market segments, 228, 231
market share, 51, 62, 208, 211,
    214, 218, 228, 230, 231
market structure, 230
marketing function, 227, 228, 229
marketing skills, 2
marketing technologies, 103
marketization of firm activities,
    51
Matsushita, 7
McDonald's, 7
means of production, 19, 31
mergers and acquisitions, 65
Merita Bank, 161
Metro, 173, 174, 175, 176, 178
Mexico, 206, 208, 210
Miller, 204, 211, 212, 213
MNCs, 7, 9
mode of market entry, 5, 13
Moldova, 189
Molson, 208
Mongolia, 197
monopolization, 24
Montenegro, 105, 108, 119, 208,
    209
motives, 49, 52, 62, 63, 64, 65,
    66, 226, 228, 231
  efficiency seeking, 63
  market seeking, 63, 64, 65
  resource seeking, 49, 52, 62,
    63, 64, 65, 66, 70
  strategic asset seeking, 63

Nanjing, 209
NATO, 23, 109
national brands, 228
natural resources, 25
Nestle, 94
Netherlands, 112, 159, 204, 206,
    208, 209, 210, 214, 215, 223,
    225, 230
Netto, 176
network spread index, 59, 74
Norway, 151
Nova Kreditna Banka Maribor
    (NKBM), 39
Nova Ljubljanska Banka (NLB),
    39
NoWe Bank, 161

OECD, 76, 82, 89
Oetker, 216
offshore countries, 157
oligopolization of market
    structures, 47
Opel, 225
operation costs, 62
Optiva Bank, 161, 163
Oranjeboom, 208, 209, 210
Oriental Brewery Co., 208
outward FDI, 48, 49, 50, 53, 54,
    55, 72
outward internationalization, 48
overcapacity, 221
ownership specific advantages,
    58, 60
Ozujsko Pivo, 208, 210

Panama, 157
parent company, 65, 66, 69, 70,
    72
past experience, 59
Pension Fund, 33, 34
pension reform, 41
PepsiCo, 94

Perestroika, 20
Philip Morris, 7
Philippines, 208
physical and cultural distance, 59
Piedboeuf, 205
Pivovar Saris A.S., 223
Poland, 7, 9, 10, 11, 12, 13, 14,
    21, 23, 31, 32, 37, 42, 53, 60,
    76, 77, 78, 79, 80, 81, 82, 84,
    87, 89, 90, 91, 92, 93, 94, 96,
    98, 99, 101, 103, 135, 136,
    138, 146, 155, 162, 169, 171,
    172, 173, 174, 175, 176, 177,
    178, 179, 180, 189, 190, 191,
    192, 193, 194, 195, 196, 197,
    215, 219, 220, 221, 222, 223,
    224
Polish economy, 76, 77, 79, 82,
    96, 97, 98, 99, 100, 103
Polish enterprises, 77, 78
Polish foreign trade, 77, 82, 83,
    85, 94
Polish retailing, 169
portfolio investment, 139
Portugal, 47, 74, 87, 159, 173
post-communist countries, 76, 77
post-communist enterprises, 78
Postna Banka Slovenia, 39
Prazske Pivovary, 222
premium brands, 216
pricing policy, 229
private sector, 110
privatization, 31, 32, 33, 34, 35,
    36, 48, 51, 52, 96, 97, 99, 101,
    103, 107, 152, 153, 166, 169,
    170, 171, 173, 221, 226
privatization investment funds,
    34
privatization process, 31, 33
privatization programs, 6, 7, 8
proactive strategy, 230, 232
Proberco, 209

product image, 206
product life cycle, 217
product portfolio, 232
production site, 185, 196
profit maximization, 228, 231
promotion, 227, 228
propensity to internationalize, 3
protectionism, 218, 221
psychic distance, 183, 184
public offerings, 34, 35
purchasing power, 220, 224, 225
Pvovar Karsay Spol, 224

Rákóczi, 208, 210
R&D capacities, 25, 26
regional brands, 228
Renault, 36
resource commitment, 183, 194
resource utilization, 115
Restitution Fund, 34
restructuring, 76, 80, 81, 99, 100,
    225, 227
retailers, 6
retailing, 169, 170, 171, 178, 179
return on investment, 228
Rolling Rock, 205, 206, 210
Romania, 7, 9, 10, 11, 12, 23,
    108, 112, 138, 155, 190, 198,
    208, 209, 210, 219, 220, 221,
    222, 223
Russia, 10, 11, 13, 32, 33, 138,
    143, 146, 147, 148, 155, 162,
    164, 165, 167, 168, 190, 191,
    192, 193, 194, 195, 196, 197,
    215, 218, 219, 220, 221, 222,
    223
Russian market, 148, 157, 160

sales office, 185, 193, 196
Sara Lee, 225
Sava Group, 36
Scandinavian countries, 48, 74

SC Ursus SA, 223
SC Vulturul SA, 223
SE Banken, 161
self-governance, 101
Selgros, 175
sequential internationalization, 48, 49, 50, 60, 231
service sector, 121, 124
Shell, 176
Slovakia, 7, 9, 10, 11, 12, 13, 21, 112, 136, 138, 155, 162, 198, 219, 220, 221, 223, 224
Slovenia, 7, 9, 10, 11, 12, 13, 14, 19, 20, 21, 22, 23, 25, 27, 28, 29, 30, 31, 32, 34, 35, 36, 37, 38, 39, 40, 41, 42, 43, 44, 45, 46, 47, 49, 50, 52, 53, 54, 59, 60, 61, 64, 66, 70, 72, 73, 74, 90, 138, 155, 219
Slovenian corporate sector, 55, 70, 73
Slovenian industry, 27
Slovenian outward investments, 49
SMEs, 55
social infrastructure, 23
social ownership, 19, 33
socially owned companies, 31, 35
Sol, 208, 210
South Africa, 204
South African Breweries, 204, 213, 217, 223, 225, 230
South America, 61
South Korea, 209
Soviet Union, 20, 133, 150, 168, 197
Spain, 87, 159, 215
Spanish compromise, 22, 45
Spaten, 208, 226
specialization, 24, 25
standardization, 115
state monopoly, 77

state owned companies, 8
state-owned enterprises, 89
Statoil, 176
Stella Artois, 205, 206
Stinnes, 173
strategic alliances, 47
strategic control, 186
strategic management, 229
strategic partnership, 206
strategic trade policy, 102
strategic priority, 206
strategy evaluation, 227, 230, 232
structural unemployment, 40
subsidiaries, 184, 185, 186, 187, 188, 189, 190, 191, 192, 194, 195, 196, 197, 198, 199, 200, 201, 205, 229
Sun Breweries Ltd., 223
supermarkets, 173, 174, 176, 177, 178
Swedbank, 161
Sweden, 143, 147, 148, 151, 184, 202
Switzerland, 112

Tallinn Stock Exchange, 153
Tallinna Äripank, 163
Tallinna Pank (Bank of Tallinn), 161
tax holidays, 89
Tecate, 208, 210
technological changes, 47, 48
technological modernization, 27
technological progress, 23
Tengelman, 174, 176
Tesco, 173, 175, 176
tolar, 20, 31
trade balance, 85, 97
trade deficit, 87, 99, 110
transaction costs, 2

transition economies, 135, 138, 155, 162
transition to a market economy, 21, 39, 43
transnational corporations (TNCs), 54
Trebjesa, 209
Tuborg, 217
Turkey, 11, 107, 112

UK, 151, 186, 206, 215, 216, 218
unemployment, 110
US, 9, 11, 23, 59, 61, 148, 151, 204, 206, 208, 211, 212, 213, 214, 225
Ukraine, 7, 10, 12, 13, 14, 162, 164, 167, 190, 198, 201, 208, 209, 210, 215, 219
Unilever, 225
Union Bank, 161, 163, 164, 165
Uppsala model, 3, 183, 185
Uzbekistan, 162

Vegana, 209
Venezuela, 209

Warsaw Pact, 8

wholesalers, 6
wholly-owned subsidiaries, 5, 119, 195, 198
Wild Cat, 208
window dressing firms, 51
World Bank, 20, 29, 30, 31, 34,35, 36, 37, 38, 39, 40, 41, 42, 43, 44, 46
world beer industry, 211
World Trade Organization (WTO), 102, 104
World War I, 19
World War II, 5, 19, 20, 22, 33, 76

Yalta regime, 20
Yugoslavia, 19, 20, 21, 22, 28, 29, 30, 31, 37, 39, 43, 45, 50, 52, 53, 58, 59, 60, 72, 106, 108, 109

Zagorka, 224, 225, 230
Zagrebacka, 209
Zemes Banka, 164
Zhu Jiang, 209
Zlaty Bazant, 224
zloty, 80, 81
Zywiec, 224

*For Product Safety Concerns and Information please contact
our EU representative GPSR@taylorandfrancis.com Taylor & Francis
Verlag GmbH, Kaufingerstraße 24, 80331 München, Germany*

T - #0118 - 270225 - C0 - 217/150/14 - PB - 9781138726444 - Gloss Lamination